'Dear BBC': Children, Television Storytelling and the Public Sphere

Drawing on the diverse views of over 1,300 children in the UK between the ages of 6–12, *'Dear BBC'* discusses key controversies in the public sphere about children's relationship with the media, especially television drama. Máire Messenger Davies draws on material gathered from an audience research project commissioned by the BBC, based on surveys, structured discussions with children and interviews with programme-makers and policy-makers. The book explores a number of complex and controversial issues. What do children think is the ideal television service for them, and for others? How should media be regulated? How is media consumption managed and negotiated in the home? How is the relationship between programme-makers and audience changing in the light of global broadcasting trends? Why are genres like animation and fantasy so meaningful for children? And finally, and perhaps most importantly, how much attention should be paid to children's views about these issues and the future of children's television? This engaging and accessible book will appeal to a broad audience.

MÁIRE MESSENGER DAVIES is Senior Lecturer at the School of Journalism, Media and Cultural Studies, Cardiff University. She is the author of *Television Is Good For Your Kids* (1989) and *Fake, Fact and Fantasy* (1997).

'Dear BBC': Children, Television Storytelling and the Public Sphere

Máire Messenger Davies

CAMBRIDGE
UNIVERSITY PRESS

PUBLISHED BY THE PRESS SYNDICATE OF THE UNIVERSITY OF CAMBRIDGE
The Pitt Building, Trumpington Street, Cambridge, United Kingdom

CAMBRIDGE UNIVERSITY PRESS
The Edinburgh Building, Cambridge CB 2 2RU, UK
40 West 20th Street, New York NY 10011–4211, USA
10 Stamford Road, Oakleigh, VIC 3166, Australia
Ruiz de Alarcón 13, 28014 Madrid, Spain
Dock House, The Waterfront, Cape Town 80011, South Africa

http://www.cambridge.org

First published 2001

Printed in the United Kingdom at the University Press, Cambridge

Typeface Plantin 10/12 pt   *System* 3b2   [CE]

A catalogue record for this book is available from the British Library

Library of Congress Cataloguing in Publication data

Davies, Máire Messenger.
'Dear BBC': Children, Television Storytelling and the Public Sphere /
Máire Messenger Davies.
    p.   cm.
Includes bibliographical references and index.
ISBN 0 521 78077 2 (hardback) – ISBN 0 521 78560 X (paperback)
1. Television programmes for children – Great Britain. 2. Television and
children – Great Britain. I. Title.

PN1992.8.C46 D37 2001
791.45′75′0830941–dc21   00-067490

ISBN 0 521 78077 2 hardback
ISBN 0 521 78560 X paperback

Contents

Tables

Acknowledgements

Many people contributed to the production of this book. Particular thanks are due to Dr David Machin, Research Fellow at the London College of Printing (LCP), and contributor to chapters 5 and 8; to Kate O'Malley and Beth Corbett, my fellow researchers and good friends in the design, fieldwork and analysis stages of the BBC-funded research project on Children and Television Drama, from which the data discussed in the book have come; to Mena Digings and Carmelina Wright for extra help with the fieldwork on this research project; to Mena and Roger Digings, Sheila Doré and Dympna LeRasle for their advice and help in the design and pilot stage of the research; to Mary O'Malley, Gwen Corbett, Cathy Grove and Cary Bazalgette for help in contacting schools; to Monica Fewins and Rachel Huntingford, former students at the LCP, for help with further analysis and transcription; to Hannah Davies for organising the Through the Square Window conference at the LCP in June 1996, which brought many of the participants in the study together and at which early results were discussed, and, also, for general intellectual stimulation; to all the staff and students at the LCP who helped with the Square Window conference; to Dr Fotini Papatheodorou and her colleagues who held the fort on the BA in Media and Cultural Studies at the LCP, while the fieldwork was carried out; and to Gill Branston, Professor John Tulloch, Roberta Pearson, Thor Ekevall, Beccy Harris and colleagues in the School of Journalism, Media and Cultural Studies who did the same during the final production of the book; to Godfrey Lee and Matt Lenny at the LCP and to Sharon McGill, Dave Ladd and John Adams at JOMEC, for help with computing; to Dr Bob Kubey at Rutgers University, New Jersey and Dr Renee Hobbs, at Babson College, Massachussetts for their support for the publication of an earlier study with children which laid the groundwork for this one (Davies, 1997). Acknowledgements also to the journals *Childhood* and *Continuum: Journal of Media and Cultural Studies*, where some of the research has been reported.

Special acknowledgements and thanks are due to the funders of the research – the BBC and the London Institute – and also to the Broadcasting Standards Commission, especially Andrea Millwood-Hargrave, whose funding for a parallel research project on the provision of children's television in the UK (Davies and Corbett, 1997) facilitated the work on the children and drama study in many ways. Special thanks, too, to the many drama producers, broadcasters and policy-makers, who agreed to be interviewed for both studies and to share so generously and fully their views about their profession and about their audience.

Above all, thanks to the nearly 1,400 children in the pilot and main studies who shared their opinions and knowledge with us, and who carried out the research tasks with such professionalism, openness and courtesy; thanks, too, to their teachers and head-teachers for all their help and co-operation.

Finally, thanks to my family, who have grown up, grown older, and, in some cases, grown away to adult lives, in the long course of this work, and who have given patient support, and useful advice throughout all of it: John; Tom; Hannah; Huw and Eli, and my mother, Margaret Messenger.

Introduction

Isn't it amazing how hard people work to raise their children? . . . For every grownup you see, there must have been at least one person to lug them around, and feed them . . . for years and years without a break. Teaching them how to fit into civilisation, and how to talk back and forth with other people, taking them to zoos and parades and educational events, telling them all those nursery rhymes and word of mouth fairytales. Isn't that surprising?
    Character in *The Clock Winder*, by Anne Tyler, 1972, pp. 258–9

If you want to know what children like, you have to think like one or base it on your small brother or your cousin, you have to base it on them.   Boy, 10, inner-London primary school

The BBC has, I think, a special responsibility that transcends, while it cannot afford to ignore, ratings and reach. Our responsibility is to supply a distinctive public service offering information, education and entertainment, which extends young people's choices and lifts their horizons.   Sir Christopher Bland, Chair of Governors, *The BBC and Children*,
    BBC, August 1996

This book has three main origins, each in some sense based on the spirit of the quotations above. To begin with the last: the practical origins of the book are an empirical study, funded by the BBC and the London Institute, with children aged between 5 and 13 years, in different parts of England and Wales, carried out during 1996 and 1997. The study's primary aim was to assess children's responses to televised storytelling, including programmes made especially for children, as well as drama programmes made for adults, which are watched by children. Its immediate goal was to inform BBC policy, and a report was delivered to the BBC in June 1997 for internal consideration.

The study was seen as necessary at the time because the BBC, as a major public service broadcaster, was, and is, having to adapt to the fact that broadcasting around the world is changing irrevocably from a channel-scarcity system to a system where viewers are promised access to hundreds of channels, via digital technology, and where the subjective experience of viewing is expected to change from 'passive entertainment' to 'interactivity' and consumer choice through new computer technology. The commissioning of this study was an example of one of the many changes that overtook British broadcasting during the 1990s – the perceived necessity to consult 'the market', as well as relying on traditions of public service, in forming editorial policy.

This book draws on data from this study to discuss the uses, pleasures and meanings derived by children of different ages from the broadcasting services they currently know, as well as their views about the new services beginning to wean them away from them. The book asks whether this relationship can survive in a new millennium when traditional forms of entertainment may be displaced, and when regulation by national governments for special children's media provision may become impossible. Changing ideas about childhood, and the increasing sophistication of children as media consumers, have also contributed to the raising of question marks over children's ideal relationship with broadcasting. The book's most central question asks: what do children themselves think that the future of media entertainment for them will, and should, be, and what can their explanations tell us about the changing nature of childhood, and its relationship with culture?

Reconstructing childhood

Implicit in the debate about what is appropriate entertainment for children in the twenty-first century, who should provide it, and who should regulate it, are changing ideas about the nature of childhood. Sociologists of childhood have pointed out that the idea of 'childhood' (as distinct from actual children) is a social construction, which varies across time and space. They also point out the powerlessness of children within complex modern societies. Paradoxically, as more institutions have come into being to protect and improve the status of children during the twentieth century, so children's lives themselves have become, in many ways, more constrained. Prout and James (1997, p. 32) point to the fact that 'almost all political, educational, legal and administrative processes have profound effects on children, but they [children] have little or no influence over them'.

The research described in this book aims to remedy this lack of consultation by putting forward a portrait of the child as citizen-in-the-making, capable of operating intelligently and purposefully in the public sphere, while at the same time displaying the more familiar characteristics of the child-as-consumer model, and the child-as-vulnerable-victim model. It suggests that none of these characteristics are mutually exclusive in any individual child or groups of children, and that debates about the nature of childhood have not always taken into account the complexity of children's lives and personalities, and their ability to move between different roles according to context – an ability which engagement with popular media is particularly well equipped to encourage. Sociological and historical debates about the nature of childhood are also conspicuously lacking in comments from children themselves.

Thus, the second origin of the book is democratic, and responds to 10-year-old J's assertion above that if you want to know what children think, you have to 'think like them'. More will be said about children as potential citizens and their rights – if they have such rights – to be heard, later in the book. Put simply, the structure of the book takes a series of topics on which adult media analysts, journalists, sociologists of childhood, historians, psychologists, teachers, parents and media professionals have been debating for years, and provides children with the opportunity to join in. In doing so, it is an attempt to bring the views of the large and diverse group of children who took part in the study into the 'public sphere'.

The public sphere

The term 'public sphere' to discuss the circulation of information as a civic function, was first used by the German philosopher Jürgen Habermas (Habermas, 1962) and ever since has served as a heuristic for reflections on the participation, or not, of various groups in civil society, including women, workers, writers and, as in this case, children and young people. Habermas (1962, p. 25) defined 'the public sphere' as a product of the rise of the literate bourgeoisie during the seventeenth and eighteenth centuries. Their conversations, discussions, printed essays, satires and journalism constituted 'a forum in which the private people, [having] come together to form a public, readied themselves to compel public authority to legitimate itself before public opinion'. Feminists such as Joanna Meehan (1995) have pointed out that this view of 'the public sphere' was a very masculine one, and marginalised aspects of the 'private sphere' which did not equate the interests of the private person (*homme*) with the public one (*citoyen*). The private person, as Habermas's use of these phrases indicates, was masculine, and he was characterised as 'simultaneously an owner of private property who, as *citoyen* was to protect the stability of the property order as a private one. Class interest was the basis of public opinion' (Habermas, 1962, p. 87).

The invention of mass broadcasting in the mid twentieth century was seen by Habermas as destructive of the Enlightenment public sphere, leading to a 're-feudalisation' of the relationships between those in power and their subjects/citizens. 'The media . . . functioned as manipulative agencies controlling mass opinion, in contrast to the early press which had facilitated the formation and expression of organic, public opinion' as James Curran (1991, pp. 38–9) put it. Broadcasting has helped to break down both the physical and discursive barriers between public and private spheres in ways which have been much lamented. Education professor Neil Postman, in *The Disappearance of Childhood* (1982), deplored the fact that television had destroyed the Enlightenment model of prolonged childhood, which originally came into being to educate *citoyens* (if not *citoyennes*) for their public roles.

When first radio in the 1920s, and then television in the 1950s, broadcast public affairs and events directly into the home, public affairs could no longer be kept exclusively outside the domestic sphere. Even more worrying from a cultural pessimist's point of view, radio, and later television, began to represent forms of private behaviour – whether in drama, comedy, gameshows or talk shows – which for American critics such as Joshua Meyrowitz (1984) and James Twitchell (1992) were vulgar, objectionable and destructive of the necessary barriers between public and private. Even the early, ostensibly democratising pioneers of cultural studies in Britain, such as Richard Hoggart and Raymond Williams, who demanded more diverse and populist definitions of art and culture than those offered by the traditional education and arts establishments, have objected to some of the material produced by popular television for universal consumption in the home.

The key implication of the development of mass broadcasting for the purposes of the topic of this book is its impact on the domestic sphere, the sphere of the home – of women, and, of course, of children. When public issues of politics, economics and cultural expression, as well as the representation of different and unfamiliar kinds of private behaviour, invade the private sphere of the home via the broadcast airwaves, children (and women) become exposed to information that they might never otherwise have encountered, and traditionally was never intended for them. With the exception of the French *salonnieres* and the educated daughters of enlightened men in the eighteenth and nineteenth centuries, such as Mary Wollstonecraft, women and children had no part in Habermas's bourgeois enlightened public sphere. And, as Neil Postman revealingly explains, so long as print was the dominant medium of communication, this state of affairs could be maintained. Until the end of the nineteenth century in Europe and the USA, the vast majority of women and children were denied formal education and hence access to print literacy, and, in large parts of the world, they still are. With radio and television, broadcasting has become the dominant public medium, and both women and children have as much access to its products – if not yet to its production – as men do. However, the more interactive products of the convergence between computers and other media are already allowing domestic consumers to have more control over the production of mass media. This, too, is generating public concern. Hence the continuing debate, which shows no signs of diminishing, about 'harmful effects' of invasive media representations on young and 'vulnerable' (including female) minds.

This brings me to the third of my three initial quotations – the one about adults' years of 'lugging' and 'civilising' children in order to 'get them grown'. Many of the debates about children's relationship with media – the moral panics, the cultural pessimism – have been conducted, as it were, high over the heads of the people responsible for looking after, working with and shaping children's daily lives – parents, relatives, teachers, childminders and professional storytellers, including those working for children in the media, as well as children themselves, who also look after each other. Children's relationships with the people who, somehow or other, 'get them grown', do not feature prominently in cultural pessimism/moral panic discourses, because the very fact of children 'getting grown' (and all the feeding, cleaning, transporting, nursing and training that go into it) implicitly denies a wholly pessimistic view of the relationship between children and adult society. As Tyler's character observes, the very fact that so many adults – even, as she later comments, delinquent ones – go to so much trouble to do all this lugging and caring, is 'amazing'. Like many amazing phenomena, the diurnal and unending effort of 'getting children grown' is not often noticed; like housework, and office administration, it is only noticed when it is not done. It is symptomatic of the dearth of academic acknowledgement of it that, in seeking for a literary quotation to represent it, I had to go to a novel, by one of the most sympathetic writers about family life currently in print, not to a scholarly textbook.

The account of the research set out in this book is an account of a relationship or, more accurately, a series of relationships, between a group of adults (the researchers), and a large number of children who were willing to confide their opinions to these adults, because of an obvious implicit trust in the grown-up organisation which those adults represented: the BBC. The comments from children in this book reflected to us, when we first read them, an 'amazing' openness, indicative of a confident and confiding relationship with the discursive public sphere as represented by the broadcasters, and also with us, whom they comfortably, and, humblingly, accepted as the representatives of these trusted broadcasters. As the title of the book suggests, these children repeatedly took the opportunity to address the organisation directly as an 'auntie' or 'grown-up brother', or occasionally a wayward parent figure, in tones of presumed intimacy, as well as adopting other kinds of tone in other kinds of discursive tasks (as described in later chapters).

The account of the research in the book is, I hope, partly an expression of the need among adults involved in 'the hard work' of 'lugging' and 'civilising' children to give a structured expression of this experience in terms which illustrate how that civilising process might work. The book describes not only the work of the various adults privileged to be co-operating with these children in the research itself, but also the work and attitudes of some of the adults who have been charged with the 'special responsibility', as Sir Christopher Bland put it, of 'extending young people's choices and lifting their horizons' within the British broadcasting system: producers, writers, directors and policy-makers. In addition to the professional storytellers, with their modern versions of 'nursery rhymes and word of mouth fairytales', the book draws on implicit – and sometimes explicit – comments from children, about the adults in the backgrounds of their lives – parents, relatives, older siblings, teachers and other people they knew, although none of these people was interviewed directly. (To preserve the confidentiality of this information, no schools or children are referred to by name.)

As children took on adult decision-making roles in designing broadcast schedules, their views of how adults both did, and ought to, behave, were revealed. In the long-running public debates and 'moral panics' about the corruption of childish innocence by cultural products, the private sphere of the caring adult–child relationship, particularly when this relationship takes a non-newsworthy, benevolent form, rarely appears. The relationship between the adult world and the child's revealed by some of the comments in this book, gives, I hope, some hint of the supportive aspects of the relationship between children and the adult world, in both the public and the private spheres – although I hope the book is not complacent about less benevolent aspects of these relationships.

The issue of direct effects, for long almost the only issue in which children's status as members of a mediated society has been recognised, will be discussed in more detail in chapters 5 and 6. Whether or not media have good or bad effects is not the issue for the purpose of this book. The starting-point for the book is the ways in which children in this study expressed their opinions on matters of public, as well as private, importance, including the question of effects, all of which constituted an assertion to the listening adults, that 'we, the children, belong in this debate too'. This book is, to an extent, their forum, and its subsequent chapters are their topics. It would be difficult to summarise the case for allowing children's voices to be heard on these topics more succinctly than 10-year-old J, and his view that: 'If you want to know what children like, you have to think like one.' If you cannot 'think like one', as he pointed out, the next best thing is to ask some children.

Constructing and disappearing childhood

As I shall discuss later, in chapter 3, childhood studies, which have burgeoned in the 1990s, do not specifically deal with children themselves (nor, for that matter, with the adults who look after them) – a development which, Neil Postman (1982, p. 5) argued, suggested that our culture has lost interest in real children. 'Of all the evidence [of the disappearance of childhood] none is more suggestive than the fact that the history of childhood has now become a major industry among scholars.' Postman (1982, p. 5) accuses Philippe Ariès, the French art historian, of 'starting the rush', since Ariès was one of the first to point out, in 1962, that 'childhood' is a social and cultural construct, with the implication that this construct may bear little resemblance to the day-to-day lived experience of actual children, and their parents. Television has played an enormously large part of the lives of Western children – at least in terms of time spent in its company – for the last thirty years – a fact lamented by scholars such as Postman. Yet, surprisingly, it is neglected by the new theorists of childhood following in Ariès' footsteps. For instance, *Theorizing Childhood* (1998) by Alison James, Alan Prout and Chris Jenks, a summary of the current state of the art of childhood studies, has no index references to 'media', or to 'broadcasting', only one to television, and only one to 'culture'.

Academic study of the relationship between children and television has fallen primarily to psychologists working within social-science traditions of research (my own discipline) in the USA (for example, Aimée Dorr), and to educationists who, in Britain, come from an academic background in English and/or film studies (for example, David Buckingham). Willard Rowland (1997, p. 103) argues that the American intellectual tradition, of applying social science to the study of meanings and texts, comes from a deep-rooted respect for science and its pragmatic application in a country 'that imagined itself as a laboratory for social and political experiments to be conducted over time in a process of competitive individual entrepreneurship'. This, says Rowland, set the dominant forms of communication research as scientific-and-effects oriented. This tradition has led to a very great number of studies in the USA (see, for example, Comstock and Paik, 1991; Bryant and Zillman, 1994) seeking to identify the primarily harmful effects of media representations and messages on children – a public health, 'hypodermic' model of media influence which continues to flourish, despite Rowland calling it 'a myth'.

The field of empirically studying children themselves and their responses to media, has been almost entirely left to the social scientists who are part of this entrepreneurial 'laboratory' tradition, and they have dominated debates about media 'effects' and set the agenda in terms of concerns such as violence, and premature sexuality, although there is a more creative and productive field of study from cognitive psychologists who have studied the ways in which children learn from media (for example, Bryant and Anderson, 1983; Rice et al., 1983; Dorr, 1986; Dorr et al., 1990; Wright et al., 1994) and psychologists and educators who have studied the meanings and effectiveness of 'media literacy' in its widest sense around the world (see for example, Kubey, 1997; Bazalgette and Buckingham, 1995). Cultural studies, deriving primarily from literary and humanities academic traditions, is more dominant in the study of media in Britain and Australia than is social science and psychology. Cultural studies scholars have paid comparatively little attention to children – particularly children under 12 – as audiences, with one or two exceptions, such as David Oswell in Britain, and Ellen Seiter and Marsha Kinder in the USA. Cultural studies, with its proliferating attentiveness to forms of popular culture such as soap opera, adult TV drama, and talk shows, has not paid much attention to cultural products for children either, including children's television. One outcome of the attention paid to children's TV drama in the study described in this book, is an attempt to redress the lack of critical attention to children's TV by producing some more critical writing about children's programmes (see, for example, Davies and Machin, 2000a, 2000b).

Cultural studies' response to psychological traditions of research, particularly studies on harmful effects, has often been oppositional. An example is the resistance of many in the field to suggestions that screen violence might be harmful to children, as discussed in chapter 6, a resistance based not so much on specific findings of social science research, as on the methods, and the credibility itself, of the whole field of social science scholarship, particularly of psychology. The possibility that children might be hurt by exposure to graphic depictions of the infliction of pain, or embarrassed and shocked by graphic portrayals of adult sex, and the desire of caring adults both to understand, and to prevent, such hurt, can become equated with an illiberal desire to impose indiscriminate censorship in all areas of public life. The resolution of this problem is not helped by the fact that the two concerns – protection of children, and protection of free speech – are dealt with in different academic domains: the care and protection of children, both of bodies and minds, are primarily the prerogative of medicine, education and the law. The care and protection of free speech tend to be the domain of philosophy, politics and the humanities. Both sorts of care and concern can produce politically liberal positions, yet they are often opposed, and this is not in the interests of children, nor of useful scholarship.

Reflexivity in research

Anxieties about validity and the importance of 'renegotiating the power relations between researcher and child' (Davis, 1998, p. 329) have led to a decline in the use of traditional social science methods for examining attitudes and behaviour, particularly in areas such as media and culture which are themselves the water in which we all swim. We can never remove children, or anyone else, from their social and cultural environment for the purposes of 'laboratory-based observation'. The laboratory itself is part of this cultural environment, and the research process is part of it too. As Buckingham, Davies, Jones and Kelley, in their history of British children's broadcasting (1999, p. 137), put it: 'the endless quest to know more about the child consumer is itself an intervention. Research does not only reflect tastes; it also subtly shifts them.' For some scholars, such as John Hartley (1992) or Ien Ang (1993, 1996), this has led to a logical stance from which they urge us to abandon all attempts to define, describe or, most impossible of all, measure, actual 'audiences' or 'real people'. However, scholarly research, too, is part of 'the public sphere' and has traditionally been called on – as were we in this study – to answer questions on behalf of public institutions. The kinds of public agencies who need to know about the relationship between children and media, such as the BBC, or national governments and their education departments, continue to want the nearest thing to reliable empirical data that can be managed, in order to inform policy.

In social science there is, in fact, an increasing demand for 'reflexivity' – an awareness of the research situation and its contribution to the interpretation of research findings. In a paper about reflexivity in research with children, Davis (1998, p. 329) argues:

[research] should empower children . . . to become active participants in the research process, employing tools which offer children the maximum opportunity to put forward their views and reducing the social distance and renegotiating the power relations between researcher and child.

As Davis points out, research with children has an extra responsibility in that, first, it must be careful not to exploit their immaturity or to undermine their relationship with the adults legally responsible for them, parents and teachers; and, second, the techniques used must be appropriate, and designed to be comprehensible. We all have to be aware that 'talking television' (in Buckingham's, 1993, phrase), whether with researchers, other children or families, is not just an objective research procedure; it is an integral part of the processes whereby cultural traditions are established, changed or continued. It is, itself, a cultural, and enculturating, process. In the study described in this book, the children learned more about themselves as media consumers, potential citizens and critics, from the research tasks they performed, as did we, and as did their teachers. Through the discussions and negotiations of the tasks they were given, this learning process became transparent and explicit.

In response to the call for more self-awareness on the part of researchers, recent texts by media scholars offer accounts of parental engagement as a starting-point for discussing children's culture and the public/private interface between it and other areas of society. Steven Kline begins his account of the commercialised culture of American children's media, *Out of the Garden* (1993), with anxieties about his own small son and the film-based toys the child liked to play with. In *From Barbie to Mortal Kombat: Gender and Computer Games* (1998), Henry Jenkins discusses his teenage son's passion for the virtual spaces of computer games and rather wistfully contrasts this with the physical freedom he enjoyed during his own boyhood. Marsha Kinder draws on the games and conversations of her young son and his friends throughout her discussion of TV cartoons, toys, advertising and postmodern intertextuality, in *Playing with Power* (1991). David Buckingham begins his book about the emotional impacts of media on children, *Moving Images* (1996), with a touching account of his little boy's fear of Big Bird in *Sesame Street*. All this is to be welcomed. As well as being of central concern to parents, the topic of childhood is one of which every human being has first-hand experience, and this experience is bound to influence adult discussions of the topic. As Carolyn Steedman (1995, p. 114) argues in *Strange Disclocations*, 'accounts of childhood space relate most directly to lost or unexplored concepts of the adult self'. James, Jenks and Prout (1998, p. 57) go further and characterise modern thinking about childhood as a rediscovery of the inner child in adults – a therapeutic enterprise: 'an analytic dimension concerning the human interior . . . emblematic in late twentieth century American quests to recover the inner child. Here we reconnect with Foucault and his views concerning the shaping of the private self.'

The members of our research team were not consciously on a quest 'concerning the shaping of the private self' – but we were all involved closely and personally with children prior to and during the study, and this constantly stimulated us to reflect on our own expectations and responses to the children we worked with in the research, as compared to our private experiences of caring for, and working with, children. Two of us were mothers with school-teaching experience, the third became a mother during the project. David Machin, co-author of chapters 5 and 8, joined the project at the London College of Printing (LCP) in 1998 and brought the experience and enthusiasms of a father and former school-teacher to bear on the analysis of the children's voices. In addition to these sources of personal engagement with the project, we encompassed different academic perspectives, all of which, in their different ways, had involved working with and studying children: two of us were psychologists including one (myself) who had worked as a journalist for many years for parental advice magazines; one was an anthropologist, one a media-studies graduate who had specialised in studying children and television.

This disciplinary variety was reflected in the differing methods used in the study, the result of a great deal of prior discussion and debate, which were chosen not only for their potential research validity, but especially so that they would best serve the needs and rights of the children and the schools taking part. In this, and in the course of conducting the study, we became aware of strong personal feelings of commitment to the project; to a sense of enjoyment, protectiveness and responsibility to the many children who shared their confidences with us. This sense of commitment could have potentially endangered scientific objectivity, had the study been one in which our subjects were not supposed to know, or share in, the aims of the project. However, this was not the case. Our 'subjects' were not anonymous, nor were we neutral in our dealings with them, because we told them that we wanted to find out, on behalf of the BBC, what they thought about television drama. The children were invited to become partners with us, not only in answering the questions required by our sponsors, but also in raising other questions, and suggesting ways to pursue answers to these too.

The study procedure and sample

Full details of the study's methods, sample, piloting and all results are given in the full report to the BBC (Davies *et al.*, 1997). However, some background information about the source of the data quoted in the book is necessary here. Firstly, throughout the book, the term 'we' is used to describe the people who conducted the research. This team consisted of Kate O'Malley, Research Fellow, Beth Corbett, Research Assistant, and, at a later stage, Dr David Machin, currently Research Fellow – all at the London College of Printing, where the director of the project, myself, was working at the time the fieldwork was carried out, and where the BBC report was written. The many others whose efforts contributed to the project are listed and gratefully thanked in the Acknowledgements, on pp. vii–viii.

The sample of children

Children aged between 6 and 12 were chosen for the study, primarily because this was the main target audience for children's programmes, and this was the group our sponsors were interested in. However there were further considerations: much discussion about the suitability or otherwise of television for children, or about children's rights, tends to focus on teenagers (12 year olds and over), who can reasonably be included with adults in terms of 'rights' to uncensored media. (Many teachers and parents, for instance, would have no problem with 12 year olds reading adult literature.) Twelves and over also have more numerous channels of access to the public sphere. They are more likely to be represented, for instance, in youth access programmes such as Channel 4's *Wise Up*, because they are more articulate and confident on camera, and in less need of supervision off it. They are also a large commercial market, with greater sources of disposable income, and hence, market power, than younger children. Younger children are less often consulted than over-twelves, yet, in terms of the function of public service broadcasting and its contribution to a liberal public sphere, it is the interests of younger children which most need articulating and representing by responsible older people (including older children – as the study revealed). Our source of children was schools, reached through a range of contacts including the British Film Institute's regional education representatives, professional colleagues and personal contacts.

Most of the Year Seven (12-year-old) children in the study were in secondary (high) schools, and, in this sense, belonged to a socially older group, which was a necessary comparison, given our goal of examining the shifting borderlines between children's tastes and adults' tastes in media storytelling. The BBC did not require a scientifically representative sample, but, within the criterion of availability of schools who were willing to take part, a quota of types of school was set, to ensure that different groups in the television audience were represented. The school quotas were: inner-London primary (one school); outer-London primary (two schools); inner-London secondary (one school); outer-London secondary (one school); inner-city primary, non-London (three schools); outer-city primary, non-London (three schools); inner-city secondary, non-London (one school); outer-city secondary non-London (one school); rural secondary (two schools); rural primary (two schools). A pilot study was carried out at an urban primary school in Colchester, Essex.

All schools were mixed boys and girls, and all classes used were mixed ability, including a number of children with special needs, and for whom English was not a first language. There were 1,332 children aged between 5 and 13 in the total questionnaire sample. Allowing for missing values in some questions, the sample was always at least 1,236 children. There were 631 boys and 645 girls; 56 children did not give their gender on the questionnaire. The number of children in each age group is given below:

Age:

5	6	7	8	9	10	11	12	13
10	119	193	194	235	193	267	110	8

Fifty-seven children did not give their age.

Schools were classified according to a special needs index, based on the number of factors in their self-description which indicated higher than the average numbers for our sample of children who, for instance, had free meals, or did not have English as a first language. At the preference of the schools, ethnic and socio-economic information about each child individually was not included in the questionnaires, but other demographic information included the children's age in months, and the size of their families. The schools were asked to classify themselves and the demographic nature of their intake, and a special needs index was drawn up for each school; the 'special needs' status of children is classified only in terms of the school they attended. There were seven special needs factors altogether, including social class; the proportions of children living in council housing; the percentage of children having free meals; and the percentage of children for whom English was a second language. Full details of the special needs categories, from the form which schools filled in to describe themselves and their intake is given in Appendix 1. There were 2 schools in the sample with no special needs on this scale; there were 3 with 1; 3 with 2; 2 with 3; 2 with 4; 1 with 5; 3 with 6 and 1 with 7. High special needs (i.e. 5–7) were primarily associated with London (inner and outer) and inner cities (Cardiff and Milton Keynes).

The basic instrument was a carefully designed and piloted standardised questionnaire, so that all 1,300+ children could be included in the study, and their responses statistically analysed within the one year time available for the study. There was a pictorial version of the questionnaire for the youngest children, which was read aloud to them by the researcher – both versions asked exactly the same questions (see Appendix 2). The use of a standardised measure was an attempt to provide both social and scientific representativeness, and, more importantly in terms of public sphere issues, political representativeness: we wanted to ensure the rights of all the children we met to have their responses included in the study, not just the talkative ones in discussion groups.

The questionnaire included a number of sections where free comments could be given, and this produced our second source of data, which was qualitative: what the children wrote in these sections. Younger children were given the opportunity of doing drawings, if they did not want to write. Most of the sample took the opportunity to make free comments on their questionnaires – a very large data source. This data-set was sampled twice. The first time was as the numerical data were entered into the Statistical Package for the Social Sciences (SPSS) programme. Whenever a comment that looked interesting or relevant, particularly about individual drama programmes, was found, this questionnaire was set aside. This process was obviously biased towards articulate and literate children, and towards drama. For the purposes of writing this book, a second sample was taken randomly, that is, every third questionnaire was selected from one age group in each school, and a quota system was used to ensure that equal numbers of boys and girls were included in this process. In the final writing of the book, quotations from these comments have had to be even more selective, both to illustrate the themes of the book, and for brevity. Inevitably, this process is biased towards my authorial arguments, and to editorial concision. To counter this, in selecting the comments, I have, wherever possible, tried to ensure that the whole age range, the comments of both boys and girls, and examples from every school used in the study, are represented as equally as possible.

Our third procedure, the qualitative discussion tasks, was necessary to address different kinds of questions, including direct responses to programmes, as required by the BBC. The design of these tasks came from a background of educational research and practice, in which we drew on the advice and practical help of experienced primary-school teachers, including a drama teacher and film-maker. The qualitative tasks were carried out in 14 of the 17 schools in the main study, and also in the pilot school. On the advice of the teachers in the schools, we did not carry out these discussion tasks with children under 8 (with the exception of the final infants' school we visited – see chapter 9). It was necessary to make these tasks as imaginative and engaging for all children as possible, not least for the sake of the schools who were co-operating in the study. One of the conditions for allowing us to come in to carry out the research was that the techniques we used should not be disruptive, should involve all children in a class, and should be educationally useful.

As a result of our preliminary discussions, and the pilot study at a primary school in Essex, a two-stage process was devised for all the tasks. The first stage involved the whole class, divided into small groups of 5 or 6, with a child from the group as 'chair' or 'leader'. The tasks varied; some required each group of children to act as schedulers, choosing programmes from a variety of titles, for a children's channel. Others took the form of debates about censorship, or reality and fantasy. These small group decision-making sessions were followed by a whole-class feedback discussion, in which each group's choice of schedule, or reasons for decisions, were announced to the class and written on the board; this all-class session was tape-recorded.

The second stage consisted of representatives from each of these groups having a later, round-table discussion in depth, at which one of the researchers was present – this discussion was also tape-recorded. The rest of the class either continued with lessons, or were shown some episodes of the programmes they had been discussing. The second stage varied with the task; in the case of scheduling tasks, for example, children were told that their channel was losing money, and that they had to lose programmes, one by one, until only one was left. The process of discarding, or defending, programmes and the reasons for doing so provided the basic evidence of children's evaluations of different kinds of programme, whether adults' or children's, drama or other genres. In reporting these tasks in this book, the children are not identified by name, but only by gender, and by whether they were the first, second, third, fourth and so on, child to speak in a particular conversation. All conversations took place between groups of 5 or 6 children, and all children in the groups spoke.

Our fourth technique and source of data was one-to-one recorded interviews with professional programme-makers and policy-makers in broadcasting, some of which were conducted during a production observation of *The Prince and the Pauper*, the BBC's adaptation of Mark Twain's novel, broadcast at the end of 1996. In his introduction to *British Cultural Studies* (1990, p. 12), Graeme Turner argued that a method was needed 'to analyze the ways in which [popular] cultural forms and practices produced their *social*, not merely their aesthetic meanings and pleasures. To reconnect the texts with society . . . one was required to think about how culture was structured as a *whole* before one could examine its processes or its constitutive parts.' One of these constitutive parts is the skills, practices and attitudes of the producers of media texts, and their reflections about what they think they are doing. Such views are absent from many critical analyses of popular media, which focus on texts, institutions and audiences, but less frequently on the agency and intentions of creative personnel. In our study, we did not want to make this omission – not least because, as the study was sponsored by the BBC, we would have privileged access to BBC (and other) production personnel, if we wanted it. This was an opportunity not to be missed. Because children are seen as an especially vulnerable audience, whose needs have to be served within some sort of special arrangements in a public service system, we wanted to know what the professional storytellers' conception of the child audience was. Producers' views were used as a background source firstly in the design of the questions and qualitative tasks in the study, and secondly as a further source of interpretation for an analysis of what children thought television drama was doing. The strand contributed by producers to the cultural fabric, of which both media texts and audiences are part, needs to be recognised, as John Corner (1991, p. 71) has pointed out: 'With the possible exception of work on television news, there is not yet the richness of intellectual agenda here which can be traced in the history of work on institutional structures, programme forms, and audiences.'

The account of the study described in this book I hope does some justice to the involvement of the adults who took part in it, and more importantly, to the contributions of the 1,300-plus children. The determination to analyse the data far beyond the requirements of the BBC's original brief, ultimately came from a belief on behalf of us all that the rights of the children in the study to have their views expressed in the public sphere, having taken part in a publicly funded exercise on behalf of a public broadcaster, should be upheld, as an aspect of children's rights more broadly.

The children, on the whole, also enjoyed themselves – a measure of validity I always take seriously when working with children. A group of 8–9 year olds in an inner-London primary school were asked whether they had found a role-playing task, in which they acted as schedulers who had to discard programmes from their schedule, difficult:

SEVERAL VOICES Yes, serious, it felt like we really had to do it. At first everyone agreed but as we had to get rid of each programme it got a lot harder . . . We had to make loads and loads of decisions and hard ones I think. We only had about four minutes but it seemed longer because we were interested in doing it.

Part I

Broadcasting institutions and childhood

1 Children and broadcasting in the 1990s

It should be mixed and something for all ages.

Boy, 9, inner-London primary school

I don't like children's television but just for little children there should be only 1 hour of children's television after school. After 1 hour you should put lots of football on the TV for 5 hours. I think you should make a new channel called BBC sport and get the rights off Sky for Aston Villa Matches. Also please get the rights off Sky for the *Goosebumps* cartoon. And *Shooting Stars* there should be more of. Please get more football. Thanks [name signed].

Boy, 11, inner-city primary school, Cardiff

I like all your programmes. I like best of all cartoon network! I would like to see more programmes please – thank-you. I am very happy [little drawing of smiley face with hair bunches].

Girl, 7, name signed, rural village primary school, Co. Durham

It's too babyish. It's starting to get really terrible. They should make grownups channels for kids too. They should stop the programme with the bus going past where a girl is and the lollipop turns over. They should stop making rude channels after 9. They should make it 12 o'clock or something.

Boy, 11, inner-London primary school

According to Gerbner, Gross, Morgan and Signorielli (1994, p. 17), 'Television is . . . the mainstream of the common symbolic environment into which our children are born and in which we all live out our lives.' Because of this, they argue (1994, pp. 23–4) 'television viewing both shapes and is a stable part of life styles and outlooks. It links the individual to a larger, if synthetic, world, a world of television's own making.' Despite the growing popularity of interactive computer activities among children, television continues to maintain its centrality in children's lives. A recent study in the UK, part of a twelve-nation, European-wide study (Livingstone and Bovill, 1999, p. 29) showed that TV was the most popular leisure-time medium for children, with an average of 147 minutes a day spent watching it, compared to 45 minutes

21

on video games, 28 minutes spent with books and 31 minutes on non-game personal computer (PC) use.

The four quotations above, from children at different ends of the age range in our study, and from widely varying geographical locations, indicate an ease in the 'mainstream' cultural environment of television for these children. Their tone is representative of all the comments that children made in the free comment section of their questionnaires – a tone of confidence in an assumed direct relationship with broadcasters. One of the issues that this chapter will address is whether the nature of this relationship is as 'synthetic' as Gerbner *et al.* suggest, particularly from the point of view of the children consulted in our study.

Two of the children above – typically – address the broadcasters directly, using the term 'you'; a third, in contrast, talks *about* the broadcasters, and addresses us, the readers of the questionnaire. He uses the term 'they', rather than 'you', and confides in the reader his feelings about the shortcomings of contemporary programming 'it's terrible'. The girl, too, writes expressively; characteristically of the younger children in the study, and in contrast to the more critical 11 year olds, she tells the reader she is 'very happy'. Her happiness is addressed directly to the broadcasters, who, for her, encompass much more than the BBC, and seem to be the whole world of television – thus, she congratulates them for the Cartoon Channel, a subscription cable channel, which is nothing to do with the BBC. The two 11-year-old boys write directively, frequently using the term 'should'; they offer advice on content, scheduling, consideration of other audience groups ('1 hour for little children) and censorship ('stop making rude channels after 9'). Common to all is an assumption that their comments and advice will be heard and accepted by people with whom they infer (rightly or wrongly) an equal, and genuine, relationship.

Children in the maw of the monster: politics and regulation

Television has been characterised as a 'one-eyed monster' (Gunter and McAleer, 1990) and adult fears of a monster snatching away their children 'in its maw', as Patricia Palmer pointed out in her study with Australian children in 1986, are ancient and compelling. Thus, the relationship of children to mass culture, and specifically television, to which nearly 100 per cent of all children in developed countries, and an increasing minority in other parts of the world, have access from birth, raises problematic issues of *adult* responsibility: who exactly is in charge of what children get to see in the media? Who should decide what is, or is not, appropriate material for them? Who decides the contents of the cultural 'mainstream' described by Gerbner *et al.*, and who should make what decisions about the positioning, or otherwise, of growing children within it, or outside it? Should children be taught to swim in this stream? Given a lifebelt? Stopped from plunging into it altogether? Fish in it? Taught how to redirect, dam, pollute, or add tributaries to it? Cut it off and dry it out completely? All of these strategies would require different kinds of action from children and the adults responsible for them: different personal choices; media education in schools and in the media themselves; direct action as citizens, with children giving information to providers, not just on their own personal tastes as consumers, but also on the institutional arrangements surrounding broadcasting in their own societies, and the rights of themselves as citizens-in-the-making to comment on, and influence these arrangements politically.

For the children in the study, the actual existence of television and other mass media was hardly an issue. Not one child in the study was unfamiliar with any of the programmes discussed in it (the names of all of which had been generated by children themselves). Television was accepted completely as a naturalised part of their world, and it seemed equally natural to them that the BBC should ask for their opinions on it. Their discussions revealed a concern with its appropriate organisation in order to benefit the maximum number of people, including minority groups. For instance, these 12-year-old Welsh children in an outer-city secondary school, which taught in the Welsh language, discussed the option of doing away with English programmes altogether, because such material did not reflect Welsh identity, but in the end agreed that this would be undemocratic. One boy said: 'We've got to have these English programmes. Even though I would not watch *Slot Meithrin* [a Welsh preschool programme, translated literally as 'Infants' slot'] some people would.'

When the children in the study discussed the possible banning of controversial programmes, adult responsibilities were invoked, for instance, a 9-year-old boy in a Cardiff inner-city primary school declared: 'If parents aren't happy with the programme they don't have to let their children watch it.' A 10-year-old girl in a Buckinghamshire primary school pointed out that protecting little children is a responsibility shared by parents with schedulers: 'You could put it on later when the little children can't watch it.' As these children, pretending to be adults, were clearly aware, implicated in questions of social control are not only the rights of children themselves, but issues of who has rights *over* children. These issues are not confined to broadcasting; the whole relationship of children to adult society, to nation states, to cultural groups and to the international community, in the fields of health, welfare, education, labour, crime and warfare, is subject to an ongoing international debate in the United Nations, UNESCO, the institutions of the European Union, and NGOs such as Save the Children. As this chapter was being written, the World Trade Organisation talks in Seattle in December 1999 broke up with no agreement, partly because poor countries could not accept the employment regulations of rich countries which restrict child-labour.

Regulation and deregulation in Western broadcasting

The characteristics of a deregulatory culture in broadcasting, as distinct from broadcasting as a public service, are commercial. Deregulatory developments have gathered momentum in the 1990s throughout the world (see Blumler and Hoffman-Riem, 1992). These trends have included: the abolition of public service monopolies, and new private commercial entrants to the sector; fewer public service obligations, such as children's provision; and fewer restrictions on advertising and sponsorship. Regulation by national governments becomes increasingly irrelevant with the access to international and global channels provided by satellite technology. In a privatised system, consumer 'sovereignty' replaces the concept of audiences as citizens and they become, not viewers of programmes, but consumers of broadcasting 'product' through paying for access to commercially sponsored and operated channels. These trends have been accompanied by a public discourse which challenges the ethos of public service in broadcasting – much of it in the form of hostile press coverage of children's programming and the contemporary child audience.

As part of our literature review for the BBC, published in 1996, we carried out a review of press articles on the subject of children's relationship with television. The articles we reviewed were characterised by two dominant themes: first that children's television (that is, programmes made specifically for children) was 'dumbing down' and losing quality, however this was defined, and, second, that the child audience had become 'adultified' (as Neil Postman (1982) put it), so that there was no longer any point in treating children as a separate group within the main audience. Adult programmes such as *The X Files* were getting high audience figures among children aged 4–15 (although not necessarily the youngest of these, who are frequently subsumed in the general category, and hence overlooked); therefore, the argument went, there is no point in making special children's shows. Such press comment absolves commercial influences from any 'blame' for these twin trends –

dumbing down, and the disappearance of childhood. A typical comment came from Cosmo Landesman in the Rupert Murdoch-owned *The Sunday Times* of 11 June 1995:

Producers and parents who worry about the state of children's television tend to blame market forces but then they have been doing this since the 1950s when commercial television was first introduced. Cultural change, and not competition, is the real reason why children's television no longer knows what its role is or what sort of service it should provide.

When our report for the Broadcasting Standards Commission was published at the end of 1997 (Davies and Corbett, 1997) showing that the influx of new commercial cable channels was associated with a decline in choice and diversity in children's programming, and arguing that public service values might need defending, there was a great deal of press comment, much of it seizing the opportunity to attack the BBC. The *London Evening Standard* (4 November 1997, p. 24) proclaimed:

The BBC was accused today of being 'lazy' and 'cavalier' in allowing its children's programmes to be dominated by cheap, imported cartoons and was warned it could face changes in the law unless it improved its service. With a stinging rebuke the Broadcasting Standards Commission unveiled the results of a detailed four-year study into all children's TV and said there was no doubt standards had dropped dramatically.

If standards 'have dropped dramatically', this has come about at the same time as the impact of the UK Broadcasting Act, 1990, was making itself felt. This Act was the first major deregulatory legislation in Britain to formalise the new trends. Under this legislation, telecommunication rules were relaxed to allow TV cable companies to provide telephone services, and ITV franchises for commercial stations were to be auctioned to 'highest bidders', not just those with the best schedules, or the most-respected track records in broadcasting. Another provision was an end to a monopoly of in-house production, especially affecting the BBC; 25 per cent of programming was to be made by independent companies. The regulatory body for commercial television in Britain, the IBA (the Independent Broadcasting Authority) was replaced by the ITC (Independent Television Commission) which had a 'lighter touch'. All of this was done in the interests of market efficiency; its goal was to increase commercial competition – including many controversial changes to the BBC, such as an internal market and a system of 'producer choice', whereby producers had to buy resources from the BBC's own departments, or a cheaper external provider.

Some attempts have been made to mitigate the perceived negative effects within the public sphere of the mass deregulation of society's primary medium of communication in the UK. ITV (commercial) companies have to meet 'quality thresholds' to win licence franchises; the commercial channels of Channel 4 and the Welsh-language channel S4C have to continue providing for minorities. Somewhat controversially, the Broadcasting Standards Council (now Commission) was set up to monitor standards, taste and decency, thus initiating a broadcasting regime which, on the one hand, was commercially liberal, and, on the other, apparently morally restrictive – a combination which many saw as the worst of both worlds. The license fee for the BBC continued, and, at the time of writing, is again the subject of public debate and controversy; the BBC are seeking a substantial increase to cover the cost of digitising their services, and, for the first time, there is public resistance to this (76 per cent are unwilling, according to the *Guardian*, 15 December 1999) as well as opposition from the right-wing press. The BBC's Royal Charter was renewed in 1996.

In the midst of all this grown-up wrangling stand the nation's children: always at the forefront of campaigns both to uphold quality and educational standards, and, at the same time, to restrict access to morally harmful material. Children's programming is protected in current British legislation. The 1990 Broadcasting Act in the USA also attempted to make rudimentary provision for 'educational' children's programming by threatening to withhold licence renewal from stations which did not provide a minimum of three hours of children's educational programming per week. It also put some limits on advertising to children. In Britain, the quality thresholds for the commercial ITV companies to hold a franchise must include:

> at least 10 hours a week of programming for children;
> programming must be diverse in genre;
> programming must appeal to different age groups;
> it must be shown at times when children are available to view.

This legislation and the spirit of public service protectionism behind it clearly influenced the discourses of the children in the study. When asked to act as though they were responsible for broadcasting scheduling, they came up with provisions and recommendations almost identical to those listed above. Why this might be so, and how the children had become so aware of the public discourse surrounding broadcasting regulation, and so adept at feeding it back to the researchers 'from the BBC', will be discussed at more length in chapter 5.

Competitive effects

Children were less aware of the commercial implications of the kinds of protectionist regulation they favoured. Even though the research tasks asked them to see themselves as commercial broadcasters, having to discard programmes 'in order to save money', they showed much less awareness of the commercial implications of regulation than of its public service aspects; the words 'money', 'cost', 'commercial', 'payment', 'advertising', almost never appeared in their discourses, despite some tasks specifically requiring them to consider costs.

Producers in the study, in contrast, displayed persistent anxiety about reduced commercial competitiveness because of legislation. Having to conform to the provisions of the 1990 Act, according to Vanessa Chapman (interviewed for Davies and Corbett, 1997), former Controller of Children's and Youth Programmes at the ITV Network Centre, had created real commercial difficulties:

I suspect if it [the legislation] hadn't been there we wouldn't have the range of children's programming that we have now . . . I actually have to fulfil some criteria and some mandates . . . Here I am looking at the coldest, hardest commercial situation, sometimes feeling as if both my hands are tied behind my back. And that's not because I think there's something wrong with regulation, the reality is that without it, CITV [Children's ITV] might not have survived as long as it has. And I think that's [true] the world over.

Chapman's dilemma is, indeed, found all over the world, where finding a balance between public service goals and finding enough money for the production of quality children's programming often seems incompatible, leading to a reliance on foreign, especially American, imports. An international attempt to formulate the ideal political relations of the child to adult society, and the corresponding responsibilities of adult societies towards children, is the United Nations Convention on the Rights of the Child (1989), ratified by 191 nation members of the UN (only two nations – the USA and Somalia – have not ratified it), which devotes a number of clauses and articles to the question of children, media and culture.

In the UN convention, parents are identified as the people with 'responsibilities, rights and duties' for the child (Article 5), and from whom the child has a right 'not to be separated' (Article 9). This suggests that parents are the ultimate arbiters of children's cultural consumption, at least for what is consumed domestically. The Convention sometimes seems to imply that state broadcasting organisations, or commercial corporations, have the right to override, or ignore, the wishes of parents when it comes to judging what is appropriate and suitable for children to see and hear. This is an issue of acute political concern in the United States, where parents' groups have successfully objected to certain kinds of teaching materials in schools and books in libraries. The Convention provides for the 'right of the child to express an opinion and to have that opinion taken into account, in any matter or procedure affecting the child' (Article 12).

Article 17 of the Convention is the section dealing with mass media and culture in most depth. It stresses the importance of 'protection' in the state's responsibility towards children:

The role of the media in disseminating information to children that is consistent with moral well-being and knowledge and understanding among peoples and respects the child's cultural background. The State is to take measures to encourage this, and to protect children from harmful materials.

Article 17 further specifies that mass media should: 'disseminate information and material of social and cultural benefit to the child'; 'encourage international co-operation . . . from a diversity of cultural, national and international sources'; encourage the production of children's books; attend to the 'linguistic needs' of minority and indigenous children; and provide guidelines to protect children from 'injurious' material. The other article concerning children's relationship with cultural forms and institutions, Article 13, further provides for the child's right to freedom of expression and information: 'This right shall include freedom to seek, receive and impart information and ideas of all kinds, regardless of frontiers, either orally, in writing or in print, in the form of art, or through any other media of the child's choice.'

The child's right to *receive* information 'regardless of frontiers', lays open the possibility of conflict between different sets of rights: between parents, charged with duties and responsibilities for children, and media regulators, charged with 'protecting' children from 'injurious' material, and media providers – global entertainment corporations, toy manufacturers, World Wide Web providers and print publishers – seeking to profit from the child's 'right' to information. It also raises challenges for media producers who, while respecting the right of the child to have his or her own cultural background respected, also reserves the right to the freedom to represent, for instance, girls in equal roles with boys (not universally culturally accepted) or to use adult language, or to deal with sensitive topics such as pregnancy or homosexuality, in certain kinds of programming.

The conflict about who is the best arbiter for what is appropriate material for children – parents or producers – has been a fault line for many of the children's producers we interviewed throughout their professional lives. Anna Home, formerly head of children's programming at the BBC, now head of the British Children's Film Foundation and instrumental in the Children and Television World Summit movement, pointed out in an interview (Davies and O'Malley, 1996, p. 140) that she often overrode potential parental objections in making editorial judgements about what was realistic in children's drama: 'Often I think parents are unaware of the world in which their kids live – and they are concerned when we talk about things in programmes which they don't think are of concern to their kids, but I think they often are.'

Global views

The debate – at least within the broadcasting industry – about the child's right to information has been taken forward on a global scale by the 'Children and Television World Summit' movement, of which Anna Home is one of the leading organisers – a group of concerned broadcasters for children, who to date have held two international meetings on children and television. The summits have been primarily industry-based – not least because the financial resources to bring delegates and technologies from all around the world are more likely to be forthcoming within the media industry, than within educational or charitable organisations. However, educators and NGOs have been represented at the two summits held so far – the first in Melbourne in 1995, the second in London in 1998. Another 'Summit', organised by The Alliance for Children and Television, The American Center for Children and the Media, The Association for Media Literacy and The Jesuit Communication Project – all North American non-profit organisations – took place in Toronto in May 2000. This had equal representation of academics, educators and industry representatives, but there was intense post-conference discussion about the level of industry sponsorship (necessary to finance any large conference) and whether this compromised the principles of media education. The issue of the world market of children's screen culture is clearly capable of attracting both a great deal of commercial sponsorship and increasing scholarly interest.

The industry world summits addressed the survival of local cultural programming, particularly in non-Western countries and the difficulty of providing home-grown, non-American cultural representations on children's television. The issue of whether special children's broadcasting services are still necessary in the multichannel age, in the age of the Internet, and in an age when children are presumed to be more sophisticated, and less in need of specialised provision, is of particular concern to people whose jobs depend on such services, and who consider that their expertise is an essential ingredient for a proper broadcasting system. As John Marsden (interviewed for the BBC study in spring, 1996), in charge of animation at Carlton UK, a commercial company, put it:

I think most of the people working with children have a discipline in themselves. We are all slightly privileged not to come from a commercially driven area, we come from a public broadcasting tradition . . . and unfortunately we are having to become a lot more commercially edged. Channel 3 [the main independent commercial channel in the UK] was almost totally funded by money from ITV [Independent Television] stations, we didn't have to look to other countries for income to make programmes, so we could actually make those programmes for children in the UK. It's changing in the fact that we can't make programmes solely for the British market.

The broadcasting model in the UK, as outlined by Marsden, has been seen internationally as a model children's service (Palmer, 1988). However, recent changes in Britain, as analysed in a study for the Broadcasting Standards Commission (Davies and Corbett, 1997), reflect accelerating international trends of change, in particular the increasing penetration of North American channels and programmes. New technologies of satellite and cable have brought specialist children's channels, such as Nickelodeon, Disney, the Cartoon Network and Fox Kids, from the United States during the 1990s, with schedules almost entirely filled with imported programming made in the USA. This is not just a matter of commercial penetration and competition, it is also an issue of different attitudes to the child audience, reflected in different styles of programming. This is especially an issue in the most universal of children's forms, animation, a form which increasingly dominates children's provision both in cable and on terrestrial channels. Marsden (interviewed for the BBC study in spring, 1996) pointed out:

The Japanese style of animation is particularly graphic; you can see people with their heads chopped off, cracked open with great hammers, etc. . . . I wouldn't want my children to be exposed to that . . . it's just not necessary to show . . . graphic . . . sexual activity . . . In a lot of countries this is an acceptable form of animation. In France they've got a series called 'The Naughty Nun', you wouldn't have seen over here . . . not for children.

Traditional children's programming in the UK

In protecting children from 'naughty nuns' and dismembered skulls, as well as in having regulations for positive educational provision, traditional children's programming in the UK has sometimes been accused of being 'paternalist' (for example, Oswell, 1995; Buckingham et al., 1997). The children in our study had absorbed these traditions. Many of their remarks indicated that they themselves required a degree of 'paternalism' in judgements about what is appropriate entertainment, and that, if it is not imposed, they may generate it, for example, this 12-year-old's comments in the free comment section of the questionnaire:

I think children's programmes should be more exciting and dramatic but should not show bad language or fighting. (Girl, 12, outer-London primary school)

This protectiveness was particularly evident when children were making judgements on behalf of younger children. Here, as above, in the case of children representing adults discussing a ban, the children in the study behaved like adult members of a distinctly bourgeois (in the sense of taste, as well as citizenship) public sphere. They demonstrated a recognition that judgements made about public provision of services required citizenship perspectives, which tended to be more conservative and consensual. Private judgements, on the other hand, could be more permissive, as, for example, that of a 10-year-old girl in Oxfordshire, writing in the free comment section of the questionnaire:

I like watching blood thirsty and action-packed films on Sky. I want the films from the cinema to come more quicker on Sky. I like watching Disney films and action-packed cartoons like *Battle Tech*.

The contrasts between these positions reflected not only differences between individual children, and groups in the study, but also children's competence in accessing different kinds of cultural representations in order to express different roles – whether a citizenship role, or a consumer role. Use of judgemental terms (reflecting adult terminology) such as 'bad language' suggested a 'citizenship' perspective, contrasting with the use of (equally adult) publicity material jargon – 'action-packed' – by the 'consumer' child who wanted films 'more quicker' on Sky.

The official child audience

According to Hartley (1992, p. 9), the whole concept of audience is 'an invisible fiction' – an unknowable entity, a social construct in the way in which 'childhood' is a social construct, for defining, and exerting power over different groups in the population. The major construct of the audience in terms of the institutional future of broadcasting in the public sphere is the child audience according to official ratings figures. Ratings are the audience numbers collected by the Broadcasters' Audience Research Board (BARB) in the UK, and by A. C. Neilsen in the USA, which determine income from advertisers. In the case of the non-commercial BBC, they are a major measure of their public support, and, hence, justification for charging a licence fee to every household owning a television set.

Ratings can be unreliable in a variety of greater and lesser ways, ranging from unrepresentative sampling, to viewer error, to statistical error, but are nevertheless accepted as a common currency across the broadcasting and advertising industries for establishing who is watching, and listening to, what programmes and when. At the time of our study, regular information about the size of the child audience was collected by BARB from a socially representative sample of 4,435 homes in the UK, including approximately 1,750 children between the ages of 4 and 15. As channels proliferate and audiences fragment into smaller groups, the sub-groups of the sample (for example, 4- to 7-year-old boys, in a particular region, in a particular socio-economic group, watching Nickelodeon) become infinitesimally small. For many cable channels, no audience sizes can be measured, because the numbers of people in the sample may be less than one. In a multichannel world, this is going to create considerable difficulties in the enterprise of 'controlling' audiences via measurement; but it will have to be done because, in a commercial media industry, measuring and evaluating the audience is a fundamental economic requirement.

The child audience in the UK, as elsewhere, is a permanent minority. In the UK, people under 16 constitute around 20.6 per cent of the population as a whole, according to 1995 estimates. Even allowing for social constructions of childhood, resting on arbitrary cultural distinctions, the official child audience of 4–15 year olds also encompasses a very wide range of human development and experience. A 4 year old is a very different person from a 15 year old. He or she is also a different person from a 5 year old, who, in Britain, will already have started full-time school, and will therefore, for instance, have more understanding of what a school-based drama programme like *Grange Hill* is about. Children's producers are faced with having to subdivide this minority audience into still smaller minorities in order to serve the assumed differing needs and tastes of these precise age/experience groups. The problem for producers in trying to attract the maximum proportion of all 4–15 year olds, is that younger children often watch programmes intended for older children, which raises problems of 'suitability' as well as of comprehension, whereas older children do not often watch programmes made for very young children, not least because they have already been young children and do not want to revisit this state. As a 9-year-old girl in a study I carried out in Philadelphia, USA, put it: 'I don't need to watch *Sesame Street* because I already know this stuff' (Davies, 1997, p. 134).

The 1990 Broadcasting Act made it a legal requirement for all commercial companies applying for a broadcasting franchise that they should include a range of programmes for children in their schedules. There is no such legislative requirement laid on the BBC. At the time of

Table 1. *Shares of the 4–15-year TV audience between 1991 and 1995 (percentage)*

YEAR	BBC	ITV	SATELLITE/CABLE
1991	44	49	7
1992	41	51	8
1993	40	50	10
1994	37	52	11
1995	35	50	15

Source: Television Quarterly, Broadcasting Research Dept, BBC.

the 1990 Act, the BBC was deemed to be providing the standard baseline of children's programme provision, as part of its public service remit. It was against this baseline that the performance of commercial companies could be measured. In the UK, BBC and ITV are thus in strong competition with each other for the 4–15 audience – and, in satellite/cable households, they are increasingly in competition with specialist children's channels, such as Nickelodeon, the Children's Channel, the Cartoon Network and Disney, as well as 'adult' channels, such as Sky 1 and the Movie Channel. The fluctuating shares of the child audience between BBC, ITV and Satellite/Cable over the five years prior to the study can be seen in Table 1.

The share of the child audience going to satellite/cable channels, with children's schedules based almost entirely on animation and imports, more than doubled in the time period up to our study, and it was mostly at the expense of the BBC, rather than ITV. However, children do not only watch satellite/cable for the purpose of watching cartoons; boys between 10 and 15, in particular, are more likely to sample adult programmes such as sport (*source*: Children's Satellite Viewing: Quarter 2, 1995, BBC Broadcasting Research Services).

Children's viewing behaviour

Children are seen as a necessary target for media producers, and worth wooing and understanding. Children are also characterised as a source of public concern in terms of feared media effects and ideological contamination. Hence, in addition to the constant monitoring of child consumption and leisure habits by market research companies, there have recently been several major publicly funded surveys of children's media behaviour – a sign that, as rapid technological innovation is forcing change, so the relationship of children to media moves into the public sphere to become a matter of social concern. The most recent large-scale analysis of children's screen-leisure behaviour in the UK has come from a study by Sonia Livingstone, Moira Bovill, George Gaskell and their team, of the London School of Economics (Livingstone and Bovill, 1999), part of a European wide survey of 'young people and new media'. The study surveyed 1,303 young people aged 6–17, including 334 diaries of detailed media use. Within this sample, 100 per cent had a TV set; 96 per cent had a video cassette recorder (VCR); 67 per cent had a video-linked games machine; 42 per cent had access to cable/ satellite multichannel television; and 53 per cent had a personal computer in the home. Livingstone and Bovill found evidence of what they called a new 'bedroom culture': 63 per cent of their sample had TVs in their bedrooms and 34 per cent had a video-games machine there. Only 5 per cent had access to satellite/cable in their bedrooms; and only 12 per cent had access to a PC in the bedroom, so moral concerns about children secretly accessing forbidden and unregulated material via new television and computer technology still only apply to a small minority of children. Of more concern, given that society is supposedly moving towards an economy and an education system reliant on access to, and competence in using, computer technology, Livingstone and Bovill also found very marked gender differences in access; 78 per cent of boys and only 56 per cent of girls had video games, and there was a huge difference in bedroom access with 48 per cent of boys and only 19 per cent of girls with PCs in their own rooms. Within this small group, girls used computers for non-game activities at home for 20 minutes a day less than boys, that is, for only an average of 11 minutes a day. There were also significant social class differences in access to computers, with 58 per cent of social grade ABC1 (professional class) children having access to a PC at home, and only 30 percent of C2DE (lower middle/ working class) children having such access.

Our study was a younger sample (primarily children aged 6–12) than Livingstone and Bovill's, but the data were gathered during almost the same time period and, although our sample was not scientifically randomised, many of our findings parallel theirs, which suggests that our sample, like theirs, was a reasonably valid representation of the child viewing population in the UK. It consisted of 1,332 5–13 year olds in seventeen schools in England and Wales, plus approximately 40 children in a pilot study in Essex, in the East of England. Further details of the sample are given in chapter 6 and in Appendix 1.

Like Livingstone and Bovill, we also asked children about their viewing behaviour, although not about other forms of screen-media use, since dramatised storytelling was not a primary function of new media

Table 2. *Proportion (percentage) of boys, girls and all children saying that they watched/had access to the following channels*

	Percentage answering 'yes'			Percentage answering 'no'			Percentage answering 'not sure'		
	All	boys	girls	All	boys	girls	All	boys	girls
TV in bedroom	53	59	46	47	40	54	0	1	0
Satellite/cable	43	46	40	43	44	42	14	10	18
Nickelodeon	38	37	39	55	56	54	7	7	7
Disney Channel	44	41	47	50	54	47	6	5	7
TCC	30	32	29	58	59	58	12	10	14
Cartoon Network	47	47	45	46	48	46	7	4	9
Children's BBC (CBBC)	84	80	88	12	15	8	5	5	4
Children's ITV (CITV)	68	68	69	24	26	23	7	6	8
Children's Channel 4	44	43	44	43	44	42	13	12	15

as yet. The viewing-behaviour section of our questionnaire asked children whether they had TV in their bedroom; whether they had satellite or cable; and whether they watched a number of channels offering children's programming, including BBC1, ITV and Channel 4, as well as the specialised cable children's channels. A breakdown of their answers, first according to gender, and then according to age group, is given in Tables 2 and 3.

Table 2 shows that over half of our sample had a TV in their bedroom. The proportion – 43 per cent – of children who said they had satellite/cable is virtually the same as the Livingstone sample of 42 per cent, which suggests that our sample was demographically not widely dissimilar to theirs. Children's BBC (CBBC) received by far the greatest number of 'yes' responses to the question 'Do you watch this channel?' – 84 per cent overall, with more girls (88 per cent) than boys (80 per cent) answering 'yes'. Children's ITV (CITV) was next with 68 per cent overall, nearly equally shared between boys and girls. Of the specialist cable/satellite channels, the Cartoon Network did best, with 47 per cent of children answering 'yes'. The gender differences in these answers were virtually negligible – it is likely that they would have been greater, as with Livingstone and Bovill's sample, in answer to questions about new media use. At the time of our study, therefore, TV remained a leisure and information medium widely and equally used by both sexes.

Table 3 shows obvious age differences in bedroom access to TV and there was a marked increase from age 10 onwards, rising from 48 per

Table 3. *Proportion (percentage) of children in different age groups saying they watched/had access to the following channels*

	Percentage of children								
	age 5	6	7	8	9	10	11	12	13
TV in bedroom	40	47	45	41	48	60	64	65	25
Satellite/cable	22	50	36	40	42	47	42	49	75
Nickelodeon	22	58	43	40	32	36	35	32	86
Disney Channel	40	62	61	46	45	36	30	38	43
TCC	50	43	39	22	31	26	26	27	86
Cartoon Network	38	69	61	51	47	41	33	36	0
Children's BBC (CBBC)	56	90	86	79	89	83	78	84	88
Children's ITV (CITV)	67	78	75	65	68	74	60	66	38
Children's Channel 4	67	66	56	41	43	41	33	35	25

cent at 9 to over 60 per cent at 10 – an age-related 'watershed' which we observed in other parts of the data, including children's opinions. Younger children – 6–7 year olds – were more likely than older children to watch the Cartoon Network and Children's ITV, and in general the figures showed a downward trend in viewing satellite/cable channels as the age range went up. None of the figures showed an *increase* in viewing these specialised channels as children got older; children's BBC held up best across the age range, with 84 per cent of 12 year olds and 86 per cent of 7 year olds saying they watched it. Thus, the evidence from our study suggests that the terrestrial networks still scored with most children in terms of regular access and familiarity over new channels – and, perhaps unexpectedly, this was more likely the older the child.

Children and channel choice

Many children in the study had absorbed the multichannel argument that, if more choice in programming was to be provided, the answer was more channels, for example, this 9-year-old girl from a suburban primary school in Oxfordshire, in the free comment section on her questionnaire:

I think there should be more children's programmes on a Sunday. I think there is too much grown ups' programmes. I think there should be more programmes for the whole family. I think there should be more channels.

Another 10-year-old girl, in a village primary school in Buckinghamshire, saw channels as ways of targeting different audiences:

I think you should have grown up programmes on the Channel 5 and Channel 6. Children's on 1 and 4 and science, the future, the past and other varieties on 2, 3, 6 and 7.

Younger children, too, were aware of the option of having a special channel for special genres of programming, as in the case of this 8-year-old girl in a rural primary school in Co. Durham:

I would like you to put on more cartoons about witches and monsters. And call it the spooky channel.

Changing choices: from 2 to 10 channels

One of the most revealing sections of the questionnaire was a simulated 'channel-choice' task in which children were asked to choose, first between 2 programmes on 2 channels, then between 3 channels, then 5, then 10. More information about the outcome of this exercise is given in chapter 4 on the child as broadcasting consumer. However, it is worth commenting briefly on the results here, in the context of predictions about what children may do in the new multichannel dispensation, and what they actually did do in this exercise. Table 4 shows how children 'voted' at the 10-channel stage. Programmes were selected by the research team on the basis of shows popular at the time, as identified in our pilot study. The final 10-channel schedule also included, as in real-world schedules, 50 per cent cartoons. Because the focus of research was on drama, we were particularly interested in the fate of drama programmes across this series of choices. We were most interested to see the fate of *Byker Grove*, a continuing drama series about a youth centre, produced in the UK by the independent company Zenith North for the BBC, scheduled in the Children's BBC 5.10 p.m. slot, and aimed at older children and early teenagers.

Table 4 shows how the spread of scores across channels, allied to the spread across age groups, produced great variability in choices. However, there were some patterns. Nearly every programme received at least some votes among some age groups, so a channel mix like this would presumably have something for nearly all children, albeit relatively small numbers of them. This spread of programmes, appealing to different age groups, looks like an argument for the apparently greater 'choice' offered by more channels. However, within the diversity of choice, there is little diversity of genre, with cartoons predominating. If further choices were made available, the spread of scores would become even thinner, with more zero scores for some programmes. Bearing in mind the hypothetical nature of the exercise, this final 10-choice stage suggested that, in a multichannel environment, boys and girls may

Table 4. *Proportion (percentage) of children in each age group for 10-channel TV choices*

Programme choice	Percentage of children								
	age 5 (base 10)	6 (base 118)	7 (base 186)	8 (base 186)	9 (base 230)	10 (base 193)	11 (base 266)	12 (base 108)	13 (base 8)
Rugrats (children's cartoon)	0	0	13	9	10	9	8	7	13
Byker Grove (UK children's drama)	0	4	4	4	5	6	5	3	0
Art Attack (UK children's art programme)	0	6	7	8	9	10	7	8	0
Friends (US adult comedy)	0	2	4	9	5	12	21	29	50
Home and Away (Australian soap)	0	5	4	7	11	13	15	19	25
Garfield (US animation)	10	1	5	4	4	1	5	1	13
Power Rangers (US children's adventure)	30	25	22	10	5	3	1	1	0
Ace Ventura (US animation)	20	23	23	28	35	27	18	20	0
Scooby Doo (US animation)	40	27	18	10	6	7	4	2	0
Ren and Stimpy (US animation)	0	7	5	12	10	12	17	9	0

polarise, with girls choosing narrative dramas – soaps, sitcom and children's drama like *Byker Grove* – whereas boys will tend to opt for cartoons and action-adventure. The programme which most sustained its appeal for both sexes throughout the exercise was *Art Attack*, ITV's art-skills programme; this magazine, 'edutainment' format seemed to be one of the safest options for attracting all sections of the child audience.

The best the realistic, UK-produced children's drama representative, *Byker Grove*, could hope for, if our multichannel simulation predicted real world behaviour, was a small, loyal core of children of both sexes, fairly stable across the age range, which would be around 4 to 5 per cent of the child audience as a whole. This finding would not be good news for those wanting to justify spending money on expensive children's drama, which would apparently only appeal to a small fraction of the available audience, unless, of course, it could be sold overseas. But a programme with such specific local appeal, set in the north-east of England, about 'a load of Geordies' as one 12-year-old boy, himself from the north-east, described it, would not have international marketing appeal. Thus, in the multichannel universe which is on the way, programmes like *Byker Grove*, which emphasise and reinforce children's local identity – as recommended in the United Nations Convention on the Rights of the Child – may have an uncertain future. This Welsh 11-year-old boy was forthright in his views that cartoons were for 'babies', and for cartoons to drive out drama would be an undesirable development for children like him:

I would like to see a lot [of] drama on telly. I hate to see too much children's cartoons because they're on every day of the week, even on the weekend. There should be more interesting programmes for children that have grown out of cartoons.

Children on the multichannel future

A group of children aged 9–11 in a Buckinghamshire village primary school, were asked what channels they normally watched and whether one was better than another. The discussion began with the subject of commercials. These were not recognised as financially necessary; they were seen, as by many adults, as an irritant and an interruption. The conversation was moved on by the interviewer to more general questions of programme financing, and Boy 1 expressed scepticism about the financial probity of the people running the system, using the characteristic voice of the disempowered. He did not use the word 'us' to mean 'us children', he used it to mean 'us' the audience, the general public. None of these children had satellite/cable at home, but all demonstrated an awareness of the impact of the arrival of new channels on the choice, range and public usefulness of programming generally:

GIRL 1   One good thing about BBC1 is that you do not have any commercials. For example they come when you are sitting watching *Coronation Street*.

INTERVIEWER   Who pays for the programmes on ITV?

GENERAL COMMENTS   Me, me, me, the managers and all that, all the people on the managing staff.

INTERVIEWER   Where do they get the money from?

BOY 1   People are willing to give the money.

BOY 2   They rob us.

BOY 3   The lottery.

GIRL 2   But the lottery is on Channel 1 [BBC1].

INTERVIEWER   And how do BBC1 get the money for the programmes?

BOY 1   From the TV licences.

. . .

INTERVIEWER   Do you think that the news is important?

BOY 2   The news is, yeah.

GIRL 1   It is important for people to know what is going on in the world.

BOY 3   They should add on a channel with just news on it.

BOY 2   They do, but it is on satellite.

INTERVIEWER   Do any of you have satellite?

ALL   No.

BOY 2   There is no point because it is just repeats. They just show the same films four times a week, it is always the same film. . .

INTERVIEWER   What do you think the people who put the programmes on think about when they are choosing the programmes?

BOY 1   They think about the other people, their age, and what they think they like.

. . .

GIRL 2   In magazines sometimes they have this poll to ask what we like and then they send them to the station and then they see what the audience like.

This conversation ranges from a degree of cynicism about the behaviour and motives of broadcasters – 'they rob us' – to a touching faith in the broadcasters' willingness to consult the needs of the general public and different groups within it – 'other people, their age, and what they think they like'. Although the children were aware that more specialised programme choices, such as news, could be offered by 'adding on a channel', comments about the existing satellite/cable provision offered more proof of scepticism: 'There is no point, it is just repeats.' In general, when children were acting as channel controllers themselves, financial considerations, and even taking systematic steps to 'have a poll' to find out what their audiences liked, were not prioritised. However, this is not to say that these children were ignorant of the different methods of financing broadcasting. This 12 year old, in his questionnaire, expressed awareness of the financial drawbacks of the universal licence fee, as opposed to advertising:

I think you [the BBC] are a bit over the top about not advertising. Why do people have to have a TV licence if they are perfectly happy not to have the BBC channels and just cable? (Boy, 12, outer-London secondary school)

Other children expressed confident familiarity with the new media landscape. A 9-year-old Asian girl in an inner-London primary was an experienced satellite/cable watcher, according to the comments on her questionnaire. She may be the voice of the future:

I watch Sky. Sky has lots of channels like Nickelodeon, Cartoon Network, TCC, Disney Channel. Sky is not like cable, because cable has a little bit more channels than Sky.

But some, unlike this girl, referred to all cable and satellite channels with the generic term 'Sky' (News Corporation, headed by Rupert Murdoch):

Please can you put more Sky programmes on CBBC and CITV because I haven't got Sky and I would like to see what is on Sky and please can you take some cartoons off. (Boy, 10, inner-city primary school, Cardiff)

This boy obviously believed that BBC and ITV had the power to put Sky (or satellite/cable) programmes in their schedules at will; and there is, indeed, an increasing cross-over, or 'windowing' of programmes made for cable channels, being shown on terrestrial channels, and vice versa, as in the case of *Rugrats*, made by Nickelodeon, shown on both Nickelodeon and BBC1. Again, this plea is a pointer to the future, although his request to 'take some cartoons off' is unlikely to be met (see Davies and Corbett, 1997).

Children in the market

What are the implications of all this? Despite ambitious predictions of a total change in the televiewing habits of the nation thanks to multi-channel digitisation of broadcasting, the children in our sample, as in Livingstone's, were still wedded to, and appreciative of, the BBC/ITV duopoly, with a taste for occasional viewing of other channels. The largest audience ratings in our sample were still going to terrestrial programming, although, obviously, as Table 4 reveals, all channel shares inexorably drop as more channels become available. This is a mathematical inevitability which should not surprise anybody, yet it often does. Anxieties about fragmenting audiences and their implications for the future of broadcast entertainment and information continue to focus on declining audience numbers, and have led to an intensification of public debate and examination of the present and future state of the electronic media, especially where children and the young are concerned.

Such has been the degree of concern over these changes that, in recent years, an unusually large number of academics have been asked by broadcasters and regulatory bodies to review the implications of the deregulatory and technological changes in broadcasting for child audiences. Broadcasters and other professional communicators are not always sympathetic to academic methods of inquiry, so this growth-industry of scholarly research is perhaps an indication of the intensity of concern felt by broadcasters and their regulators both for the future of their livelihoods, and for their traditional public service responsibilities. This applies both in Britain and elsewhere in the world, including in the USA. Public service broadcasting (PSB) responsibilities were compara-tively simple to defend in a monopolistic, or duopolistic system where most decisions could be taken centrally; public service for children becomes much harder to define, and defend, in a free-market multi-channel global system. Hence, children as broadcasting consumers and citizens have become a much-researched topic in the last decade.

Studies carried out to review deregulatory trends and their impact on children include those by Palmer (1988) and Kline (1993) in the USA, Blumler (1992), in the UK, on behalf of the Broadcasting Standards Commission; Davies and Corbett (1997), who did an update of Blum-ler's study, also for the Broadcasting Standards Commission; Buck-ingham, Davies, Kelley and Jones (1999), in a study funded by the British Economic Social and Research Council (ESRC); Lohr and Meyer (1999), on German and other European children's current media use and Keys and Buckingham's 1999 Australian-produced collection, *Children's Television Policy: International Perspectives*. There was also the study reported in this book, funded by the BBC. The most extensive of all these scholarly researches is the Livingstone and Bovill study quoted above – part of a twelve-nation review of children and screen media across Europe. This was funded by a number of commer-cial and public organisations including the Advertising Association, the BBC, the Broadcasting Standards Commission, the ITC and the Eur-opean Parliament.

Reading these reports, including one of my own (Davies and Corbett, 1997) one becomes aware of some disagreement among media aca-demics about the value of public service broadcasting, about broad-casting generally, and about the nature of children's 'needs' in the area of screen entertainment. American scholars such as Edward Palmer (1988) are concerned to campaign for good educational programming as a compensatory right for the poorest children in American society – something which, Palmer argues, the exclusively commercial American broadcasters owe to the culture which, from the outset in the 1920s, had handed them free use of the airwaves and made them rich. British scholars, on the other hand, writing within a society which remembers the BBC as an organisation which used to require radio announcers to wear evening suits and black ties, are much less exercised about children's 'rights' to compensatory education, or the need to soften the excesses of commercialism in the system as a whole. They have expressed much more concern about the dangers of the 'worthy, paternalistic constructions of childhood' (Buckingham *et al.*, 1999, p. 189), which can be seen as representing undesirable conservative attitudes, and a lack of respect for children's populist and, to adults, vulgar tastes.

Concerns among media scholars about a lack of recognition of children's needs and tastes, have converged with concerns in sociological childhood studies about the constructed nature of childhood itself, and the importance of recognising cultural diversity in children's experiences, including the fact that, for many children, childhood (in the sense of being a protected space) ends early. Such arguments can lead to a view that there may be no need for regulation protecting child television audiences, or for any kinds of special programming provision for children at all. If this were so, it would certainly save the BBC and the ITV network centre a great deal of money, and would provide golden marketing opportunities for purely commercial organisations such as Disney to fill the gap in provision for children's entertainment left by the departure of the protected PSB networks. As Buckingham *et al.* (1999) point out, this is where another set of interests start converging with those of media scholars and childhood theorists: the interests of the marketplace – an alliance they describe as potentially 'unholy'.

The polarity between paternalistic public service/education and unfettered marketing, is in practice often an artificial one. In Britain, ITV, Channel 5 and especially Channel 4, because of its minority remit, fulfil public service obligations, as the BBC is required to do. A further argument for PSB is, and always has been – particularly in the USA – that the market does not provide some kinds of minority-interest programming, such as shows aimed at Hispanic children, or Welsh children, or programmes about esoteric interests like classical music, or 'unpopular' topics, such as the news. The special argument for a public service model of children's broadcasting is that children do not yet have enough experience of all kinds of cultural products to know what they most like, and what they most dislike; a range of material needs to be made available to them in order for them to decide, if only to become effective cultural 'consumers'. Because of their rapid developmental changes, too, what children like and dislike will vary at different stages of their growing up. There is, finally, the paternalistic, and maternalistic, case that, whether children like things or not, some things are good for them and they should have them anyway: this is the case for special news programmes for children, for instance, and for programmes in which minorities are equally and sympathetically represented.

Representation

Politically, the argument for PSB representing a diversity of interests is a democratic one: that all children should have the opportunity to access the accumulated hoards of cultural capital, which are usually reserved primarily for middle-class children, including literature, music, the arts, current affairs and general knowledge. This can be seen as élitist, but, given that children are not forced to watch or listen to anything, it can only be seen as élitist if children have no access to other kinds of material as a corrective. Providing access to 'high culture' capital does not logically preclude children, including middle-class ones (and adults), from enjoying more demotic pleasures such as the frenetic game show, *Mad for It* (Carlton) which parodies adult programmes like *Blind Date* and *Stars in their Eyes*, and includes regular baths in 'gunge' for the participants (Davies and Andrewartha, 2000). Neither did access to an élite, middle-class culture on the Home Service of BBC radio or BBC TV, in the 1950s, prevent working-class children from enjoying other lower-brow pleasures at the time. In the days of the BBC monopoly, working-class children who were bored with the Home Service's middle-class representations, could listen to BBC radio's Light Programme with its offerings of popular music and vaudeville variety shows. If they wanted to escape the radio and television at home, they had many opportunities to go out by themselves and enjoy populist entertainment, such as Saturday morning cinema clubs (see Staples, 1997), a wide range of cheap comics, cheap access to professional sport, and plenty of public play spaces, including the streets and the fields – pleasures and freedoms long since vanished from the lives of most working-class children.

The issue then, is not whether children are unjustly denied access to representations of working-class life – which for working-class children is their own life; they are not, nor were they in the past. The issue is the presumed power of broadcasting to normalise certain kinds of cultural values and standards and to 'make' working-class children (or other groups, such as ethnic minorities, or girls) feel marginalised and excluded from the mainstream of society. This is clearly a political issue about the constitution of the public sphere, which should extend beyond the values of the bourgeoisie. But, where children are concerned, the issue is also one of 'effects' and 'impact'. With children, there is often an assumption that they are being harmed in some way by media representations: in this case, by having only a narrow, élitist range of cultural representations made available to them by broadcasters. Like all claims for effects, this is very much harder to 'prove'.

Public service for children also includes a recognition of their needs and rights to childish entertainment – to 'fun'. The market *may* provide shows such as *Mad for It*, which are commercial and down-market, but the very continuation of Carlton's children's service, including its down-market game shows and its cartoons, as Vanessa Chapman pointed out, is dependent on regulation and a public service ethos. The essence of a PSB schedule, as many of our interviewees argued, is not to rule out commercially attractive genres such as gunge-dunking games, but to provide a framework which can guarantee diversity – a diversity both of genre, and of audience-appeal.

These were the values most frequently expressed by the child-schedulers in this study. The following comments from a group of 12-year-old boys in an outer-city secondary school in Cardiff, give an example. Their schedule began with the comedy drama for young children, *Fudge*, followed by the cartoon *Rugrats*, with two factual programmes – *Live and Kicking* and *Newsround* – in the middle, and ended with the more adult cartoon *Ren and Stimpy* and the pop-music show, *Top of the Pops*. They justified it as follows:

We came to a decision that we should put programmes for younger children, e.g. *Fudge*, first and then work up through the ages gradually and finishing with *Top of the Pops*, with *Newsround* in the middle because we think it's important for children to know what's going on in the world.

The desirability of diversity as a primary need for children was the implication of the analysis of programming provision between 1992 and 1996 in our Broadcasting Standards Commission report (Davies and Corbett, 1997). The ideal schedule is one in which drama, factual, entertainment, preschool and animation are broadly balanced, and in which there is diversity of origin – that is, home-grown and regional programming, and programming from Europe, Canada, Australia and other parts of the world, as well as from the dominant USA. The report, when it was published in 1997, was controversial because it implied that the new multichannel era was reducing choice on all channels, including the terrestrial PSB broadcasters, which were overdominated by car-toons. The broadcasters were not happy with this apparently critical message, and neither were our fellow-scholars, who pointed out, some in letters to the press, that the cartoon form contains some of the great art works of our civilisation – the *Guardian* cartoonist Steve Bell produced a half-page cartoon on the topic himself, to illustrate the point.

The difficulty of putting children's storytelling or other kinds of entertainment into rigid generic categories, for the purpose of this kind of analysis, was also pointed out. The all-purpose category 'children's' is as problematic as any – and is a problem for children's literature too. As Peter Hunt (1992, p. 6) argued:

Children's literature is a maverick . . . it is generally defined in terms of its audience, and the concept of that audience shifts with time and place; and it is written for a subservient audience, which has led to a good deal of definition by *use* . . . and of course, that use is generally to serve the dominant culture.

More will be said in later chapters about 'definition by use', and also about the unfair equation of the cartoon form with low quality. In considering the role of televised storytelling in introducing children to, and allowing them to be included in, any kind of cultural public sphere, the central question is one of participation. Although it can be difficult for scholars to agree on what exactly constitutes a preschool animation, or an 'entertainment' as distinct from a 'factual' non-fiction programme, most childhood media scholars do agree that children should have their own needs, tastes, wants and identities acknowledged in their entertainment media, and that this is potentially a question of 'rights'. What arrangements can any society make to guarantee these rights? Who should be responsible for making sure that these guarantees are fulfilled? Children, not being citizens, cannot do it for themselves. Again, as always, we have to return to the responsibilities and roles of adults.

Adult intervention

Media scholars involved in campaigning for children's programming, such as Edward Palmer in the USA, or those who have worked within a social science tradition with its continuing interest in effects and audiences, such as Sonia Livingstone in the UK, and the present writer, do not take a purely relativist 'constructedness of childhood' position. They have argued that there are aspects of childhood that, for practical purposes, need to be seen as unchanging, particularly the continuing need for responsible adults to represent and protect the rights and needs of children in social, economic and cultural arrangements, however these rights and needs are defined, and however cultural arrangements may vary. Children need special services and attention from adults and adult institutions, including broadcasting, and are likely to go on doing so. There are aspects of the experience of childhood in the twentieth century, with its increasing dependence on technology, which make special provision for children, through the design and regulation of this technology, even more necessary than it might have been in the past. Such questions are raised, for example, by the increased accessibility of adult material like paedophilic pornography, through interactive video and the Internet.

As in this example, much of the public and academic debate about children and media has focused on negative 'effects', where the majority of research funding has tended to be concentrated in the past. However, this neglects other uses of media as a valuable and necessary means of introducing children to the ways of the adult world. There are plenty of aspects of adult life (leaving aside sex and crime) about which children need to be informed and which therefore need to be addressed in terms which are appropriate to their understanding and social and emotional status. These include the later stages of education; health; politics; citizenship (see, for example, Criticos, 1997); finance; employment; relationships with adults, parents, siblings, peers; and the culture generally – including the arts – the whole cultural capital of the society in which they live. What are the appropriate vehicles for giving children this information? Children's broadcasters would argue that this is a major function for their specialised role. Our study indicates that children, too, see television drama as a vehicle for social learning.

These are particularly relevant questions when it comes to drama, since drama is a favourite genre for children – not least because it usually deals with issues that are of relevance to their own lives, in forms which are accessible and entertaining. It is also the genre most likely to 'push the envelope', to use a phrase popular with producers, in dealing with socially sensitive and even taboo subjects, such as sexuality, relations with authority (parents and teachers) and – as in the case of the early *Grange Hill*, the realistic children's drama serial, based in a London secondary school – social class, especially as expressed through children's accents and speech. This inevitably brings children's drama producers into conflict with parents and other authority figures, including politicians, who may argue that such 'adult' subjects are not suitable viewing for children, especially in view of the numbers of very young children watching children's programmes. The concept of children's TV as trusted babysitter is a highly valued one in the UK, in contrast to the USA where 'TV babysitter' is a much more pejorative term.

Many current concerns about children watching adult programmes, or children being exposed to 'unsuitable' material, were prevalent forty years ago, as now. Himmelweit *et al.* (1958) revealed an earlier state of anxiety among policy-makers and opinion formers about the impact of new technology – in this case the new commercial TV channel, ITV. Would television move down-market, become more commercial, less qualitative, less sensitive to children's needs, would children be 'corrupted' by these new values? The same questions are being asked again. Our study set out to discover whether children perceived their concerns to be adequately addressed in the programming they are offered at the moment, in particular, by television drama – and also to find out what they expected in the future. We got a foretaste of the kinds of concerns these were likely to be in the first school we visited, where we conducted a pilot study, and asked children to choose programmes to take in a space capsule to another civilisation which did not have children's television. This was the first group's choice and rationale:

999 is very good. It's educational as well. We chose *Songs of Praise* for religious people, *Animal Hospital* for the people who like animals. We didn't really want *Man O Man* but we thought it wouldn't be really fair on the girls if we didn't have it.

This language echoes the language of campaigners for children's broadcasting and broadcasting regulation. Even the dating show, *Man O Man*, is discussed as a matter of 'rights', not of 'fun' or of commercial competitiveness. A group of 12 year olds in Middlesbrough also used the language of rights, and argued for specialised programmes for 'little kids':

Little kids don't want to watch *EastEnders* because it is boring, it hasn't got children in it . . . It has smoking and drugs . . . Children want to watch their own programmes, that is their right, what they are interested in, they like magic and things [that are not] realistic . . . *Grange Hill* tells us about smoking and drugs and stuff, but they get punished.

As with the campaigners for special provision, so these children presented the case for specialist children's broadcasting in public-sphere terms – 'needs' and 'rights' – similar to those employed by adults: the need for identification ('children in it'); rights (to 'their own programmes'); age-specific needs (for 'magic'); and the necessity of setting good examples ('they get punished'). Other children argued for rights, including the right of different, more vulnerable, unrepresented groups in the population, to be catered for, for instance, a 10-year-old girl, of Asian origin, from an inner-London primary school:

You are not thinking about yourself, in fact you are thinking about the other people who are going to be watching this children's channel. You have to think about little kids and not just about kids of your own age.

These were the keynotes struck repeatedly in the study: 'educational'; 'for the people'; 'really fair'; 'thinking about others'; 'little kids'. This is not what might have been expected from putting primary school children in charge of their own children's channel. But perhaps their attitudes would be different when it came to the discussion of storytelling and the pleasures of fantasy.

2   The importance of television storytelling

Once you get into it you are just, like, hooked.

Boy, 10, rural primary school

Broadcast drama is an art-form in its own right – the most important of all the new forms made possible by radio and television.

People and Programmes: BBC Radio and Television for an Age of Choice,
BBC, 1995, p. 54

In British television, drama is a 'flagship' genre both in the main schedules, and in schedules for children, and its survival as a staple ingredient of children's schedules has been seen as a mark of quality by Blumler (1992) and Davies and Corbett (1997), as well as a central ingredient in a public service system like the BBC (Home, 1993; BBC, 1995). According to *People and Programmes* (BBC, 1995, p. 54) British television drama is 'the most influential and, at its best, the most original source of dramatic fiction. It has its own forms – the soap, the series, the serial.' These forms have been inherited from earlier media – the soap from radio, the series and the serial from literary fiction. Television drama also includes the single play (not included in the list above) with its antecedents in live theatre.

In its early days, in the 1950s and 1960s, the single television play was produced live in a studio, and its outstanding practitioners were writers such as Paddy Chayefsky in the USA, and Dennis Potter in the UK – who claimed in his McTaggart Memorial Lecture in 1993 that the medium of television was the true 'national theatre'. Nowadays, single TV plays have more in common with the other major twentieth-century dramatic art-form, the full-length feature film, and both the BBC and Channel 4 have become partners in film production. All of these forms continue the ritual, theatrical tradition by presupposing drama as a performance event, taking place at a scheduled time, with the whole audience in position for the start of, and throughout, the performance. Indeed, such was the perceived importance of viewers being able to see an unbroken performance of dramatised screen narrative, that the

49

British commercial channel, ITV's, News at Ten was moved to 11 p.m., so that prime-time movies would not be interrupted, except by commercials.

In future, as the outgoing Director General of the BBC, Sir John Birt, pointed out in his New Statesman lecture in London in July 1999, the experience of viewing television drama, as with other kinds of TV programmes, will be different. Breaking with the historical tradition of theatrical performances as specific communal occasions, attended by specific audiences, digital technology will permit viewers 'to call up programmes and services on demand at a moment of choosing, rather than sitting on the couch waiting for our chosen programmes to begin' (Birt, 1999, p. 2). Digital technology will also 'unleash the past', using 'different performances of the same Shakespeare play from the BBC's archives' (*ibid.*, p. 4).

Birt's view of a world in which drama is no longer a shared, ritual, performance event is shared by other commentators we interviewed for both our BBC and Broadcasting Standards Commission study (see Davies and Corbett, 1997), but the children we interviewed were more sceptical, pointing out that viewing always has to take place within the other routines in children's and their family's lives, for example, these two 12-year-old girls from an inner-city secondary school in Middlesbrough:

GIRL 1   They shouldn't change children's programmes with adults, because the adults are probably going to miss them anyway because they are at work, and [have] got things do . . .

GIRL 2   They are normally cooking tea at that time . . . When I get in it is 4 o'clock and I do a bit of my homework.

These comments were typical of children's opinions when consulted about possible changes to the schedules, including the disappearance of special time-of-day children's slots. For them, TV viewing was part of a complex domestic social fabric which could not easily be unilaterally unpicked. Their primary consideration was what else they and their families might be doing at the time. Some daily activities were movable; others, like parental employment, tea and homework, were not.

The cultural value of TV drama

In the UK, as Birt's remarks indicate, television drama is positioned within a primarily literary theatrical tradition which includes the ultimate literary cultural icon, William Shakespeare, and is seen as having a central part to play in literary education, 'a civilising influence'. Elsewhere in the world, including in the United States, such claims for the cultural élitism of the genre are less likely to be made by those in charge of broadcasting institutions. In the USA, television has always been wholly commercial, funded by advertising, intended to make money for corporations, with the exception of the non-popular PBS channel, much of whose drama output on 'Masterpiece Theatre' consists of prestigious British imports. Despite early attempts to give American television a more élite literary function, as in early live broadcasts of literary dramas, the medium has stayed with tried and tested audience-winning formulas for long-running drama series such as the cop show and the hospital drama, and the commercial influence on the structure and function of television storytelling is accepted as inevitable. Jane Feuer (1986, p. 114) in an essay on 'Narrative form in American network TV', argued that TV storytelling was primarily characterised, not by any cultural or traditional value, but by its 'need to repeat, and need to contain' – above all to sustain its audience for advertisers. Feuer argues that all TV drama is serial in its form – its segments are not necessarily causally connected with each other – and contrasts this with linear form, as in cinematic storytelling. Although cinema is a commercial medium too, its need to attract and sustain audiences for commercial purposes is not always part of the way in which its narratives are analysed. This is not so in the case of television; Feuer's comparison suggests implicitly that, because of its transparent commercial origins, television narrative forms are culturally less interesting or valuable than those of cinema or literature, a suggestion that could be challenged.

Despite inevitable fluctuations in quality because of the demands of generating weekly outputs for half a year, many television dramas (*Homicide*, *ER*, *The X Files*) in their best episodes have standards of production, writing, performance and innovation as high as some Hollywood movie 'product', and higher than much of it. Where comparisons are possible between televised and filmed versions of dramatic narratives, as in series such as *Star Trek: The Next Generation*, it is arguable that the televised version provides greater opportunities than the film versions, for the kinds of character-driven, literary storytelling, including innovation and experimentation with form, which usually earn the label of 'high quality'. Broadcast drama, despite its achievements, and perhaps because of its popularity, lies uneasily low down within the cultural league table of canonical literary value – and hence, its value for children, the vulnerable and impressionable young, has often been seen ambivalently by adult critics.

There is no denying that, questions of élite cultural value aside, a major source of broadcast drama's influence is the fact that it is watched by enormously large numbers of people, compared to the audiences for previous dramatic media. However, the focus on the 'mass' audience brought into being by television, and its presumed irredeemable vulgarity of taste (see, for example, Twitchell, 1992), has meant that cultural debates around the value of television have polarised around concepts of élitism versus populism, as if the two were mutually exclusive. Popular television certainly is, has long been and, despite predictions of its replacement by interactive computer narratives, will probably continue to be. The currently top-rated soap in Britain, *Coronation Street*, regularly attracts around 14 million viewers and will reach many millions more in the course of a month. But in 1999 *Coronation Street* also won BAFTA (British Academy of Film and Television Arts) awards in every creative category. Other more prestigious categories, such as costume drama, have commercial as well as artistic, imperatives. TV drama in Britain, as well as in the USA, is not only 'important art', as the BBC claimed, but also big business. Publicly funded broadcasting organisations, such as the BBC, can more easily justify their funding by pointing to the widespread popularity of dramas such as *EastEnders* (soap), *Casualty* (series) and *Pride and Prejudice* (costume drama serial). As *People and Programmes* (BBC, 1995) put it: 'a channel's drama output is an important influence on the perception of the channel as a whole'.

When the study described in this book was undertaken in 1996–7, there was some concern about the survival of drama as a genre because of its expense, because of its local particularity in an increasingly global broadcasting market, and because of the fragmentation of the audience, due to new channels and new leisure activities such as computer games and the Internet, which, in the case of children, were supposedly leading to a loss of the ability to concentrate. This was particularly seen as a cause of concern for children's drama, because of the statistical fact that the biggest audience ratings in the 4–15 age group, that is, the 'child' audience, go to adult programmes. This is not always true for the younger age groups in the audience (that is, under tens), and it is never true for preschool children. Catering adequately for this very young audience with programmes designed to stimulate learning, social skills and imagination, has been characterised as another of the primary hallmarks of a public service system, in addition to quality drama (Palmer, 1988; Blumler, 1992; Davies and Corbett, 1997).

Children's sources of dramatic storytelling

In contrast with earlier generations, children now get most of their stories from television or film (often in the form of video). In Livingstone and Bovill's 1999 study, as mentioned, 100 per cent of all the households surveyed owned at least one television set. Their study was partly prompted by an expectation within the industry, and also among politicians, that children will begin to prefer new interactive computer technology as their main source of screen leisure in the future; this is driving new developments in broadcasting, such as BBC Online and other children's TV websites like Nickelodeon's. However, the replacement of television by computers has not happened yet. As noted earlier, Livingstone and Bovill found that children, on average, spent 147 minutes a day watching TV and only 12 minutes a day 'interacting' with non-game computers. Looking at the relative popularity of media technologies also does not give any indication of children's taste in genre, nor in different kinds of storytelling. In our analysis, drama was the most popular genre in the Top Ten ratings among all programmes and also for children's programmes. Livingstone's analysis produced a similar finding. Children in her study were asked to name their favourite programmes, and of all programmes mentioned – which showed a very wide range of individual titles, with none particularly dominant – the most frequently mentioned genre was the dramatic one of soap opera (26 per cent of responses) with other drama series/serials being chosen by 13 per cent.

Children's drama

Analysis of audience ratings in the period of our BBC drama study (1992–6) showed (as studies such as Himmelweit's in 1958 also showed) that large numbers of children watched adult drama such as *EastEnders* and *Casualty* and *The X Files*, and the children's qualitative comments reinforced this. But a further strand in the BBC's reputation for high-quality public service broadcasting, has always been its children's programmes. Providing children's programming continues to be part of its public service remit, although there are no regulatory obligations to provide quotas of different kinds of programming at particular times for all ages of children, as there are for the ITV and Channel 5 commercial terrestrial channels. *People and Programmes* (BBC, 1995, p. 159) acknowledged the strength of contemporary children's series dramas such as *Grange Hill* and *Byker Grove*. 'They are rooted in the lives which modern British children live and have proven to be among the most successful of all the BBC's contemporary naturalistic dramas.' Children's drama, like adult drama, is thus officially, at least, seen as making an important contribution to British broadcasting's role as the patron of this most culturally significant of the arts. However, among the changes to the structure of the BBC announced by its new Director General, Greg Dyke (spring 2000), was the announcement that there would no longer be a separate Children's Department, responsible for the BBC's children's programming, within the BBC. One of the most revealing aspects of this change, from our study's point of view, was that children's programming has been included under one of four new programming departments – not under 'Factual and Learning' (as it almost certainly would have been in the USA) but under 'Drama and Entertainment'. The implications of this change for the BBC's commitment to quality children's programming and drama remain to be seen.

British children's television as a separate department was abolished once before, in the 1960s (see Home, 1993; Buckingham *et al.*, 1999). It was folded into what were called 'Family [a euphemism for 'women's'] Programmes' – but, as Buckingham *et al.* comment (1999, p. 31), 'feeling grew in the BBC that the Family Programmes experiment, at least as far as children's television was concerned, was in overall terms a failure'. As Buckingham *et al.* point out, when children's programmes are included in the same structure as adult programmes, 'in the contest between "child" and "adult" demands there [can be] only one winner' – that is, adults' programmes. One of the casualties of the last period of abolition was specialist drama for children, which virtually disappeared – so it may be reassuring that, at least this time around, children's programming has been included in a Drama and Entertainment grouping. However, some children's drama producers among our interviewees, such as Roger Singleton Turner, now freelance (personal communication, April 2000), fear that 'it will be harder to build a career as a specialist children's drama (or even general children's) programme-maker' as a result. 'The trend will be to use people from the mainstream drama pool.'

The last period of abolition, having failed to deliver what it had promised, came to an end in 1967, with the appointment of Monica Sims as the head of a new, resurrected Children's Department, and the start of what many see as a 'golden age' period in British children's television, at least in terms of increased resources and diversity and originality of output. Many of the strengths of this period, including the 'CBBC' identity and special CBBC time-slots; long-running audience participation and informative programmes like *Blue Peter* and *Live and Kicking*; serious news and documentary like *Newsround* and *The Lowdown*; and a diverse children's drama tradition, including *Grange Hill* (starting in 1978) and *Byker Grove*, were introduced during this period. It remains to be seen whether history will repeat itself in the form of a failure of the merger, and the reintroduction of a separate Children's Department. A number of our interviewees mentioned the possibility of specialist children's digital channels being set up by the BBC; however, such channels will still require specialist children's programme-makers, who will need to acquire their skills and experience in the present system, including the commercial and independent sectors. These sectors may well become more influential as a breeding-ground for children's storytellers than the once-dominant BBC, which was left alone in the 1990 Broadcasting Act requiring commercial television to provide quotas of children's programming, because it was 'trusted' to provide a full public service for children, without the need for legislation.

The best children's television drama schedules, whether on the BBC, or within the commercial system, have traditionally attempted to provide a microcosm of adult schedules in television storytelling. Such schedules have displayed, in Caughie's terms (1991), the dual emphases of British broadcast drama: realistic authenticity, based on drama's origins in live studio production, and prestigious literary 'heritage' drama, as in costumed adaptations of classic books, which was originally a way for the new medium of television, like film before it, to stake its claim to cultural respectability in Britain. These twin criteria for British TV drama are reflected in children's drama too. Shows such as the BBC's *Grange Hill* and *Byker Grove*, and ITV's *Children's Ward* belong in the tradition of dramatic realism, which has its roots in early *Coronation Street*, the nearly 40-year-old soap opera, set in a working-class community in Salford, near Manchester, and regional, realistic, social-problem dramas such as the Liverpool-set police series, *Z Cars* in the 1960s. These, in turn, owed much to the 'kitchen-sink' dramas of the 1950s and 1960s in British theatre, and to the work of social–realist directors such as Anderson, Reisz and Richardson, in 1960s British cinema.

From the point of view of the more prestigious literary heritage strand, children's drama schedules have been one of the most favoured homes for classic serials, although recently the expense of these has resulted in such adaptations being positioned as 'family' shows and scheduled at family viewing times such as Sunday 'teatime', or at Christmas and Bank Holiday special occasions. Recent examples of the 'family' quality book-adaptation, were 1996's *The Prince and the Pauper*, 1998's *The Children of the New Forest* and, a new departure by ITV in winter, 1998, an adaptation by Carlton of *Goodnight Mr Tom*, shown during early evening prime time, rather than in the afternoon – a scheduling departure which may be increasingly repeated since the programme got high ratings and BAFTA awards. The reliance on literary adaptations continues a tradition begun when the BBC Children's Department first started, when it produced *Little Women* (1950–1) and *The Railway Children* (1951) and, through the 1950s and 1960s, *The Black Arrow, Treasure Island, Great Expectations, Katy, The Cabin in the Clearing* and *The Secret Garden* (Home, 1993).

The history of children's broadcasting as discussed by Oswell (1995, 1998) and by Buckingham, *et al.* (1999) argues for a strong ideological underpinning to the movement to provide classic storytelling for children – what Oswell calls 'programming for a liberal democracy'. Buckingham *et al.* (1999, p. 36) call it 'a core of values in which middle-class attitudes and universal moral principles had come to be seen as one and the same thing' – an issue which will be discussed in more detail in chapter 7. As Home (1993), in her history of children's broadcasting pointed out, there were pragmatic, as well as ideological, reasons for early children's broadcasting services relying on children's classics for their output: many were out of copyright and they provided ready-made narratives for a voracious new medium. The need for pragmatism, in a medium whose survival depends on mass support, was expressed by Edward Barnes, Home's predecessor as head of BBC children's programming, quoted in Buckingham *et al.* (1999, p. 37). He pointed out that children's storytelling programmes provided 'training in narrative [which] will bring them to the drama of ideas in [the adult] *Play for Today*'. Buckingham *et al.* characterise this type of comment as a desire to enable 'the development of a mature citizenship' – a presumably laudable desire in a publicly-funded PSB organisation. Again, there are pragmatic motives behind this training in narrative; child audiences need to be sustained to help maintain the size of the adult audience, and ultimately to help guarantee broadcasters' economic survival. Alan Horrox (interviewed for the BBC study in spring, 1996), of Tetra Films, producers of *The Tomorrow People* and *Mike and Angelo*, both broadcast on ITV, and exported internationally, summarised the case thus:

Broadcasters need children because they grow up into adult audiences . . . Fox [producers of *The Simpsons*] in the US have demonstrated how lethal it is to the other networks to say 'children don't matter to us'. That's why the networks have haemorrhaged in the USA and allowed Fox to build into a rival channel . . . It's also a fundamental fact for all channels to feel young, including middle-aged audiences like myself; youth is a tremendous asset. If you put these two things together – the desperate need for new audiences and the need to feel like a young channel – networks need children.

The value of children's drama

With limited budgets, but the same requirements for the same high production values as for adult drama, children's television drama has usually been the poor relation in the prestigious British tradition, and there is no tradition of critical writing about children's broadcasting, with one or two minor exceptions, one of which was the present author's review columns in *The Listener* in the 1970s and 1980s. The lack of serious critical esteem for children's programmes continues despite the fact that well-established writers have worked for children and children's programmes have been produced by subsequently well-known directors. Andrew Davies, the adapter of classics such as *Middlemarch* (1994), *Pride and Prejudice* (1995), *Vanity Fair* (1998) and *Wives and Daughters* (1999), began his TV career writing the anarchic ITV children's comedy, *Marmalade Atkins* in 1987–8. Anthony Minghella, the multiple-Oscar-winning director of *The English Patient* (1996) and of *The Talented Mr Ripley* in 2000, was one of the first directors of *Grange Hill*.

This lack of recognition of children's drama as part of the great TV drama tradition, is part of a general critical tradition which does not take seriously material specifically labelled as aimed at children. Peter Hunt (1994) has pointed out how literature for children written by adult authors – Thomas Hardy, Graham Greene, Leo Tolstoy – becomes something other than literature once it is labelled 'for children', and it becomes invisible to critical attention. Children's television drama has suffered very much from this invisibility; much of it, even from as recently as the 1980s, does not survive at all. Marilyn Fox, a former executive drama producer at the BBC, now retired, was interviewed for the BBC study, and talked about two serials she had directed in the 1980s – *Running Scared* and *Break in the Sun* – which dealt with respectively, crime and racism in the East End of London, and child abuse and neglect – subjects that were difficult and disturbing in ways that had not been possible before. She also pointed out the stylistic innovation of these series, which made considerable use of realistic location shooting. Such 'groundbreaking' work was a brief high point of contemporary radicalism in children's drama, of which only *Grange Hill*, the school soap, begun in 1978, survives; the short-run drama serial, once a regular weekly offering, is virtually defunct. Such adventurous programmes as *Running Scared* do not survive on video either, so an important period of children's television's output is unavailable either for the public, or for scholars and historians to review. In this, children's television differs markedly from children's literature; its supposed middle-class values have not been sufficient to guarantee its physical, and cultural, survival.

The uses of television storytelling

Part of this lack of prestige and seriousness for children's television, is that, as with children's literature, it is defined by use, not by standards of canonical cultural value, however much such standards may shift with changes in public taste. Children's drama is expected to serve functions over and above aesthetic excellence, entertainment and narrative engagement for its audience; it has to help children in the task of growing up. As the title of Bruno Bettelheim's 1976 book about fairy tales indicated, even 'enchantment' has to have 'uses'. The need to take children's fictional material seriously has been a challenge for literary critics attempting to draw children's literature into the mainstream of literary theory. Children's literature raises what Peter Hunt (1991, p. 127) calls 'the problem of audience' for narrative theory – the fact that children's readings of texts and adults' readings may be different, and the fact that children's literature, unlike much adult literature, has traditionally been both produced and evaluated by adults for specifically didactic purposes.

Children's storytelling is seen as having a role in aiding the child's development, however development is defined. As the film classification system recognises, adults (over the age of eighteen), in whom the processes of biological growth are virtually complete, are assumed to be capable of deciding for themselves what they should and should not experience, and to be able to cope with any adverse consequences of their own choices. The didactic requirement for art to teach the good life to all, not just to children, and to show the 'best that has been thought or said' (Matthew Arnold, 1896, p. 6) has disappeared with postmodernity – and in our anxiety not to impose middle-class ideologies, or any other kind of culturally hegemonic values, we appear to have accepted Oscar Wilde's dictum that 'All art is utterly useless'.

This will not do for children's material; stories for them are expected to teach social values – to promote values of which adults approve, and to suppress those of which adult society does not approve. Children's material follows the Brechtian edict (quoted in Willett, 1964, *Brecht on Theatre*, p. 186) that:

The theatre can only adopt . . . a free attitude . . . if it lets itself be carried along by the strongest currents in its society and associates itself with those who are necessarily most impatient to make great alterations there . . . straight into the suburbs, at the disposal of those who live hard and produce much.

The usefulness of 'making alterations' in 'the suburbs' may be out of fashion in adult art and literature, but has proved to be a function that is very resistant to changes in literary and cultural fashions for children. Hunt (1991, p. 127) talks about the need for reassurance for child readers/audiences: 'Children prefer stories with an element of closure that is, where there is a sense of an ending. Normality is restored, security is emphasised. The strong resolution is important to certain kinds of texts for it provides comfort.'

Alison Lurie (1990) does not accept that the ideological values of children's literature are an imposition of adult hegemony. She argues that, despite the undeniable, and for some commentators such as Jacqueline Rose (1984) problematic, fact that children's literature is produced by adults, the most enduring children's stories are valuable and popular with children because they are subversive of the status quo of adult society. Lurie argues that classics such as *Alice in Wonderland*, as well as traditional fairy tales, with their empowerment of the poor, the young and the female, teach children to be sceptical of the world of grown-ups – the foolish giants, spiteful witches, foolish Dodos. There seem to be some grounds for this view given the popularity of anarchic and politically-challenging children's stories (see chapter 8's discussion of *The Demon Headmaster*), but it is still a functional view – the uses not just of enchantment, but of subversiveness.

Bruno Bettelheim (1976), from a psychoanalytic perspective, stresses the functions of fairy tale in promoting psychological health through allowing children to address at a safe distance, fears of their own interior 'monstrosity', and of the overwhelming power of adults. Such power, as stories like 'Hansel and Gretel' and 'Jack the Giantkiller' show, can be combated through children's discovery of their own virtue, wit and courage in vanquishing the powers of the wicked adult, restoring relationships with the good adult, and eventually becoming the good adult themselves, through winning the partnership of the good 'other' and marrying the prince/princess. The common ground of these analyses of children's material – whether questioning the middle-class morality of early children's television, or championing the radical icono-clasm of *Alice* – is that children's material is seen as having a social, and socialising, effect from which children either 'need' to be protected, or to which they 'need' to be exposed.

Children's television drama producers, too, subscribe to the discourse of 'need'. In our interviews with them, when discussing narrative development, they stressed the importance of the restoration of the status quo as a psychological necessity for children – especially when storylines which were potentially morally controversial were introduced.

In the case of the long-running school serial *Grange Hill*, a pregnancy storyline was run in the 1995 season. The producer at the time, Steven Andrew (interviewed for the BBC study in spring, 1996), pointed out:

We have a responsibility within those stories to be informative and to have a clear moral guideline as to why we are doing the stories and the outcomes, so that if we are doing something that could be perceived as ambiguous, the kids are not left wondering what should have happened; they can clearly draw their own conclusions, and know which way they should have gone.

Andrew worked for the BBC and is now Controller of the Children's department of Granada Media – such attitudes are not unique to the BBC. In the UK, at the time of the study, there still existed a generation of children's producers both within the BBC and in the commercial system, who, in the years before the 1990 deregulation, were interdependent in the cultural and professional values they shared. Many of them are now independent commercial producers serving both publicly funded and commercial television, and, despite reduced budgets and increased competition, claim to be continuing to promote these shared values. Alan Horrox (interviewed for the BBC in spring, 1996) emphasised particularly the social learning aspects of dramatic narrative on TV:

What children learn from television is much broader than what can narrowly be defined as educational television. It is learning about relationships, the kind of things you learn from drama, about how to transact a relationship, relationships of power, family tragedies . . . that is what retelling of stories does for you.

The survival of children's television drama

Children's drama has constantly to make a special case for its continued existence and being useful in terms of teaching about relationships is one strand of this case, a strand that children themselves recognised. A further strand, as Buckingham *et al.* (1999) argued, is to make explicit what they describe as the 'middle-class values' of upholding literary heritage traditions. Thus, appeals to cultural élitism, and the sustenance of the high literary tradition, can be a survival tactic for children's programming. Lewis Rudd, formerly Controller of Children's Programming at Carlton TV, after a long career in commercial children's programming, pointed out in his interview with us (Davies and O'Malley, 1996, p. 162):

At the moment [in 1996] ITV can afford £120,000 or a £150,000 for an episode of children's drama but if there are loads of channels . . . maybe everyone will be able to afford £30,000 for an episode but nobody will be able to afford £150,000 . . . Period drama has an enormous advantage because it doesn't date.

Another justification of children's drama as a specific category within broadcasting has been the general cultural value attached to the imaginative value of storytelling in aiding the child's intellectual and emotional development. Hilton (1996, p. 42) argues that dramatic fictions allow children 'shamelessly to address and repeat the dream themes which allow the pleasure of organising growing sexual identity with its intense anxieties and repressed material'. The educational value of dramatic storytelling was also stressed by producers. Peter Tabern (interviewed for the BBC study in spring, 1996), an independent producer, with his own company, Childsplay, producers of BBC1's *Pirates*, pointed out that:

[storytelling] certainly sets out the basic principles of causation . . . it teaches you about identification, by placing yourself inside the story . . . A good strong story with a beginning, a middle and an end, and a bit of ingenuity . . . children are learning the ground rules of how a good story works.

Richard Callanan (interviewed for the BBC study in spring, 1996), a former executive drama producer with the BBC, responsible for adaptations of *Little Lord Fauntleroy* (1995) and the original *Demon Headmaster* series, saw beneficial similarities between traditional forms of storytelling and television storytelling, including popular storytelling for adults which children enjoy:

It is something they [children] really need, and they find their own path through . . . as we sat around the tribal fire, and sat around talking about battles etc., the kids in those days would identify with sections of those stories, similarly kids will watch through *EastEnders*; two thirds will mean nothing, one third will ring a bell.

Here, there is dissonance between what the producers see as the integral and historically based cultural value of their craft and criticisms made of electronic storytelling by communications theorists. A major difference between traditional storytelling and TV is, as George Gerbner has pointed out, that the stories of the mass media of film and TV, are industrially produced, according to Hollywood-dominated narrative and stylistic formulas, and mass-circulated for profit, by rich industrial corporations. Pre-industrial stories and fairy tales were generated by people themselves and passed on orally, from generation to generation, which allowed children's own communities to be the primary instruments of socialisation through culture and narrative.

This view is a somewhat oversimplified one given that certain kinds of narrative, such as the Cinderella story, have turned up in many cultures, and given that they have common formulaic structures (Propp, 1968). However, from the child's point of view, the most significant change from community-generated storytelling, within an oral tradition, to 'industrialised' storytelling, is the change from being an audience receiving information directly from a known storyteller, to being an audience buying and consuming reproduced copies of a strange story-teller's work, at a distance of both time and place. In this sense, the industrialised mass-production of children's culture began, not with Disney, nor with television, but with printing, and with the accelerated development of special books for children in the eighteenth and nine-teenth centuries. Printing and book-selling meant stories came from professional writers and publishers, and, once produced and written down, their forms stayed fixed. Although public concerns have been expressed about some forms of print aimed at children, for example penny dreadfuls in the nineteenth century and comics in the twentieth (see Barker, 1989; Starker, 1991), the anonymous and depersonalised aspects of print as a medium for storytelling do not seem to have aroused the same degree of concern as the concern aroused by television and film. In fact, new developments in the technology of storytelling do not abolish earlier forms; oral, printed, screen and interactive versions, can all exist in a child's life together, and, as Livingstone and Bovill's study of children's media use (1999) suggests, for many children they do. The fact that stories are mass-produced does not mean, either, that children's tastes are not highly individualised.

The diverse individual

If children's storytelling is to be characterised by use, and if one of its uses is 'enchantment', then we would expect children to choose fa-vourite texts on the basis of meanings and emotional impact which are personal to themselves. Given the diversity of a child's personal experi-ences, both over time and from one individual to another, it would be surprising if loved texts were universal, despite some texts undoubtedly being popular with large numbers of children. Evidence for this comes from recent studies about children's media tastes. Livingstone and Bovill (1999) pointed out that no single programme was named as favourite by more than a quarter of their sample of around 1,300 children. Diversity was greater among younger children: 103 different programmes were mentioned by 6–8 year olds, with *The Simpsons* (boys) and *EastEnders* (girls) being the most frequently mentioned. By the age of 12–14, 82 programmes were mentioned, with *EastEnders* being chosen by 23 per cent of all children. Similar diversity was found in the programmes mentioned by the children in our study. Individual variation is masked by ratings analyses and the discourse of 'size' and 'mass' which dominates discussion about popular media. Aggregates of overall numbers in the audience mask the fact (Barwise and Ehrenberg, 1996) that these numbers are always different combinations of individuals. Individuals' tastes and habits vary unpredictably, and the TV audience, in this sense, is not a mass at all. This was illustrated by a particular example of individual diversity in our own sample of children.

One group of forty-two children in our study were unusual in a clearly identifiable way. They were the group who, in the 2, 3, 5, then 10 'channel choice' exercise, showed consistent loyalty to one drama programme – *Byker Grove*, the BBC's continuing drama series about a youth centre in the north east of England. At each of the four stages of this range of hypothetical viewing choices, starting with 2 choices – between *Byker Grove* and the universally popular American cartoon *Rugrats* – and ending with 10, including cartoons, soap opera and sitcom, the forty-two children in the *Byker* subset continued to choose *Byker Grove* against all alternatives. At the 10 channel choice stage they ignored more glamorous offerings such as *Friends*, and still opted for their favourite children's drama.

Identifying such loyal groups is going to become the key to audience research in the future, as channels proliferate. However, how to identify them is more problematic, because even among such a precisely defined group as '*Byker Grove* fans', there was great individual diversity in these children's questionnaire comments about other programmes. Generally, the forty-two children were fairly representative of the sample as a whole, with most school-types and age groups represented and similar terrestrial viewing patterns. The two major differences between the overall sample, and the *Byker Grove* subset were first, that the subset contained more girls, and second, this group was less likely to have satellite/cable. This demographic breakdown is shown in Table 5.

This subset's qualitative comments on the questionnaire were analysed too, and their tastes were not particularly homogeneous. Seventeen different titles were mentioned by the seven children who wrote comments. A 9-year-old girl from a rural primary in Co. Durham (north-east England) liked *Home and Away* and *Neighbours* (both Australian soaps); a 10-year-old girl in an inner-London primary 'never missed' *Recourse* (ITV factual) and *The Queen's Nose* (BBC children's drama); a 12-year-old in a Co. Durham rural secondary school liked *EastEnders* (adult soap) and *2.4 Children* (adult British sitcom, based on the American *Roseanne*); a 6-year-old boy in outer London loved *The Demon Headmaster* (BBC children's drama); a 10-year-old boy in outer London wanted more of *The Bill* (ITV adult police drama) and *The Biz* (a BBC children's drama about a stage school). Two children set out ideal schedules – all titles not mentioned by others in the *Byker* subset:

Table 5. *Demographic comparisons between children in main sample (All) and in* Byker Grove *subset (* BGS*)*

	All (base 1,332)	BGS (base 42)
Number of age groups represented	9 (ages 5–13)	8 (no 5 year olds)
Number of schools represented	17 altogether	15 altogether
Number of school types represented (urban/rural etc.)	10	8
percentage of boys in group	49.5	32.0
percentage of girls in group	50.5	68.0
percentage with cable satellite	43.0	29.0
percentage watching CBBC	84.0	91.0
percentage watching CITV	68.0	71.0
percentage watching C4	44.0	48.0

My favourite TV programme is *Byker Grove*. I watch Channel 2 [BBC2] the most. *Ren and Stimpy* is Rubbish. *Scooby Doo* is a funny programme so keep it. *Rugrats* is Rubbish. *Friends* is boo! *Home and Away* is my 2nd favourite programme. *Art Attack* is brilliant! (Girl, 7, suburban primary school, Buckinghamshire)

Put more funny things on for older kids. E.g. *Byker Grove, Grange Hill* . . . Make things exciting and indulging. Bring out new characters. Put things on about other things. E.g. cars, motorbikes, computers. (Boy, 11, inner-city secondary school, Middlesbrough)

From this analysis, the *Byker Grove* fan cannot easily be identified as a demographic with a taste primarily for youthful, regional realistic drama; indeed, a comparison between this group's and the whole sample's answers to questions about the kind of drama they liked, showed that the subset children were less likely to want more programmes for their age, and less likely to want stories set in the past, stories from books or science fiction. Their only common characteristics were that they were slightly more likely than the whole sample to want programmes about teenagers, and they were also more likely to come from the proportion of children who did not have access to satellite/cable. The *Byker Grove* fans thus cannot easily be pigeonholed into a niche target audience group.

Children's definitions of drama

The fortunes of children's programming, including drama, have fluctuated historically, and are currently caught up in the larger debate about

Table 6. *Proportions (percentage) of boys, girls and all children combined defining drama according to the following definitions (base 1,182)*

Drama is:	All	Boys	Girls
a. someone telling/reading a story	7	6	8
b. a story with actors/people dressed up	49	48	50
c. an exciting event	13	14	12
d. something that couldn't happen in real life	17	18	15
e. your own idea (children's free response)	15	14	15

the future of public service broadcasting and television generally, given new digital technology and the rise of interactive forms such as the Internet, with its scope for media-convergence, and its threat to linear storytelling and narrative closures of the kind seen by critics as necessary for children. Because of this unpredictable future, the views of children themselves may turn out to be crucial in deciding how these new technologies develop and are socially managed. In the public service tradition, drama is seen as a necessary part of the child audience's television 'diet', and, as discussed, the imaginative identification required by the reception of stories is seen by producers and educators as continuing the traditional value of literary education. We were interested to find out whether children, too, thought that drama had wider social and cultural functions, but first we were curious to know what children thought this widely discussed term 'television drama' *meant*.

In the questionnaire, there was a multiple-choice question in which children were given the option of choosing 1 of 5 definitions of drama. The results are shown in Table 6.

The largest proportion of children – 49 per cent – chose 'b' – a story with actors. In the sense that this recognised the performative element of drama, it was the nearest thing to a 'correct' definition. 'Something that couldn't happen in real life' was the next, most frequently chosen option, quite a long way behind, with 17 per cent. However, our opposing of 'real life', 'something that could not happen in real life' and 'a story with actors', led to a number of children objecting to being forced to choose between these overlapping definitions. An 11-year-old girl from Cardiff pointed out that drama could be 'someone telling something that *could* happen in real life'.

Table 7 shows that the majority of children in every age group chose the performance definition, but that the proportion of children dissatisfied with our multiple choices, and choosing their own definition, went

Table 7. *The proportions (percentage) of children in each age group defining drama according to the following definitions*

Drama is:	age 5 (base 6)	6 (base 102)	7 (base 168)	8 (base 170)	9 (base 199)	10 (base 182)	11 (base 246)	12 (base 101)	13 (base 6)
	percentage of children								
a. someone telling/ reading a story	33	21	17	6	3	4	2	1	0
b. a story with actors/ people dressed up	17	31	47	54	47	51	53	50	50
c. an exciting event	0	20	12	14	16	13	9	9	33
d. something that couldn't happen in real life	50	26	19	16	16	18	15	6	0
e. your own idea (children's free response)	0	2	5	10	18	14	21	34	17

up steadily with age. Younger children were more likely to equate drama with 'something that couldn't happen in real life' and with 'an exciting event', without the reservations and provisos about the *representation* of real life put forward by older children. These responses show that the majority of children recognised the performative and fictional aspects of drama, but many wanted to stress that such 'made-up' events can represent 'real life', and as such have value – or 'use' – in offering social lessons to audiences.

In discussion, realism turned out to be a prime value in judging the worth of TV drama for many children, for example this group of 8–11 year olds from a suburban primary school in Oxfordshire, deciding what to get rid of from their children's schedule, in order to save money. This group was noteworthy in their rejection of currently fashionable reflexive and alienating camera techniques in which the performers draw attention to the fact of performance by addressing the camera directly:

BOY 1   [Get rid of] *Clarissa* because she always has newsflashes and things like that and looks at the TV and she is always talking to the camera and . . . I do not like that, it is really stupid.

The final choice in this group's schedule was between getting rid of *EastEnders*, the realistic adult soap, or *The Queen's Nose*, a BBC children's fantasy drama. The group was asked which they would keep:

ALL   *EastEnders.*

GIRL 2   I like *The Queen's Nose* but it is just imagination, it is good but not as good as *EastEnders.*

A group of children in an inner-city primary school in Milton Keynes also reduced their schedule to a choice between the same two programmes, and came to a rather different decision. Despite one girl defending *EastEnders*: 'it's about people, it's a drama . . . and you learn things when you're older about growing up', they got rid of *EastEnders* because of its 'romance' (an unappealing aspect for many children). It also had, at that stage, a very violent storyline (an assassination attempt on a regular character, Ian Beale) which they thought would set a bad example to younger children – 'aged about five'. This group preferred *The Queen's Nose* because, in the pragmatic view of one girl, 'it's for girls and boys', in other words, it had general audience appeal. But she also pointed out the reason for its popularity – the value of wish-fulfilment: 'kids just like wishing things, and she wishes for things'. This group stressed pleasurable aspects of the story: 'It's more funnier' (Girl 1, aged 10). 'It's more exciting. and everyone's saving their 50 p coins now' (Girl 2, aged 10). The same girl pointed out that *The Queen's Nose*, despite its fantastic premise of a girl being able to wish for things by rubbing the queen's nose on a 50 pence coin, did combine realism with the fantasy: 'she [the heroine] always wishes things for things that'll happen to you'.

A number of children defined drama without any reference to production features, such as narratives, genres, acting or performance – they simply defined it as an exciting, usually violent, or frightening, event.

Drama is kids trying to save people. (Girl, 11, inner-city secondary school, Middlesbrough)

Drama is where someone gets shot or something happens to them. (Girl, 12, inner-city secondary school, Middlesbrough)

Drama is murder I think. (Girl, 7, inner-city primary school, Cardiff)

Drama is a car crash where the driver turns out to be a drug smuggler. (Boy, 9, rural primary school, Co. Durham)

There is no suggestion here that drama is the *representation* of dramatic real-life events, although the 'car crash where the driver turns out to be a drug smuggler' has a parodic flavour, suggesting its author is an aficionado of TV police series. Nevertheless, many children did specify that drama had to include an element of representation and constructedness:

Drama is something that might have happened, but reconstructed. (Girl, 12, rural secondary school, Co. Durham)

Drama is a real event that is acted out again in a series like *London's Burning* and *EastEnders*. (Boy, 12, inner-city primary school, Milton Keynes)

The degree of realism was sometimes evaluated by using modality judgements (Hodge and Tripp, 1986; Davies, 1997) – with children referring to structural features of a programme to evaluate its relationship with reality, and the credibility, or otherwise, of the events in it. For this boy, the characteristic multiple-storyline structure of soap/drama reduced its level of realism:

Drama is a number of storylines going on at once and probably would not happen in real life. (Boy, 11, inner-city secondary school, Middlesbrough)

A major modality cue for the constructedness of drama is the fact that it is performed by actors. Some children did not mention this as a feature of drama at all. Many others referred specifically to acting, or 'pretending', or, in one case, 'dressing up', as the primary ingredient of the genre:

Drama is where you act out stories sometimes. You don't talk, just mime. (Girl, 9, outer-London primary school)

Drama is a mime. (Boy, 11, inner-city secondary school, Middlesbrough)

Drama is pretending to be someone else. (Boy, 8, inner-city primary school, Cardiff)

For these children, the mimetic form of the genre was its central component, not aspects of content. Thus, although 'real life' was repeatedly mentioned as a necessary ingredient of drama, many children insisted that, for instance, 'drama documentary' – the representation of real people living their lives on television – was not the same as drama. Drama required construction, pretence, performance and mimetic representation: drama, however real, always had an element of 'art'.

Setting good examples: the socialising function of drama

Drama serves many public purposes for broadcasting organisations, but, for the children in the study, one of the prime 'uses' of television drama was socialisation: setting good examples; wrongdoers being punished; the good being rewarded. Rarely was drama described by children as 'an important form', that is, as having cultural prestige value, when it came to justifying a place for it in the schedules they designed. Children emphasised the social and psychological value of the genre. This social role was partly within the personal and family sphere, but they also saw television storytelling as having a moral function in the wider public sphere too.

A group of 9–11 year olds in an inner-city primary school in Milton Keynes, discussed how to get rid of programmes in their Children's Drama Channel in order to save money:

BOY 1   Who votes for *Soldier Soldier*?

GIRL 1   I think we should get rid of it. Most kids don't know about things like that.

BOY 2   It's about war. Most kids don't know about war.

BOY 3   People who go to church don't really like things – people fighting and getting killed . . .

BOY 1   We've seen how people die in the war, so we don't like it.

In this emphasis on the moral responsibility of television drama, trying to keep children from knowledge of 'things like that' and the kinds of things disliked by 'people who go to church', children differed from producers. Buckingham *et al.*'s (1999) account of the history of children's television makes it clear that producers do, indeed, analyse and discuss the public impact on the child audience of the values represented in their programmes, but children's producers in Britain, unlike those in the United States, resist the label 'educator', preferring to be seen as 'entertainers'. As such, few producers seemed comfortable about saying that they were trying to 'do good' or to teach. For example, Alan Horrox (interviewed for the BBC study in spring, 1996), working in the commercial system, valued the creative freedom permitted by children's drama, which specifically meant *not* 'being done good to':

> You can work in genres that perhaps don't exist in adult television. You can mix fantasy and comedy in ways that are generally seen as iconoclastic in adult television. These are totally normal in children's programmes . . . I'm not a great devotee of social realism for kids . . . I link it in my mind with this adult feeling that kids have to be done good to . . . I'm much more the Roald Dahl school, which is a mixture of delight and savagery.

The following discussion from a group of 11–12 year olds in an inner-city secondary school in Middlesbrough, shows a different perspective. The group contrasted the morality of the children's school drama series *Grange Hill*, with the adult soap *EastEnders*. Both were seen as 'realistic' but the children's drama was defended as superior for a children's schedule, because its moral message was unequivocal:

GROUP 1 SPOKESPERSON, 11-YEAR-OLD BOY   *EastEnders* encourages smoking, violence, gives children a bad example, they might copy the language . . . *The X Files* is about murder and violence and gives our children horrific nightmares and very disgusting ideas . . .

SPOKESPERSON, GROUP 2   Little kids don't want to watch *EastEnders* because it is boring, it hasn't got children in it . . . *Grange Hill* tells us about smoking and drugs and stuff, but they get punished.

For these children, a crucial distinguishing characteristic of children's drama was not the fact of its representation of forbidden behaviours – 'smoking, drugs and stuff'. Such representation was seen as unproblematic. What made the children's drama preferable was the fact that wrongdoers were punished for doing wrong. The second spokesperson also stressed another important ingredient of programming for young children: having 'children in it'. Some producers were aware of these expectations in their audience and expressed a sense of direct moral responsibility towards them, in a way which would be unlikely to be required of producers of adult drama. This moral responsibility was not conceived as a requirement to censor and prohibit 'bad' behaviour, but, on the contrary, to discuss such behaviour and the problems arising from it openly. Lewis Rudd of Carlton said (Davies and O'Malley, 1996, p. 159):

> I think the two messages from the more serious children's television are: one, you are not alone, and two, there is someone you can go to for help . . . you are not setting out to preach, but if you have a moral question, your good characters always behave morally in these situations.

This is a continuation of the paternalist tradition of the early BBC's attitude to child audiences, but the difference with the kinds of modern storytelling referred to by Rudd is that, in these programmes, forbidden behaviour, such as sexual relationships, homosexuality and substance abuse, is openly represented in a way that many parents find threatening, but is intended to be *reassuring* to children. Controversial representations are seen as offering 'help' to children who find themselves in positions of danger, isolation or public ostracism. This is a paternalist role, continuing what Buckingham *et al.* (1999, p. 37) call 'a submerged metaphor of rescue'. But the homosexual kiss in the 1995 series of *Byker Grove*, or the alcoholism storyline of the 1998 *Grange Hill* are a very far cry from the boarding-school sagas of *Billy Bunter* or the genteel struggles of the Edwardian family in *The Railway Children*, staples of the 1950s children's schedules. Earlier programming discharged 'paternal' responsibilities to children by shielding them from realistic aspects of contemporary life; programmes such as *Press Gang* (ITV, 1985–92) or *Children's Ward* (ITV, still running), as well as *Byker Grove* and *Grange Hill* on the BBC, claim to protect children by showing them uncomfortable truths about the world that many parents would rather children did not know. In Anna Home's words (in Davies and O'Malley, 1996, p. 140): 'In the end, good always triumphs over evil. But you can't be simplistic either, you have to hold a balance. If you're too simplistic your audience won't believe you because, for heaven's sake, they live in the real world.'

Fantasy and alienation

A 10-year-old girl in a rural primary school in Buckinghamshire, taking part in a debate to ban the fantasy science fiction series, *The Demon*

Headmaster, which was set in a school, described her feelings about the programme, in defence of keeping it in the children's schedule:

It is not like normal life as you go to school; there is a strangeness about it which makes you want to watch more – it's sort of weird and different from what we do.

Here, televised storytelling was not a matter of institutional kudos, nor of setting good social examples; instead it permitted a private psychological transformation, what Bettelheim (reprinted in Lohr and Meyer, 1999), in an essay about the psychological advantages of television drama, describes as 'day-dreaming'. The experience of drama for the child quoted above was an opportunity for everyday school life to be remade as 'weird'. It was its 'strangeness' that made her 'want to watch more'. In a sense, this child was describing alienation – 'a representation that allows us to recognize its subject, but at the same time makes it seem unfamiliar', as Bertolt Brecht put it (in Willett, 1964, p. 192).

Because the exercises in the study were a form of public behaviour, taking place in the classroom – with children acting as schedulers, censors, regulators, teachers, parents and so on – such private reflections on the experience of spectatorship were less common than they might have been with a different kind of exercise. However, in some cases, where the children appeared to be very comfortable with each other, particularly in the second-stage, small group discussions, these kinds of private revelations were sometimes made – providing evidence for the Bettelheimian view that 'imagination' and 'remaking' are psychologically and educationally necessary aspects of engagement with dramatic storytelling. One group of children in an inner-city primary school in Cardiff discussed 'scariness'. This led to speculations about the impact generally of children's early experiences of fear, of their own private experiences of fear, and of the ways in which dramatic storytelling could generate useful recognitions of, and reflections on, these internal experiences:

GIRL 1   The first five years of life could make you or break you really. If you – I'm not sure how to describe it.

INTERVIEWER   If you see something very scary or frightening in your first five years, are you saying that could affect you for the whole of your life?

GIRL 1   It could . . .

GIRL 2   I've been scared of certain things.

GIRL 3   I used to be scared of shadows, I used to shut my eyes, and sometimes I'd never get to sleep. Now I love the shadows.

BOY 1   By the time children are old enough to fully understand the programme, they're too mature to be that frightened by it . . .

BOY 2   For older children its not really scary, it's just like interesting to watch . . .

GIRL 1   I think people who believe in demons and such would be really frightened by *The Demon Headmaster*.

This group were acting as a 'committee' of regulators, charged with the job of arbitrating on the proposal to ban the BBC's science fiction drama, *The Demon Headmaster*, because complaints had been received by the BBC about its scariness, including the use of hypnotism. After allowing these private revelations, they were able to summarise and finish their discussion with a characteristically pragmatic conclusion, based on the importance of recognising the needs of the whole audience, and not just the vociferous minority who make negative complaints:

GIRL 1   Can I just say that, say we get quite a lot of letters complaining about *The Demon Headmaster*. If you ban it you're going to get more than ten times the amount of letters that you get now. They'll be complaining that it's not on.

Despite, then, the emphasis on social value in drama, many children were capable of acknowledging its escapist and psychological pleasures at the same time. One 10-year-old girl from Middlesbrough gave a definition of drama as both pure entertainment, and as universally accessible: 'drama is something fun for everyone'. Between them the children in the study summed up many of the uses and pleasures of dramatic entertainment described by adult scholars and critics. Clearly they had learned from the drama offered to them by the broadcasting system they knew and had grown up with. The question for the industry now is: how can these pleasures and lessons continue to be offered when locally produced drama may be a threatened genre?

The future of children's television drama

One source of survival may be the professional pleasure derived by the makers of children's programming, despite the structural changes in media institutions which constantly seem to threaten their specialism. Because of its diversity, many producers expressed 'delight' in working in the field, because it permitted a greater creative range (if less money to support it) – including science fiction fantasy (*The Demon Headmaster*; *The Tomorrow People*); pantomimic comedy (*Mike and Angelo*; *Clarissa Explains it All*; *The Wild House*; *Microsoap* – a BBC co-production with the Disney Channel), realistic soap (*Grange Hill*; *Degrassi High*; *Children's Ward*) and classic costume drama, such as *The Prince and the Pauper*, shown in 1996 and which our study was able to observe in production. Producers were also all too grimly aware, as children were not, of the commercial and competitive pressures of making drama a non-cost-effective form of entertainment for children. As several producers pointed out, competition between terrestrial channels themselves and between the terrestrial channels and cable/satellite was having a painful effect on children's production. According to Lewis Rudd (Davies and O'Malley, 1996, p. 149):

We have turned from the cosy duopoly of BBC and ITV to a commercial system, particularly in children's programmes. There are only two sports channels and they are both run by Sky, while you have got four [terrestrial] children's channels competing with each other and competing with [each other]. You have got ITV and BBC and to some extent Channel 4, and GMTV which pulls in a lot of children's advertising.

Peter Tabern, an independent producer with his own company, Childsplay, producer of *Pirates* (BBC), emphasised the importance of the regular schedule, which John Birt predicted would disappear, favourably comparing the British system of protected afternoon slots to the more specialised provision of children's television in America. Tabern (interviewed for the BBC study in spring, 1996) argued that the children's channels in America are essentially pitched at adults:

They will run crowd-pleasing quality . . . that has nothing to do with the children but is based totally on what their perception of what their adult audience wants for their children . . . doing things *for and to* children rather than trying to get alongside where the children currently are. . . When you involve huge numbers of countries and huge global markets . . . you are bound to end up by making a programme which is least offensive to the greatest number and you are not going to make a programme that any one person out there actually wants.

Not all our interviewees were so pessimistic about transatlantic influences. Alan Horrox (interviewed for the BBC study in spring, 1996) believed that British broadcasters who have not come up with the kind of programmes for young people that he and his own family admire, should not be patronising about the Americans:

My So-called Life, Party of Five, that's some of the best drama I've seen, terrific stuff . . . I think those things find their audience and have much more impact than a million *Baywatches*. How many things that are as good as *My So-called Life* are there on UK television?

One of the children in the study agreed with him, identifying a category of programming of particular appeal to pre-adolescent and early adolescent girls, which US programming appears to have identified more successfully (despite the fact that *My So-called Life* was cancelled in the US after two seasons):

Children's television is OK for children aged about 2–12 but it ends there. There should be more programmes for pre-teen kids e.g. *My So called Life* on

Channel 4. Also *Hollyoaks* on Channel 4 and *Heartbreak High* is good on Channel 2. There *should* be more programmes for my age like there is children's television. (Girl, 12, secondary school, Middlesbrough)

This girl, aged twelve, clearly illustrated the distinction which many children in this age group made between themselves and 'children'; programmes for 'my age' were not the same as 'children's television' – and not the same as adults' television either.

The producers we interviewed identified a number of structural changes which they expected to take place in the commissioning of children's drama, made in response to new commercial and competitive pressures. These changes included extending the length of drama runs, with a minimum of twelve episodes, which are more economical in their use of actors and resources and sell better abroad. Adapting children's books was expected to continue, but no longer books such as William Mayne's *Earthfasts*, one of the last dramatisations directed by Marilyn Fox in 1996, which was seen as a ratings failure, despite the fact that she (and a number of other people, including myself) considered it an artistic success. Books like *Earthfasts* were seen as intellectual books and a minority choice for good readers. 'Simpler' books which would appeal to more children across the age and social range of the audience, like Gillian Cross's *The Demon Headmaster* series, are now seen to be a better bet for adaptation. Drama will have to get used to economising on setting, numbers of characters and the use of children. Using child performers is costly because child actors have to be legally licensed under terms which limit their working hours, and they must have an average of three hours a day tuition – a requirement which cost-cutting accelerated shooting schedules is now making nearly impossible (see Singleton Turner, 1999).

Schedules are changing so that the most expensive period drama is shown on Sunday afternoons, to a family, rather than an exclusively child audience. There are also an increasing number of international co-productions, such as the recent hybrid *The Magician's House* (1999) co-produced by the BBC with the Canadian Broadcasting Corporation, set in the UK, shot in British Columbia, and starring both British and North American actors, and *Microsoap* – a show about families in which the competing value-systems of the BBC, with its public service tradition of educational and therapeutic realism, and Disney, with its happiness-related determination not to offend, sometimes sit uneasily together. Under these new dispensations for drama, we were told, there will be more dubbing, and recycling of programmes and non-popular genres, such as ITV's factual programmes, may be squeezed out. Our analysis of children's provision in the UK between 1992 and 1996

(Davies and Corbett, 1997), carried out for the Broadcasting Standards Commission, showed that ITV's factual programming in the four sample weeks in each year of the analysis declined from 605 minutes in 1992 to 250 minutes in 1996. Lewis Rudd (Davies and O'Malley, 1996, p. 163) also predicted that programmes 'which are quirky or . . . very specific to a particular country, which are not international' would cease to be produced. Anna Home (Davies and O'Malley, 1996, p. 143) believed in 1996 that drama programmes would polarise: 'There will still be your big expensive costume pieces, and then I think there will be a lot of much cheaper things at the other end, and the middle may erode.'

In 1999/2000, most of these predictions have come to pass, along with 'history repeating itself' in the form of the ending of the BBC Children's Department as an autonomous entity within the BBC. It has now (spring 2000) become part of a large, reorganised adult programme grouping within the BBC, called Drama and Entertainment.

Inevitably, producers' analyses of the functions and future of television drama focused more on costs, marketing, production constraints, coping with new technological and economic demands, and less on broader cultural, sociological and psychological issues. It was an awareness that these technical–economic constraints were dominating the public debate about the future of broadcasting, which led to the main qualitative task of our study being an exercise in which children acting as channel controllers were required to choose (and lose) programmes on the grounds of cost. Despite this (see chapter 5) it was noteworthy that economic considerations rarely came into their discussions, although they were aware of them. Given the chance of defining, analysing and scheduling broadcast drama for their fellow children, the 'narrative training', which Edward Barnes argued was offered to them by public service broadcasting, continued to produce arguments for traditional socialising and aesthetic functions. Like many adult critics before them, children emphasised performance, social modelling, entertainment and, above all, the compelling structural power of narrative. As this 10-year-old boy in a Buckinghamshire suburban primary school put it:

Once you get into it and the characters get introduced, you are just like hooked on it . . . At the end, when all is finished, there is something happening, so you *have* to watch the next episode.

3   Changing childhood

How old are big people? Ten.   Girl, 7, outer-London primary school

Should we be doing things like this [*Teletubbies*] for 2-year-old
children? . . . they're missing out on the next level up – the 3, 4, 5 [age
group] . . . If we had enough space within the schedule we would
define the age groups . . . we could get away with having a strand for 7
year olds, and a strand for 9 year olds.
                    Producer, BBC, on preschool TV for under-threes.

In 1982, an American education professor, Neil Postman, famously
declared that, thanks to television, childhood had 'disappeared', and
wrote a best-selling book to this effect, reprinted in 1994. (Eighteen
years later, David Buckingham, too, has announced that we are now at a
stage 'after the end of childhood', Buckingham, 2000b.) For Postman,
television's weapons in the final destruction of childhood were twofold:
it 'banished shame' by making adult sexual knowledge available to the
very young, and it superseded literacy as the primary means of communication. Once television became the primary deliverer of information and entertainment to the young, the age-related and gradual
acquisition of knowledge required by learning to read complex written
texts was brought to an end.
     According to Postman, childhood ended at 7 years of age in pre-
literate societies. It was only the introduction of general schooling,
which, in turn, only arose after the invention of printing made the
widespread teaching of reading and writing possible, that brought about
what he calls 'the tie between education and calendar age', that is,
'childhood'. In industrialised societies, childhood then became a prolonged state of dependence and non-citizenship, not ending until the
age of 18, the age set for the start of adulthood by the 1989 United
Nations Convention on the Rights of the Child. Elisabeth Eisenstein
(1979, pp. 133–4), the historian of the social impact of printing, argued
that the technology of printing was directly responsible for 'youth
culture' – but she used the term in a positive sense: 'Newly segregated at

schools, receiving special printed materials geared to distinct stages of learning, separate "peer groups" ultimately emerged, a distinctive youth culture . . . came into being.' For Postman, the technology of television has been directly responsible for engendering a very different and more deplorable sort of youth culture – one in which premature adult, especially sexual, knowledge has brought what he calls childhood to an end.

Postman follows Philippe Ariès (1962) in arguing that childhood was an invention of the seventeenth-century enlightenment. It was in the seventeenth century that the first childhood slang and jargon was recorded, and parents began to give each child unique names. Arising from these developments, the 'modern family' began (Postman, 1982, p. 44):

The social requirement that children be formally educated for long periods led to a reorientation of parents' relationships to their children . . . with books on every conceivable topic becoming available . . . parents were forced into the role of educators and theologians.

This enlightened construction of prolonged, literate, family oriented childhood, argued Postman (p. 79), is being swept away, by the universally-accessible medium of television – a medium which, in its reliance on images, makes

the rigors of a literate education irrelevant . . . Unlike books . . . the TV image is available to everyone, regardless of age . . . TV presents information in a form that is undifferentiated in its accessibility and this means that television does not need to make distinctions between the categories 'child' and 'adult'.

The quotation from a children's producer above indicates that Postman's strictures are not entirely justified: television systems have, to a considerable extent, adopted the Enlightenment model of childhood and built an Enlightenment view of stage-related development into their structures. Even audience and market research, such as the Neilsen and BARB rating systems, divide the young audience into narrow age groups: children are people aged 4–15, and, for scheduling and advertising purposes, these age groups are further broken down into 4–7, 8–11 and 12–15s. Different kinds of programmes and commercials are made to appeal to these age groups. The idea that certain kinds of material, including television viewing itself, needs to be confined to specific age groups is powerfully embedded in public discourse about children and television.

The quotation from the producer at the head of this chapter refers to an international public controversy about the preschool programme *Teletubbies*. Made by the independent producers Ragdoll Productions (based in Shakespeare's birthplace of Stratford-upon-Avon) and first broadcast on the BBC, it is now the most profitable BBC programme ever made around the world. It was controversial because it was targeted at children younger than three, including pre-linguistic children, and it was accused by a Norwegian producer at the 1998 Children and Television World Summit, held in London, of being little more than an exploitative piece of international marketing. Its much respected (and recently honoured with an MBE) creator, Anne Wood, defended the educational value of the image over words in an interview (Davies and Corbett, 1997, p. 232): 'We make work to nurture the imaginations of different ages – a child of 2 is not a child of 12. Visual comedy . . . appeals to the very young. Words are no good.'

Partly prompted by this public debate, and the view that in devoting so much of the preschool budget to the non-verbal *Teletubbies* other preschoolers were losing out, a new series for a very precise age band of slightly older children, the 3–6 year olds, has now been produced for the BBC: *The Tweenies* which began in the 1999–2000 season. Like the American *Sesame Street* and also *Teletubbies*, *The Tweenies* uses adults dressed as felt-headed muppets to create a non-culturally specific group of creatures, living in a self-contained childish world of games, stories and film inserts. The programme is educationally designed to introduce children to school and other features of the public environment beyond their homes, and clearly targets people who are old enough to follow narratives and listen to direct address, but not yet so mature and sophisticated that they will resent being addressed by walking toys. Both *Teletubbies* and *Tweenies* show evidence of having been designed with reference to public and cultural ideas of stage-related progressions in childhood

The Enlightenment model of childhood as calendar-related age progression is further built into the scheduling of British television. Both the BBC and ITV in Britain are required to keep protected early afternoon slots for children's programmes, and there are special 'teatime' slots for children, and families at weekends. The concept of stage-related childhood, taking place in a family presumed to have the moral and intellectual education of their children at heart, which Postman argued could only be guaranteed by a book-based culture, is actually preserved in many of the present structures of broadcasting and the philosophies underlying their regulation. These paternalistic structures may well be swept away by developments that even the pessimistic Postman did not anticipate – the multichannel digital world of viewing on demand, in which such concepts as 'the watershed' (adult viewing after 9 p.m.) become meaningless; there is also the new cultural 'threat' of interactive computers, which allow children the same degree of control as adult users, and access to wider worlds of 'shamelessness' in the form of pornography and paedophilia on the World Wide Web.

For the time being, however, the age and stage-related organisation of television was a model that had been internalised even by the youngest group in our study, a group of 6 and 7 year olds, who were given the task of discussing the cartoon genre, with particular reference to the American children's show *Rugrats*: Asked what age group the programme was aimed at, a discussion began in which age categories were seen as both central, and flexible, in defining the appeal of the programme:

GIRL 1   About our age, because babies wouldn't like it as much, because they wouldn't understand, and big people would find it babyish for them.

INTERVIEWER   How old are big people?

GIRL 1   10.

INTERVIEWER   So it is too babyish for 10 year olds?

GIRL 1   I would have thought it would be from about 7 to about 11, because my brother is 11 and he still likes it . . .

GIRL 2   I think you can watch it from any age under 12 years old, because you can watch any time really, you don't have to watch it when you are this age or that age.

INTERVIEWER   OK, any age.

BOY 1   From 4 to 8.

GIRL 3   I think about two and a half, if they were just running they wouldn't like it, but if they were two and a half they would.

GIRL 1   I would like to change that one, because my sister, she still likes to watch it, so I agree with M. [girl 2], any age.

Postman's view that children of any age can understand everything on TV will be returned to; as the comments above suggest, it was not a view shared by all the children in the study, although they were prepared to negotiate different criteria of age-suitability, based on different personal experience. Other theorists have debated the cultural construction of childhood, historically, sociologically and discursively, but Postman is rare in addressing one of the most significant influences in the lives of modern children: the electronic media. Most other theorists of childhood say surprisingly little about it.

This chapter discusses these theories and also discusses children as audiences with reference to developmental psychological models of cognitive and linguistic development (for example, Gardner, 1991) and the work done in the USA on children's developing comprehension of television (for example, Bryant and Anderson, 1983; Dorr, 1986) – a tradition of study which is less popular in media studies in the United

Kingdom. The American tradition of studying media effects, both social and cognitive, on children, and the broadcasting system in the USA which has given rise to this tradition, contrast with the more literary traditions of analysis in both British scholarship and in British broadcasting. This contrast means that the international scholarly debate about the relationship between children and media often finds itself putting forward very different, and somewhat conflicting, models of childhood. The model of media literacy and use in the USA is a 'public health' model, requiring protection for children, especially the very young, from violence and aggressive advertising. Children are seen as vulnerable and impressionable, and hence in need of adult intervention, whether in the form of political regulation, or in the form of protective teaching of media literacy skills, in order to help them withstand the seductive techniques of commercial entertainment (Brown, 1991).

Scholars and educators in the UK, such as Barker (1989), Hilton (1996) and Buckingham et al. (1999) take a more libertarian view of children's 'rights' of access to modern media texts, no matter how popular and 'vulgar', and are optimistic about children's ability to negotiate with and benefit from such texts. This optimisim partly derives from recent sociological and anthropological models of childhood, which emphasise its cultural and historical constructedness, and de-emphasise views of the child as inevitably vulnerable and in need of protection. This redefinition of childhood is linked with broader trends in the British academy, especially in the field of cultural studies, which are devoted to rejecting middle-class élitism in the British cultural establishment, including broadcasting. British Cultural Studies (see Turner, 1990) is characterised by demands for recognition of cultural diversity, from working-class self-improvement (Hoggart, 1958) to the semiotics of popular fashions like jeans (Fiske, 1989). The rejection of cultural élitism generally has embraced a rejection of British broadcasting's paternalist attitudes to children, embodied in BBC Controller of Television Cecil McGivern's comment to Owen Reed in 1956, when the new commercial channel, ITV, 'stole' most of the child audience (quoted in Buckingham et al., 1999, p. 14): 'You have got to recover the lost child audience without sacrificing standards.' Writers such as Barker and Petley (1997) equate the child audience with working-class audiences; both groups, according to them, are victims of middle-class patronisation by cultural providers, and both are therefore equally in need of defending from overprotective regulation.

Implicit in these arguments is a rejection of Postman's idealisation of the Enlightenment model of childhood as a prolonged, and necessary, period of insulation from adult influences and knowledge. However, an area of concern which unites Postman with some of his opponents is another, and very powerful, source of construction and reconstruction of childhood: commerce. As Kline (1993) has described, the definition of the state of childhood in the late twentieth century has become the responsibility of global media conglomerates, such as Disney, and toy manufacturers such as Mattel, who operate sophisticated market research in order to define and provide ideal 'childhoods' for their customers. They have done this, as Kline (pp. 18 – 19) points out, by paying 'more diligent attention than educationists to children's active imaginations and incidental cultural interests':

Marketing's ethnography of childhood has validated children's emotional and fantasy experience, which the educational researchers have by and large avoided and derided . . . Identifying the basis of children's daily [cultural] experience provided the means for transforming them into a market segment.

The commercial institutions dedicated to providing resources for caretaking families, include the babyfood industry, the snack and confectionery industries, toiletries, technology, clothing, transportation devices, and the huge, converging variety of entertainment industries – books, cinema, video, computer games, toys and TV, many of which unite in joint marketing campaigns to promote their linked products. The implications of this, as McNeal (1992, p. 250), points out are: 'that children are very much alike around the industrialised world . . . they very much want the same things . . . it appears that fairly standardised multinational marketing strategies to children around the globe are viable'.

Such a universal view of childhood homogeneity contrasts with culturally constructivist views of childhood, which emphasise cultural variation, but it obviously works effectively for marketers and businesses, such as Disney. This suggests that some forms of cultural expectations in children are, if not universal, at least capable of being universally activated by globally circulated stories and messages – a problem for countries outside the United States who are struggling to preserve local cultural traditions in the face of Hollywood dominance. This struggle is found even in the relatively media-powerful UK, although some commentators in Britain believe that the élitist tradition of British broadcasting has enculturated the British public, from childhood, into preferring certain kinds of locally produced programming, and that this – despite its traditional failure to recognise class and minority diversity – is a safeguard which renders audiences capable of resisting wholesale Americanisation. Claire Mulholland, a regulator at the ITC, in an interview for the Broadcasting Standards Commission study (Davies and Corbett, 1997) argued:

If you look at cinema, it is dominated by Hollywood, as is every country in the world, because they produce more films and you can get them more cheaply and that applies to a certain extent to TV . . . Even people with cable and satellite, their first choice remains home-produced product . . . even with the American competition, [they prefer] terrestrial only because it's British original. I think that is because people here have expectations that the Americans never had, because they never knew it.

Ages and stages: biology and development

In a society in which families in the UK, like many other families in the developed world, spend on average £150 on toys and games for each child at Christmas (source: Head of Planning, UK Children's Society, *Guardian*, 22 November 1999), it can be easy to overlook the fact that child survival, child growth and child health are the most important prerogatives in a world where many children continue to die before their first birthday. Inequalities between prosperous and poor children have been increasing in rich countries too, and children from social classes D and E in Britain are still more likely to die or suffer from ill health than are children in social classes A and B. According to a report by researchers at Bristol University, reported in the *Guardian*, 2 December 1999, the number of deaths of babies under 12 months is at least twice as high in poor areas of Glasgow, Manchester and other big UK cities, as it is in the prosperous Home Counties (the south-eastern counties surrounding London). The nineteenth- and early twentieth-century discourse of 'child rescue', with middle-class crusaders attempting to improve the lot of working-class children by giving them, for instance, access to gardens, fresh air, and healthy food, has provoked some scepticism about motives among childhood theorists (see for example, Steedman, 1990, on the subject of Margaret McMillan, founder of the Deptford Centre open-air nursery movement) similar to media scholars' suspicions of the early BBC's do-gooding élitism. Nevertheless, underlying all discussions about childhood, and what treatment or information is appropriate to people of different ages, is the biological experience of each human individual of growing up, and growing older through time – an experience which is subjectively very central to the active business of being a child.

Assumptions about 'age' and what is appropriate for children of different ages is obviously culturally bound. As Hendrick (1997, p. 36) put it, childhood has been 'made' into a 'very specific kind of age-graded and age-related condition' as it has gone through various levels of 'construction' by sociologists and other theorists, and this, for Neil Postman, is what was valuable about it. For the purposes of deciding what was, and was not, appropriate for children's entertainment, this construction was also seen as useful by the children we spoke to; for example:

I think that children's BBC can entertain children of different ages. There are some adult programmes that children enjoy watching too. Some programmes some older children find babyish, but they are on during school time. (Girl, 12, outer-London secondary school)

'Age' was a cultural representation which children in the BBC drama study drew on very freely in guiding their decisions about what was, and was not, appropriate material for audiences. Theories of the difference that age can make, and perceptions of 'big', 'small', 'babyish', 'my age' were a constant theme in their discussions, and a central way of establishing their identity as broadcasting consumers.

Physical growth and health

In *The Sociology of Childhood* (1982, p. 12) Christopher Jenks asserted that 'childhood is not a natural phenomenon and cannot properly be understood as such. The social transformation from child to adult does not follow directly from physical growth . . . Childhood is to be understood as a social construct.' Nevertheless, an understanding of biology – physical growth – is a necessary, if not sufficient, foundation for discussions about the nature and needs of children. Biologically, human childhood is characterised by extreme immaturity and extreme length, compared to the infancy of even the most nearly related species, such as the great apes, which means that human adults' physical, emotional and economic investment in nurturing their young to maturity has to be very prolonged. From this basic biological fact flow many implications for the organisation of human social institutions, including the status and function of women – the people who physically produce children – in society.

Human babies are born well before they can properly move, feed, clean or defend themselves, partly to allow the (relatively) safe passage of the baby through the mother's birth canal. As this point indicates, women's health is closely linked with that of their children – a fact not much discussed in histories of childhood such as that of Philippe Ariès, and not at all (as Meehan *et al.*, 1995, have pointed out) in Habermas's account of the bourgeois public sphere. The interlinked well-being of children and their mothers (see, for example, Lewis, 1980) inevitably requires any discussion of childhood, and of children's culture, to consider gender issues too. Children's health, welfare and physical survival are closely linked with that of their mothers. According to a *Guardian*/Marie Stopes International, 1998 report on reproductive health in the developing world, the cost of the 'transformation from child to adult', in Jenks' phrase, for women, girls and children around the world, is considerable. Each day, 1,600 women die in pregnancy and childbirth; every year 1.4 million infants are stillborn and 1.5–2.5 million infants die in the first week of life from mothers' pregnancy and birth complications; two-thirds of all deaths in developing countries are of children under 1 year old; 1 million or more children are left motherless each year by these deaths; motherless children are 3 to 10 times more likely to die within 2 years than children who live with both parents; complications of pregnancy, birth and unsafe abortion are leading causes of death in adolescent girls; in Ethiopia alone, 1 woman in 9 will die in childbirth. Each woman there has an average of 7 children.

Feminists like Meehan have criticised Habermas' account of the bourgeois public sphere for failing to take account of women's experiences, and they might well criticise sociologists such as Jenks on the same grounds, since this holocaust of maternal death, child death and orphanhood becomes peripheral when cultural aspects of childhood are stressed over physical and 'natural' ones. An exceptional example of childhood studies recognising the separate physical realities of children's lives, and the social necessity of accurately measuring them apart from those of adults, is Jens Qvortrup's analysis, in James and Prout's edited collection of essays, *Constructing and Reconstructing Childhood* (1997), of Danish social statistics on the family. Qvortrup demonstrates, for example, that, although unemployment among Danish adults may be 9 per cent, when the statistics are re-examined to find out how many children have unemployed parents, the answer is 13 per cent – in other words more children than adults are affected by unemployment when a system of social accounting is used which acknowledges children's separate existence and status. Qvortrup argues (p. 90) that 'there may be a reality which is *common for children* [his emphasis], irrespective of their parents' backgrounds'.

Meehan (1995, p. 7) argues that Habermas's concept of public space (and she could also apply this to Jenks' rejection of physical growth in defining childhood)

suffers from a gender blindness that occludes the differential social and political status of men and women . . . he does not recognize that this relationship is affected as much by gender as it is by money . . . if capitalism has assigned the role of the 'worker' to men, it has assigned the role of consumer, which links the economy and the family, to women . . . [and] the tasks of childrearing and household maintenance.

As this comment indicates, another unrepresented group in Meehan's network of economic, social and political relations is children. The existence of childhood is intimately linked with women's health and status, and gender politics are inseparable from discussions of the public sphere and the rights of women (and children) to be represented in it. However, there is a sense in which children need to be seen as a group within the public sphere in their own right; the adults responsible for them, their mothers, fathers and parent-substitutes can never provide alone all that is required to ensure the safe arrival, growth, health and development to maturity of every baby born.

Institutional responsibility for the young

In order to facilitate the nurturing of the young by caretaking adults, industrialised societies have developed institutional arrangements such as maternity provision; paediatric health care; developmental check-ups; schooling; day-care for children whose parents are employed outside the home; and a range of legal provisions which can allow the state to take over the caretaking role of the parent in some circumstances. Among these institutional arrangements are publicly funded educational and children's broadcasting. The establishment of such institutional arrange-ments within public culture has been instrumental in creating new scope for the ring-fencing of childhood as an area separate from adulthood. As Buckingham *et al.* (1999, p. 9) put it:

The separation between adults and children is being *reinforced* [their emphasis] both as a result of the increasing fragmentation of the audience and through the emergence of new and distinctive modes of address in children's programmes . . . [they] appeal on the grounds that they *exclude* adults and everything that they are seen to represent.

Part of the institutionalisation of this culture of childhood through broadcasting has been the development of a new specialism – people whose professional expertise is dedicated to providing audio-visual education and storytelling for children – a group whose work we examined, and whom we interviewed as part of our study (see chapter 2). This group can be seen as influential in helping to create new public definitions of childhood, because the material they envisage as appro-priate, necessary and entertaining for child audiences and consumers is pervasive through film, television and their related cultural products, and because it reaches the majority of children in industrialised societies from birth (a source of Postman's anxieties).

Sociological theories of childhood and culture

Despite the historical centrality of storytelling in the socialisation of children, sociological studies of childhood have so far had little to say about cultural experiences. In *Theorizing Childhood*, by some of the most influential sociologists of childhood in the UK, Alison James, Christopher Jenks and Alan Prout (1998), there is only one index entry for 'television'; none for film or cinema; none for books or literature; one for art (children's); none for entertainment or leisure; none for theatre or pantomime; none for toys; and the only references to 'play' concern its 'adaptive potentiation' and its role in education and gender formation.

The authors (p. 56) express concern about the movement of childhood from public to private space, one example of which is the 'banishment' of children to bedrooms by the 9 p.m. watershed in British broadcasting regulation, after which 'adult' material can be shown on television because children are presumed to be in bed:

We have moved then from a collective to an individual space, with the public and external experience of shame and degradation transformed into the private and inner experience of guilt . . . From the 9 o clock watershed on TV viewing which, in Britain, postpones certain kinds of programme to later in the evening when children are supposed to be in bed, through to the more rigid enforcement of legal age limits for entry into cinemas, the child gets to know 'its place'.

The shameful banishment of the child to the bedroom by the 9 p.m. watershed, is seen by these authors (p. 57) not only as an adult colonisation of the child's physical space, but also as an invasion of the inner, psychological integrity of the essential child, 'conspiring tactically for the child's own good . . . the culmination of a nineteenth century trajectory towards, finally, regulating the space within the child'. Childhood in this 'socially-constructivised' account, with its lack of any positive reference to publicly provided entertainment or amusement, looks rather grimly like the version invented by Mr Gradgrind, with his disapproval of the circus and his emphasis on 'Facts', in Charles Dickens's *Hard Times*. To the extent that it does this, the sociology of childhood presents a view of childhood which, in its failure to acknowledge the centrality of leisure activities, is at variance with the actual practices of people responsible for the socialisation of children.

In sociological childhood studies, the idea that children's development is a 'natural rather than social phenomenon' (James *et al.*, 1998, p. 17) is also severely criticised. Particularly out of favour is Jean Piaget

(1896–1980), whose theory of progressive cognitive development, from babyhood (sensori-motor learning) to adulthood (formal operations) was proposed as part of the biological programming of all children, and has been the basis of much educational curriculum planning, including that of educational broadcasting. Piaget's developmental model of childhood supports Neil Postman's cultural/literacy model of childhood in that it is based on principled progression, with full maturity being delayed until a series of intermediate stages have been passed. James *et al.* (1998, p. 17) call Piagetian cognitive psychology 'an unholy alliance between the human sciences and human nature'. They point out, and deplore, the fact that the mature adult thinker towards which the Piagetian model of the child is supposedly developing is a peculiarly Western one. They condemn the discipline of psychology for not being 'reflexive about its own practices', and lament the fact that psychology has 'colonised childhood in a pact with medicine, education and government agencies. This has led in turn to enhanced prestige, authority . . . and a continued high level of public trust and funding.'

The model of a gullible public, and an easily duped education system and government, allowing themselves to be 'colonised' by unreflexive psychologists taking up more than their fair share of public funding is, to a psychologist (and indeed, to a member of the public), a somewhat offensive one. Assumptions about stage-related development, similar to the models proposed by cognitive psychology, underlie much of the 'common-sense' thinking of parents and quasi-parental figures such as teachers and television producers. These assumptions also underlay many of the judgements made by children in our study, which raises the question of who has the right to decide which assumptions about childhood should be permitted to circulate, and by whom, in the public sphere. An example of such 'common-sense' theorising is this 12-year-old boy's account of the cognitive and emotional limitations of a 5 year old, confronted with adult science fiction:

The X Files is too scary and a bit hard to understand, like doctors and autopsies, a 5-year-old kid is not going to understand something like that. (Boy, 12, inner-city secondary school, Middlesbrough)

Such common-sense assumptions could be resistant to change, as James *et al.* lament, partly because they provide workable models for the task of rearing and living alongside growing children, including children living alongside other children. From such accounts, it could be the case that what works in one generation, usually works, with some contemporary cultural adaptation, for the next, and the next. A key mechanism for these workable practices, despite family fragmentation in modern societies and the greatly expanded provision of 'expert' advice, continues to be intergenerational advice, and peer group support. An example of child-care cultural adaptation is the various ways in which a practice like the lullaby has been adapted over the centuries, with modern children being soothed, not only by parental voices, but also by special musical boxes or their own cassettes of music. Another is the success over the last forty years of the mother-to-mother advice movement for breast-feeding in groups like La Leche League and the UK National Childbirth Trust (see Davies, 1982, reprinted 1993). These groups have been instrumental in the education of health professionals, not the other way round.

Goodnow and Collins (1990) are among the few researchers in this area to study systematically the ways in which childhood is theorised, described and constructed through practice by parents. In their book *Development According to Parents* (p. 24), they point out that:

ideas about the course or timing of development have attracted attention both because they seem to influence the timing of parents' actions and because they seem to provide the basis for assessment, for noting whether a child's progress, or one's own progress as a parent is 'on time' or 'off time'. As long as children are 'at an age when they don't know any better', for instance, a variety of misbehaviours may be excused.

Parents' and children's ideas about 'on' and 'off time' are not only based on their own 'common sense', as Goodnow and Collins acknowledge. They come from other parents and children, and also indirectly from published academic knowledge via parentcraft classes during pregnancy, or from popular magazines, or TV programmes, in which professionals such as midwives, doctors and psychologists give advice. Buckingham (1995, p. 17) points out the historical origins of these developments in 'the removal of children from the workforce and the imposition of compulsory schooling during the nineteenth century':

these developments were accompanied by a veritable explosion of discourse about childhood and the production of knowledge about 'the child' was inextricably implicated in the operation of adult power and in the regulation of children's everyday lives . . . parallel developments can be identified in the growth of the human sciences (notably developmental psychology) and in their application through popular advice literature.

This model of a public uncritically absorbing 'popular advice literature' and helplessly acceding to meddlesome political insistence that their children should stop working in factories and go to school, has echoes of the 1930s Frankfurt School notion of the passive 'mass' audience. If children are to be 'constructed' as active and autonomous audiences, capable of independent agency, then it seems reasonable that so should their parents be. If health and psychological professionals have 'earned the trust' of parents, this could be because parents reading child-care magazines, like readers of romance and soap opera, are not dupes of professional propaganda, but are 'active audiences'. Much of the advice given to parents based on psychological research, is acceptable because it is obviously intended to be personally supportive and often accords with, and pays respect to, parents' own experiences and feelings. The same trust from parents is accorded by extension to the kinds of psychological support-systems provided for quasi-parental figures, such as teachers, and, in the case of the subject of this book, cultural providers for children, such as the BBC. I was asked to do the study because I am a psychologist, with experience of working with young children, and of finding out how they think and feel about television, and this was what the BBC wanted.

The sociology of childhood may be reflexive about its own practices, but, inevitably, this reflexiveness is of most interest to other sociologists engaged in the same practices. The practices engaged in by parents and quasi-parents need different sorts of reflexivity, which is why the analysis of parenting carried out by Goodnow and Collins is useful, and why studies of the processes of production, as well as of reception, are necessary in television and media studies. New theorisations of childhood, and the postmodern insistence that childhood, like most other social categories which people may take for granted, is culturally constructed, are intellectually valuable realisations. However, such theorisations need to find a way of being translated into constructive practical systems for supporting those outside academic disciplines who confront the problems of defining childhood every day as part of their lives or jobs. These groups include children themselves.

James et al. (1998, pp. 57–8) characterise modern thinking about childhood as primarily a means of recovering adults' own experiences of being children: 'Childhood is simultaneously our fond, adult rememberings of a time past and the immediacy of our own children's lives.' This places more emphasis on adult reconstructions of childhood than on childhood as something that children themselves experience – not as a memory, nor as an observation from the outside by parents, but as a lived state of being. Nevertheless, these authors (1998, p. 57) do call for accounts of childhood in which children speak for themselves, and which 'stress the significance for our understanding of childhood of the experiential accounts to be gleaned from the changing biographies of young people themselves'.

Our study took up the challenge of these sociologists to allow information to be 'gleaned from . . . young people themselves' – and one of the findings to emerge from this was the fact that childhood was constructed subjectively by children, as a state about which the people undergoing it had sufficient expertise to constitute themselves as spokespersons for children as a whole. As one boy in an inner-city primary school in London asserted: 'I think they [broadcasters] should look at children's opinions and figure out what they would like.' Children in our study frequently used the term 'I'; but just as frequently they used the term 'we', meaning 'we children', as distinct from 'you' grown-ups. Another 9-year-old boy from the same inner-London primary school, was quoted in the Introductory chapter, about the necessity of 'thinking like children': 'if you want to know what children like, you have to think like one or base it on your small brother or your cousin'. Thus children as individuals expressed a sense of their own age or youth, but they also expressed a sense of the differentness of children as part of a bipolar category in opposition to adults, which could be expressed through choice of programmes for their schedules, for example:

We tried to think of the age of the children. *Live and Kicking* was our age and *999* and *The X Files* was for older people and children. (Girl, 9, inner-London primary school)

The contrast between the two disciplines of sociology and psychology, while it may seem an academic diversion in the context of the topic of children's attitudes to television drama, is of relevance here, because, when it comes to answering questions about children's use, enjoyment and understanding of media, psychologists have carried out the majority of studies which can be practically applied by those charged with the responsibility of 'educating, informing and entertaining', that is, producers (see, for example, Singleton Turner, 1994, who discusses how academic research on children's attention and comprehension has influenced his own professional practice as a children's director).

Cognitive differences in childhood

If cognitive difference between children and adults is an invention of Western psychology, then children generally may not be cognitively different from adults and it follows that they can understand and enjoy the same kinds of cultural products as adults do. But there is another position – the one espoused by most of our interviewees: a pragmatic view that many children (particularly the very young) *are* different from adults, and that all children's experience of life generally, regardless both of their cognitive competence and their cultural circumstances, is different from that of adults in the fundamental sense that children as a social group are dependent for life-support on adult society, a case that never occurs, in any human society, the other way round. The experience of being dependent, whether on kindly, or on arbitrarily unjust, adults, is the universal experience of childhood – and it is this that many children's stories and dramas deal with: as Bazalgette and Staples (1995, p. 96) put it: 'children's films foreground the problems of either coping with adults, or of coping without them'.

Children's understanding of media

Aimée Dorr, a psychologist at the University of California has characterised three important aspects of the child TV audience which make it 'special' (1986, p. 16). The first is that 'children are lacking in knowledge of their physical and social world'. The second is that children are 'eager to learn about it'; the third is that children are 'only partially equipped with the needed learning tools'. The desire to remedy their own perceived lack of knowledge of the world around them is the fuel driving the engine of children's biological development, leading to their first attempts to sit up, reach, grasp, stand, walk, run, climb and develop language. Children's curiosity about other living beings and their environment generally has made television a magnet for them, but there are many aspects of the information given by television, and the forms in which this information is constructed, which are puzzling for them. This is why Dorr's third characteristic – children's 'partial' access to 'learning tools' – needs to be recognised by media practitioners, educators and media policy-makers.

This recognition is not a matter of preventing children's access to forbidden information, but a matter of recognising young children's (temporary) limitations – what Howard Gardner, of Harvard University (1991), calls 'developmental constraints'. As the children in our study also pointed out, forbidden information is not the problem, since it cannot do much harm to young children who cannot understand it. The issue is one of cognitive competence:

You shouldn't ban it [*The Demon Headmaster*] because little children wouldn't really understand what was going on anyway. Until they're about seven they wouldn't really understand it and they'd get scared then.

INTERVIEWER   So you need to understand it to be scared?

SEVERAL CHILDREN   Yes.
                                    (Group of 10 year olds, inner-city primary school, Cardiff)

These children pointed out that the stylistic, or 'modal', features of *The Demon Headmaster*, a science fiction fantasy, requiring knowledge both of real-world science, and of the generic conventions of sci-fi (the mixture of the impossible with the mundane), are not sufficiently familiar to young children for them to read the content appropriately and hence to be truly frightened of it. In this, the children were drawing attention to one of the most fruitful areas for research on children's understanding of screen media – research on 'modality' awareness, an approach first taken by Australian semioticians Bob Hodge and David Tripp in their study of children's readings of cartoons, described in *Children and Television* (1986). Modality awareness is the ability to 'read' the forms, conventions and stylistic techniques of a medium in order to establish the extent of – nearness to, or distance from – its relationship with reality, the degree of closeness of the 'signifier' to the 'signified', in the language of semiotics.

The cues for evaluating the reliability, or truth value, of a proposition in spoken language are grammatical forms; for instance, saying that something '*might* be the case' is weaker modality, indicating a further remove from the actual, than saying that 'something *is* the case'. In the case of moving-picture media, like television and film, modality cues are aspects of design, narrative structure, editing, sequencing, shot-composition, word/picture relationships and so on, which indicate the realism, or lack of it, of the representation. An example of the ability of television-literate young children to make modality judgements was given by a group of 6 and 7 year olds in our study, who applied their knowledge of animation technology to assess the degrees of reality of the programme *Rugrats*:

The difference between cartoon characters and real people is because cartoon characters are like drawings and real people are like me and you. You can make them move with computers and they look like they are moving but they are really just drawings. (Group of 6–7 year olds, outer-London infants school)

The study of children's ability to 'read' audio-visual media has been more extensive in the USA, where children's media behaviours and competences are more likely to be studied empirically by cognitive or developmental psychologists. Perhaps partly because of the kinds of professional suspicions in sociology and cultural studies described above, insights from psychology are less often deployed in British and Australian media research about children's understandings of film and television, which, as with Hodge and Tripp's work, come mainly from a tradition of literary and language studies, and draw on cultural analyses of children's learning processes. This division is a pity, because there are many ways in which the different traditions converge, which could usefully inform policy and professional discussions about children and their media.

Modality studies tend to find evidence of a Piagetian process of stage-development. A particularly strong finding in cognitive developmental studies, which also occurred in my own research with 6–11 year olds in Philadelphia (Davies, 1997), is that children under the age of 7 or 8 seem to find it difficult to make 'meta-judgements'. Meta-judgements require us to be reflexive, to think about thinking, or to talk about talking; metalinguistic ability enables children to understand puns, double entendres, metaphors, paradox and irony, the ways in which language can create layers of meaning, some apparently contradictory, many funny to adults, but often baffling to young children. Psycholinguistic research on children's 'theories of mind' – their ability to understand the thought processes of themselves and others, as in being able to recognise when someone is lying – or, indeed, acting – indicates that some of the techniques of both verbal language and television/film language, can be difficult to appreciate for under-sevens (see, for example, Harris *et al.*, 1991; Moore and Frye, 1991).

Aimée Dorr (1986, p. 15) describes Piaget's account of the difficulty that preschool children have in dealing with multiple levels of classification – another form of meta-cognition:

For them [young children] several subordinate classes cannot all belong to the same superordinate class . . . many reversible processes cannot be reversed; and visual alterations in materials are wrongly associated with alterations in other qualities of the materials (for example, changing the shape of a ball of clay changes its weight).

She points out that many adults have the same problems, so these limitations are not exclusive to children; nevertheless, as she says, they are found generally in children. In an example from her own work, she illustrates how a lack of knowledge in young children can create problems of understanding. In a story about 'lost binoculars', preschool children who did not know what binoculars were for, 'believed they were used for two purposes, to make things big and to make things little'.

Similar theoretical assumptions were made by children in our BBC study in assessing the ability of other, younger, children to make sense of television narratives. The older children in the discussion tasks had a model of young children as being in need of help to understand basic information which children of their own age had matured sufficiently to master, for instance, these children from inner London:

INTERVIEWER   Can you tell me how young you think young is, when you say young children?

GIRL,12, INNER-LONDON SECONDARY SCHOOL   Seven.

A 10 year old made the same point:

Sesame Street is only about teaching little children about the number 10 and the ABC and it's about Big Bird and things like that and it is just people dressed up.

Most people understand that and little kids love it, but for older people it is not fair, it is not for all ages. (Boy, 10, inner-city primary school, London)

A group of 10- and 11-year-old children, acting as 'regulators' in a village primary school in Buckinghamshire, also expressed an appropriately adult conception of the limitations of young children, especially the fact that young children do not know what is, or is not, real:

It [*The Demon Headmaster*] should be banned because of the hypnotising which is not good for the younger children.

It should be put on for the older children at a different time so the parents would be at home.

It should be banned for the 4–8 year olds because they wouldn't know it wasn't real . . . And the sound effects would scare younger children.

An 11-year-old boy in the same school, pointed out that 'little kids' could be helped by a form of 'modality training' to cope with programmes that were potentially scary:

It would be OK for younger children to watch it because . . . when they had *Power Rangers*, at the end they say this programme is done by specially trained people, so if they just give a little notice at the end saying this programme is not for you, or something like that.

Characteristically, some groups in the study, while recognising that particular allowances had to be made for small children and that older children have different tastes and cognitive requirements, recognised that youth was not the only determinant of somebody's enjoyment of a programme. A group of 11 and 12 year olds at a Middlesbrough inner-city secondary school was asked what age group was likely to watch the fantasy drama, *The Queen's Nose*, and they said it was 'probably 8 and 9 year olds'. One girl had shown great familiarity with the programme, and was asked:

INTERVIEWER   Emma [not her real name] you watch it, how old are you?

EMMA   12.

INTERVIEWER   So we are saying it's for children from 6 to 12?

EMMA   My mum watches it and she is 33.

Imaginative theorising

In general, a recognition of age variation, especially young children's idiosyncratic 'theories' about reality, and their 'misreadings' of texts, whether verbal or pictorial, is not to insult them; indeed, many of these misinterpretations reveal resourceful theorising, as in the case of some of the youngest children in my Philadelphia study. One 6-year-old boy, when asked how he thought blocks could move by themselves (he was watching a stop-frame animation) said: 'they have a little invisible string and they can pull it on the ground' (Davies, 1997, p. 185). Another child, a 7-year-old girl, used a mixture of technical knowledge and a belief in the marvellous, to account for the sudden appearance of a character 'out of nowhere': 'They shot one scene with the time machine there, and then they stopped and moved it, and then he appeared' (Davies, *ibid.*, p. 114).

Recognising the 'constraints' of these children's mental processes, is not to belittle young children, nor to deny them the rights that belong to other members of society; studies which reveal that children's ways of thinking, interpreting and discussing cultural representations might be systematically different from those of older people can only be useful if they lead to society's treatment of children becoming more sensitive and appropriate to their needs. Studies about children's thought processes can also be pragmatically applied by people who are charged with teaching and entertaining the young, and whose professional responsibilities are to understand and be sensitive to the expectations of their audiences. If magic is what young children want to believe in, then magic is what the adult world should supply them with in their stories, as one 11-year-old girl from a village primary school in Buckinghamshire eloquently argued:

Children don't just want to watch what is real they want fantasy, they don't just want to watch what happens every day – they know what happens because they see it in their own home – they want to see something that is really unbelievable.

The view that young children, particularly, believed in magic was a working theoretical assumption about developmental constraints produced many times by children in the study, for example, this group, from a suburban primary school in Oxfordshire, discussing the inclusion of *The Queen's Nose* (BBC1) in their drama schedule and its use of magic:

INTERVIEWER   When do you stop believing in magic?

GROUP LEADER   When you get older, when you are about seven.

INTERVIEWER   What happens when you stop believing in it?

GROUP LEADER   I think you would be unhappy that you believed it and someone comes up to you and tells you, oh, that is not true.

The testing of the bounds of reality, as in fantasy drama, makes it easier for children to reflect on alternative modes of existence, compared to the realities of life as it is lived. In doing so, they are able to compare these alternative modes with the realities of their own experiences and to understand the forces shaping these experiences. The true 'uses of enchantment' begin to become apparent in such reflections, as we found in discussing the reality and fantasy of a popular children's drama with a whole village school, thirty 5–11 year olds in Co. Durham, in which themes about the nature and purpose of childhood were central to the story.

Children on the nature and meaning of childhood

These children were taking part in a discussion of the second series of the fantasy drama series *The Demon Headmaster* (BBC1, 1997). In the first series, the Demon Head was the head teacher of a school who had used hypnosis to force dull facts and figures into his zombie-like pupils, as a preliminary to political domination, and who was successfully resisted by the child heroes of the story. In the second series, the Demon Head was now using genetic technology to 'bypass evolution' and to 'get rid of childhood'. In a number of scenes, the Demon Headmaster set out his philosophy that childhood was unnecessary, frivolous, disorderly and threatening. It was also, as revealed by the triumph of the children in the first series, a serious threat to his totalitarian Project.

In the course of discussing the degrees of reality and fantasy – the modality – of the programme, the Durham village children discussed the Head's view that 'childhood was not necessary'. One 9-year-old girl argued: 'I think that's not very real because he was a child once.' For her, childhood was an unavoidable biological reality undergone by every human being – hence, for a person who had been a child himself, getting rid of childhood could not be 'very real'. Her argument was that no adult could deny the experiential evidence of having been a child. Like other children in the group, this girl resisted the distinction between childhood as a biological state and childhood as a political/cultural construction made by both childhood theorists and the putative dictator in the story. Neil Postman pointed out in the 1994 version of his book, *The Disappearance of Childhood*, that a number of children had written to him making the same point.

Asked whether they approved of the plan to get rid of childhood, the Durham children produced a chorus of 'No, No':

GIRL 1   It would be impossible to get rid of childhood.

BOY 1   It's necessary to start your life. It gives you things like . . .

GIRL 2   Freedom.

BOY 2   You'd have to get rid of every child in the world as well.

EVERYBODY   Yeah, yeah.

BOY 1   With every child it would be impossible.

GIRL 1   You'd have to get rid of everybody on the other side of the world.

INTERVIEWER   So we think it would be a bad idea?

GIRL 1   A totally bad idea.

For these children, too, childhood was equated with real children – 'every child in the world'. They obviously felt that a plan to get rid of childhood was personally threatening to themselves, and accordingly they opposed it. But they were also capable of seeing that childhood as a state served necessary social functions as a preparation for adulthood, most significantly, through being a time of freedom and playfulness, as well as training (one child pointed out that in childhood, you learn to run fast). In emphasising the Enlightenment value of 'freedom' as an essential characteristic of childhood, they appeared to have absorbed *The Demon Headmaster*'s basic ideological premise. In the story, childhood was represented as the most dangerous opponent of totalitarian authority: something to be destroyed by brutal dictators seeking absolute power, and therefore something to be vociferously defended by children – society's potential liberators. In this, they supported the revised views of Neil Postman himself, who, in the reprint of his book in 1994 (pp. viii–ix), more than 20 years after he originally claimed that childhood had disappeared, admitted: 'Children themselves are a force in preserving childhood . . . American culture is hostile to the idea of children. But it is a comforting, even exhilarating thought that children are not.'

4 'Dear BBC': children's relationship with broadcasters – the consumer child

Dear Children's Television, could you please put more programmes about art on television. I really love art and I want to improve my art skills. Can you also put *Ace Ventura Pet Detective* on another day because on Monday and Wednesdays I have swimming lessons.

Boy, 9, inner-city primary school, Cardiff

The quotation above raises a number of questions about the preoccupations of the child as consumer of media. This 9 year old was taking the opportunity, offered by our questionnaire, to make his needs and desires as a consumer known. However, given that he addresses 'Children's Television' as 'dear', and then goes on to confide, with intimacy, his loves and aspirations to this 'dear' entity, the perception of the relationship he has with 'Children's Television' is not that of a customer ordering a desired object from a sales representative. 'Children's Television' is addressed by this child as a person in whom he feels he can trustingly confide, capable of understanding allusions to swimming lessons, and interested in hearing about his love of art, as well as being able to meet media consumption demands. The provider of children's television appears to have a quasi-parental role and is thus seen as a provider for other kinds of needs as well, including intimacy and mutual trust.

Problems of the child as consumer

Despite the benevolent perception of the broadcasting provider revealed above, the child's role as consumer has been the subject of adult contention since the early days of television, although most research has focused on the impact of television advertising rather than on the child as a consumer of the medium itself (see, for example, Gunter and Furnham, 1998). The model of the consumer in market research is someone who can choose between competing brands; the word 'choice' is the mantra of its exponents. It is now the dominant model of the television audience member, driving expensive new technological developments, such as digitisation in the UK, which promises greater 'choice' for viewers to select between hundreds of channels. In 1999, the British Minister for Culture, Heritage and Sport, Chris Smith, announced that the analogue signal for broadcasting would be switched off in 2006, and that digitised programming would become the norm. The resulting multiplicity of channels will, it was argued, give consumers more power to decide what they will and will not view, and it will be up to individual users to decide how to construct their own viewing schedules. Institutional schedulers and regulators, necessary in an era of spectrum scarcity, and making decisions on behalf of the public, will thus become outmoded and redundant.

In this new world, with the possibility of calling up programmes from digital menus, as well as the possibility of using video for 'time-shifting' (already well established in homes with children), the public service idea, embodied in the ITC regulations, that the period between 4 and 5.30 p.m. is a special, after-school 'slot' during which all children in the country can 'consume' specialist programming, will supposedly become outdated. Shari Donnenfeld, the American in charge of marketing at Nickelodeon UK, interviewed for our Broadcasting Standards Commission study (Davies and Corbett, 1997), was enthusiastic about the commercial opportunities this would create for children's providers:

The whole emergence of digital will offer a whole world of opportunities as well as video on demand. [This] creates more air time for us, producing more, making sure it's quality and the quantity will need to be there as well . . . There will be more available to kids – there will be a kids' sports channel . . . Today children are watching television because they want to, not because there is nothing else on.

Children are thus seen as very important consumers in this new expanding market, both for niche channels – and five new cable channels for children have been set up in the UK between 1993 and 1999, the time of writing – and as consumers of new technology in the future. Children's individual opinions have come to be increasingly valued by broadcasters trying to maintain a competitive advantage in this marketplace – indeed, this was one reason the BBC commissioned the study described in this book. In this new, fragmented environment, how will the 'person' embodied in 'Children's Television' be perceived by children? Will 'television' be perceived in a personalised way at all?

Public versus domestic space

Studies with children, including my own research in Philadelphia (Davies, 1997), have shown that younger children, broadly under 8 years of age, have little grasp of media providers as institutions: their accounts of the nature of television providers tend to focus on persons: 'the writer'; 'the guy on the camera'. Their relationship with television is formed in the home, along with other early social relationships: they are introduced from birth to it, and become familiar with the persons encountered in media products. The TV screen, what Steven Kline (1993, p. 17) has called 'the modern matrix of civilisation [sitting] in most living rooms', is found not only in nearly 100 per cent of all households in the USA and UK, but also in the majority of British children's bedrooms (Livingstone and Bovill, 1999). As Livingstone and Bovill comment, there is no doubt that the screen is seen as a friendly and welcome presence there.

Thus, institutionally, the broadcast media coexist in both the private and public domains, with a tension between publicly funded broadcasting (seen, particularly in the USA, as having the main, if not only, responsibility for serving children) and commercial broadcasting, whose primary purpose is to make money for shareholders. The model of the child as future citizen, with a role to play in the public sphere, and thus the responsibility of the state, can be more easily sustained when broadcasting is regulated according to socially agreed ideals of how the children of a given society should be treated.

A site of tension between public and private in the consumption of television consists in the fact that broadcasting is an arrangement whereby large, economically and politically powerful public institutions deliver a service, frequently consisting of controversial meanings and representations, which is consumed privately, domestically and often uncontrollably. Nowhere has the boundary between these public and private functions been more contested than in the relationship of children to television. In our study, over 50 per cent of our 1,300-plus children had televisions in their bedrooms; in Livingstone *et al.*'s nearly contemporary study, also of 1,300-plus children, 63 per cent did, including 50 per cent of 5–7 year olds. Livingstone and Bovill (1999, p. 34, summary version) describe the children in their study as having 'a bedroom culture' – 'a social place where they can combine friends and media, establishing a life style away from parental monitoring'. Livingstone's findings indicate some ambivalence in parental attitudes to this state of affairs: 'Parental beliefs about the effects of television programmes have little to do with whether or not the child has their own set' (1999 p. 35). Nevertheless, large numbers of parents obviously do collude with the child's private access to broadcast media, not least – as Livingstone and Bovill point out – because it is a 'safe' form of leisure activity, which enables them to know where their children are.

The British 9 p.m. broadcasting 'watershed' illustrates the uneasy nature of this public/private interface; the public institutions of broadcasting are regulated by the state so that no material deemed to be disturbing to children can be shown before 9 o'clock in the evening, after which time children are assumed to be in bed, or 'the responsibility of their parents'. However, there is no guarantee that children *will* be in bed by 9 p.m., and the state lays no legal responsibility on parents for making them go there by this time. The fact that television is increasingly likely to be in the bedroom when the child gets there, further complicates this assumption of the bedroom as a place safe from possible harmful influences of media.

The watershed has provided a disciplinary backup for concerned parents and represents an attempt at a public/private contract. It is sometimes violated by broadcasters with extreme violence, or bad language, or explicitly sexual behaviour taking place in early evening programming, resulting in complaints. Nevertheless, it has traditionally provided the basis of a partnership between broadcasters, government and families in managing the access of children to television in the UK. No similar regulatory arrangements exist in the USA; however, 'adult' (meaning sexual) programming is usually shown after 10 p.m. The genre which has managed most successfully to evade this protective approach to children's viewing is the daytime talk show. It is possible for children to watch adults discussing their sexual relationships, and to witness adult conflict, both in Britain and the USA, in the middle of the day, and in the early evening – traditional 'children's time' – via programmes such as Jerry Springer's and Rikki Lake's.

The watershed contract is further becoming unstable with the advent of new technology – multichannel choices, with material on satellite/cable not covered by watershed regulations, as children in our study were aware:

It's people like Sky and cable who are making all these gruesome and bloody films and putting them on at 4 or 6 where the kids are getting into watching television before dinner . . . It's like, on Sky, I was flicking through the channels and *Pulp Fiction* was on at 8 o'clock and some kid could be watching this and think, 'yeah'. (Boy, 12, outer-London secondary school)

Dedicated children's channels, mainly featuring imported programming, and special children's videos, which substitute for broadcast TV in many homes, allow more parental control over viewing. Ironically, parental control over viewing may well be more limiting to the child's access to a range of different forms of content, than the control of a BBC or ITV scheduler would be. When children's channels are primarily subscription-based, and hence paid for by parents, and intended to be profitable for other adults – the channel's shareholders – then the direct contract between producers and children offered by a public service system, is dissolved. As Peter Tabern (interviewed for the BBC study in spring, 1996), a British independent producer, put it:

[The schedule] is quite different in this country from the experience that you might find in America, of having totally dedicated children's channels . . . It [American children's programming] is based much more on previous perceived success than our programming. It is much more ratings driven; you just *have* to get viewers and if it doesn't keep children sitting watching it, for whatever reason, that show just cannot survive. You will find on those stations things that are of genuine worth and value, but that is not chiefly why they are there.

The increase in channel choice (if not programme choice – see Davies and Corbett, 1997) is certainly conferring on the child the sovereignty of the consumer, one who decides from a range of options what he or she will view, and when. However, not only is subscription to new channels dependent on parental choice, but the child's choice is further limited by the fact that all new TV equipment sold in the UK has a parental control mechanism attached to it.

The decision about what these viewing options will be is thus shifting from public to private – from broadcasting schedulers, participating in a public sphere determined by government, professional and institutional policy considerations, many of them with élitist, conservative and paternalist tendencies, to parents in the home, choosing which videos to buy, and which channels to subscribe to. Giving parents more choice was seen as perfectly reasonable by many children in the study, for example:

I think there should be more teenage programmes on more often and not so late like *The X Files*, because it could be on at 8.30 p.m.; then parents could choose if they wanted their children to watch and we don't have to go to bed so late then, if we watched it. (Girl, 12, outer-city secondary school, Cardiff)

Commercial models

The public service ideal sees the child as a potential citizen who needs to be informed, stimulated, included in the social world, and – increasingly – consulted through, for example, the Children's BBC and Children's ITV websites and email addresses, as well as demanding to be entertained. The model of the child is somewhat different in purely commercial television, as in the USA: in commercial television, money has been raised traditionally by 'selling audiences to advertisers', and audiences of children have to be sold too. The notion of selling children in this way has often prompted some public uneasiness, for example through parents' and citizens' groups such as Action for Children's Television in the USA, and Voice of the Listener and Viewer in the UK. There is no such uneasiness inside the American children's television industry, or even among regulators, as Kline (1993) has documented in his account of what he sees as the primarily malign relationship between television and other children's consumer products, especially toys, *Out of the Garden*. He asserts (p. 277) that 'Contemporary children's culture [in the USA at any rate, which is the only system he discusses] exists because merchandising interests are willing to invest in the production of children's television.' The Reaganite deregulation of all television, including children's, in the 1980s, resulted in a situation where 'toy marketers' enthusiasm for character promotions resulted in an enormous boom in children's television production activities' (p. 278). The overriding need to serve the marketing priorities of Care Bears or Dyno Riders (toys based on dinosaurs), argues Kline, not only was a marketing strategy for selling toys, it also had a negative impact both on consumers and on storytelling quality. Narratives were distorted to make sure that key characters were of sufficient appeal to make children want to go and buy the models in the shops, hence 'dinosaurs must talk for there to be a bond between the audience and the characters' (p. 281).

His concerns are mocked by some representatives of the children's toy and television industry. Cy Schneider, a former toy-marketing executive who also worked for Nickelodeon in the US, wrote a book called *Children's Television: The Art, the Business and How it Works* (1987, pp. 5–9) in which activist groups' concerns about the wholesale commercialisation of children's culture were breezily dismissed:

What these people fail to realize is that commercial television, even for children, is just another business . . . The television business works on three simple principles: keep the audience up, the costs down, and the regulators out. The reformers forget that television's first mission is not to inform, educate or enlighten. It isn't even to entertain. Its first mission is to entice viewers to watch the commercials . . . Advertising is part of a child's socialization process in our culture and protecting him from it does no good in the end.

UK commercial producers are less overt in justifying the training of children to be consumers.

Commercial television, as in the case of Nickelodeon, raises funds through audience subscription, as well as advertising, and both commercial and public television (such as the BBC) raise money through sales of programmes abroad, marketing programme-related consumer goods, such as the highly lucrative Teletubbies, and other spin-off commercial activities. Children are aware of some of these commercial ramifications, but, in our study, they were not in the forefront of their thoughts when discussing how television 'ought' or 'ought not' to be organised. Most of their comments referred to content or scheduling, with little awareness of how content and scheduling could be affected by economic and institutional considerations. This was quite striking in the scheduling exercises (see chapter 5) where children acting as schedulers, and forced to jettison programmes to save money, rarely argued for keeping a programme because it would be economically more profitable. Considerations of content and audience were usually paramount, although, within the general context of concern for the audience, some children did show awareness of economic considerations and the chain of connections between profitability and serving, not the child consumer (significantly), but the parent:

You see *The X Files*, if a child was watching it, they may scream and then their mums would come and phone up our company and we would get bad business and we would probably be in the newspapers for scaring little kids and then all our business would go down. (Girl, 10, inner-London primary school)

Other children in the study showed awareness of how the competitive economics of a world in which 'choice' is the selling-point, can actually restrict the choices of the 50 per cent of the population who only have access to terrestrial television:

Well, Sky Sports have taken all the football and other sports. The same thing happens with the children's channel, Sky have taken them too which is unfair to people like me who do not have Sky. As you saw on page 12 [of the questionnaire], BBC just normally show repeats which I find silly. Our family thinks that when we pay our TV licence we should get the same amount of programmes as Sky. WHY SHOULD WE PAY MORE? [his emphasis] as Tesco say!! (Boy, 12, inner-city primary school, Milton Keynes)

The notion of child as consumer needs to take account of the fact that the consumer role coexists within the citizen role and the vulnerable juvenile role, and that children themselves will express these multiple perspectives in their perceptions of how media function. For instance, children in the BBC study, although supportive of public service ideals of informing and protecting, were aware of the wider functions of advertising on television as a potentially beneficial way of funding programme-making:

I think you are a bit over the top about not advertising. Why do people have to have a TV licence if they are perfectly happy not to have the BBC channels and just cable? (Boy, 12, outer-London secondary school)

Enhancing status

Furby (1991) has pointed out the importance of objects for children's identity – as having either instrumental or symbolic power in their lives.

The use of media products – the programmes themselves – can also be instrumental or symbolic, with goals of either learning, or of enhancing, status. Children acting as schedulers heavily stressed the instrumental aspects of TV programmes – the need for them to do good, and to teach. Speaking individually as themselves, in the 'free comments' section of the questionnaire, children were more likely to stress programmes' self-expressive functions, although these were sometimes linked with instrumental goals, including the expression of identity. One girl asserted her identity in the questionnaire by writing her entire comments in Welsh. Repeatedly, identification with programmes was expressed in a desire for programmes for 'children my age', enabling children both to identify with older audiences, and to distance themselves from what they described as 'babyish', for instance:

I'd also like *Red Dwarf* to be on two times a week. On programmes like CBBC the presenters treat you like babies, it really annoys me. (Girl, 12, outer-city secondary school, Cardiff)

One inner-London 11-year-old boy took the opportunity to assert a whole range of different positions: enjoyment ('love'); instrumental uses ('recipes'); ethical judgement ('I do not approve'); a hypothesis of media modelling effects, based on observation of a sibling, a demand for censorship ('it should be banned') and a straightforward consumer demand:

I love art programmes and simple cooking recipes. My favourite programs are *TRANSMISSION IMPOSSIBLE* [spelling and capitalisation retained] I love that and old detectives such as *Man from Uncle, The Avenger, The Champions*, that sort of thing. As well, I like *How 2* and the Children's *Newsround*. I do not approve of hospital programmes or *999* or *The Ward*. I've got a brother who's three, he likes guns and swords and fighting because of *Power Rangers* – that should be banned. And there should be more football on. (Boy, 11, inner-London primary school)

Another boy illustrated the point that, even in a digital era of unlimited 'choice', programme executives will still need to take account of children's availability to view. No children will be available during school hours, regardless of digital profusion:

I wish children's BBC and CITV started at 4 p.m. because it takes me forty minutes to get home and I miss half the programmes. (Boy, 11, primary school, Exeter)

For many children in the study, as with the Welsh girl, regional identity was also important: children wanted to see people from their own home towns, or districts, who looked and sounded like them, for instance, this 12-year-old girl from Middlesbrough, in the industrial north-east of Britain:

Children's television is good to watch – things like *Ace Ventura, Live and Kicking* and *Byker Grove* [set in the north-east]. But maybe it would be better if children could be on it and people from Middlesbrough, we don't really get the chance.

There followed a long list of programme likes and dislikes, ending with the following wish-list:

I'd like more music programmes and more programmes to have a moral to them as well. There should be less violence on TV.

The consumer model

The consumer child, especially when demanding morals in the same sentence as more music programmes, poses a challenge to theorists of childhood. Advertising executives, in contrast to some academic theorists, promote a model of the child which is not local or culturally specific, but universal. McNeal (1992, p. 250) states: 'before there is a geographic culture there is a children's culture; . . . they generally translate their needs into similar wants that tend to transcend culture'. This contrasts with approaches to childhood which stress cultural specificity. For example, Bazalgette and Buckingham (1995, p. 96) point out 'Ideologies of childhood stress that children are all the same, and are all the same the world over.' They add:

This idea is not exclusive to right-wing or romantic notions about the purity and innocence of childhood; the idea that children can transcend or ignore national, ethnic and religious boundaries has an obvious appeal to anyone wanting to prove that such boundaries are unnatural constructs.

They could have added that the idea of transcending national boundaries also has an obvious appeal to international marketers. If 'standardised marketing techniques' *do* appeal to children in many different cultures, as they do, this would appear to provide some empirical evidence for the universality of childhood, at least in children's attitudes to the consumption of goods and services in the marketplace. One universal construct which could explain the general susceptibility of children to marketing techniques, regardless of cultural environment, is the developmentalist notion of cognitive limitations during early childhood – in other words, it could be hypothesised that children everywhere are more easily swayed by commercial persuasion, because of their developmental immaturity. In a world of global marketing, media educators who want to help children in different cultures to be suspicious of Western marketing techniques, and to appreciate specific local cultural traditions and products, will need to find ways to overcome such developmental limitations through media literacy programmes.

Targeting children through advertising

Controversies about the impact of television on children have often focused on the undesirability of targeting very young children as consumers of goods, through advertising, before they are presumed to be capable of understanding, or resisting, sales techniques. In the USA, commercial children's network television consists of blocks of fast-moving animation, frequently interrupted by advertisements for toys, sweets and other appealing things to eat and drink, with the obvious intention of delivering child audiences to the advertisers of these products. In the UK, commercial television has a public service role laid upon it; it is regulated by the Independent Television Commission, and, until recently (1999), has not been allowed, for instance, to interrupt children's programmes with commercials, nor to include in commercials products which may have featured in programmes. It partly concerns deregulated international penetration of children's audiences and markets which has led the European Union to consider banning advertising in children's programming altogether as I write – something which British commercial programme-makers have argued will result in no more children's programming being made.

An assumption of cognitive incompetence lies behind many of these concerns about advertising, as well as about screen culture generally – a view that children are too immature, or cognitively undeveloped, to understand the persuasive intent of commercials. There is evidence that children can be confused by, for instance, cuts from mid-shot to close-up, thinking that the object in close-up is a different, larger object than the one seen in mid-shot (Acker and Tiemans, 1981). Hence, for instance, ITC regulations require commercials for toys to have a child's hand in shot, so that the true scale of the toy can be understood by young audiences.

Child viewers are not alone in being characterised as vulnerable to deception. Early theories of the television audience invoked 'the mass', unthinking, susceptible and swept along by propaganda. More recently, 'resistance models' of audience research have put forward the idea that by understanding the techniques involved in the deceptions of the medium, viewers, particularly immature ones, are enabled to resist its ideological persuasions. Resistance models have been invoked by a wide range of scholars studying this topic: Hawkins (1977); Hodge and Tripp (1986); Kubey (1997). The resistance model of the viewer, some of it derived from ethnographic work with households (for example, Morley, 1980) implies greater respect for viewers' powers of negotiation and opposition than earlier experimental research traditions, which tried to measure direct imitative effects on passive receptors, for example Bandura *et al.* (1963); Wolfe and Cheyne (1972). More recent research uses techniques similar to those used in our study, treating children as partners in inquiry about the effects of media on the young, for example Marion Tulloch (1995).

However, resistance models as applied to children continue the derided tradition of behaviourist 'magic-bullet' view of effects in another form. Media education programmes, which teach children, for instance, how to understand the constructed nature of toy advertising, in which models look life-size, but are not, are characterised as a kind of armoured vest, standing between the magic bullet of television propaganda and child. This assumption, as media educators have also found, does not always take into account that children may fully understand deceptive techniques, be quite capable of deconstructing camera angles, soft focus, the effects of music, or the halo-effect of glamorous sports stars, but still be willing to buy. Some scholars, themselves champions of media literacy's equal value with print literacy, have become uneasy about the apparently 'unholy' alliance between media literacy scholars and the needs of marketing. Buckingham, Davies, Jones and Kelley (1999, p. 128) quote an Association of Market Research Report in 1988: 'All our experience demonstrates that it is this age group [children] which is consistently ahead of technological developments and as such constitutes a powerful force within the family unit in terms of establishing ownership and usage patterns.' As Buckingham *et al.* (1999, p. 129) comment, 'the emergence of research proving the existence of the media-literate child served as a useful means for the industry to allay anxieties about commercialism and to reject the charge that making money out of children was simply a form of exploitation'.

The work of Brian Young (1990) has illustrated how pragmatic linguistic competence is the key competence needed for understanding the persuasive intent of commercials. This pragmatic approach underlay the study I carried out with 6–11 year olds in Philadelphia (Davies, 1997) about their understanding of what was 'real' and 'not real' in television material. One 10 year old in this study, when asked to identify aspects of a commercial for toys that 'could not happen in real life' said: 'All commercials are fake – they are just for advertising.' This view did not at all stop him wanting to own toys, however.

Child and adult

Other adult concerns about consumption and the role that television plays in its construction (for example, Postman, 1982) emphasise the undesirable blurring of boundaries between adulthood and childhood caused by children's access to adult products, including cultural products, and adult ways of behaving. This, too, rests on an assumption of children, particularly the youngest, as needing special protection because of immaturity and hence, vulnerability. Buckingham *et al.* (1999, p. 9) point out that, in fact, new technological developments in broadcasting, far from breaking down boundaries between child and adult, are now busily re-erecting them. They question whether this is indeed a desirable development, and link this separation with other developments, taking place in both Britain and the USA, such as nighttime curfews for children under 12 years of age:

children are increasingly being defined and addressed as a group that is quite distinct from adults, with its own unique characteristics and vulnerabilities. As in some areas of social policy, the separation between adults and children is being *reinforced* both as a result of the increasing fragmentation of the audience and through the emergence of new and distinctive modes of address in children's programmes . . . appeal on the grounds that they *exclude* adults and everything that they are seen to represent.

The ownership of space

James, Jenks and Prout, in *Theorizing Childhood* (1998), address the issue of consumption through a consideration of children's social space and how it is restricted. Unfortunately, their treatment of this important issue has a significant lack; there is little acknowledgement of screen culture and its influence on the organisation of children's spatial environments, except in familiar dystopic terms. In their chapter on childhood and social space, James *et al.* (p. 51) characterise the public space of the city as a place of risk and moral temptations to the young, partly because of the 'dangerous' forms of entertainment to be found there. Quoting Connolly and Ennew (1996, p. 134), they report:

located at the heart of the urban system, [the city streets] offer a number of consumer and entertainment possibilities: fast food outlets, restaurants, gambling arcades, cinemas and video stores, all with easy transport access. For young people these attractions are multiplied by the apparent lack of structure and schedule in these areas.

This negative view of the city does not take account of the city as a public place where children live, travel to school and do errands to local shops and meeting places, sometimes accompanied by older people, occasionally alone. These activities were reported by many of the older children in our study, who referred to walking and cycling backwards and forwards to school and elsewhere as one of the constraints on their viewing behaviour, for example, the 11-year-old boy in Exeter quoted above, and this 9-year-old girl in a primary school in Buckinghamshire:

I think that they [children's programmes] are too early, because you come in from school and you may want to go out for a bit or have something to eat so you miss it.

Dens of uncontrolled gambling and entertainment venues constitute a romanticised view of the urban scene, which also feeds into populist fears of uncontrolled young people roaming the streets in search of sensation and vice. This dystopic view sits oddly with generally liberal sociological views about the autonomy and independent agency of childhood. Fast-food outlets and cinemas, too, whatever their nutritional and political/economic drawbacks, could hardly be said to 'lack structure and schedule'. The view that young people are 'attracted' to a 'lack of structure and schedule' contrasts with Livingstone and Bovill's observations about the attraction of the bedroom, including the media contained in it, as a social space which can be organised according to the child's own requirements. Reference to domestic space in James *et al.* (p. 56) makes no reference to the ways in which relationships with screens – TV and computers – have influenced the organisation of children's domestic environments. Their only reference to television is to comment adversely on the 9 o'clock watershed in British broadcasting, which assumes children to be in bed, thus indoctrinating children into knowing their 'place' – which, they imply, is an inferior and excluded one. But, in Livingstone's mediated 'bedroom culture', this place – the bedroom – is not a place of banishment, it is a new children's domain. To be confined to private and virtual spaces may be a loss, as Henry Jenkins laments (1998) in comparing his son's explorations of cyberspace with his own rural boyhood. However, such a life style does not necessarily lack structure, schedule or order, nor does the child necessarily lack empowerment within its physically-limited confines.

Over half of the sample in our BBC study had a TV in their bedroom; in their comments, children demonstrated a confident ability to navigate their way around the proliferating channels, and the children's provision, on offer. The proportion – 43 per cent – of children in our sample who said they had satellite/cable was similar to the proportion in Livingstone and Bovill's sample of 6–17 year olds (42 per cent). A number of the children in our sample had access to local cable too. In terms of what children said they regularly watched, CBBC (Children's BBC) received by far the greatest number of 'yes' responses – 84 per cent overall. Children's ITV was next with 68 per cent of 'yes' responses. Of the specialist cable/satellite channels, the Cartoon Network scored highest, with 47 per cent of children answering 'yes'. Although Channel 4 did not have a recognisable schedule in the way that BBC and ITV did, nearly half the children in our sample (44 per cent) were clearly finding the children's fare that was there. The spread of scores suggested that children were adept at finding what was available and attractive to them – an ability which, though not equivalent to finding one's way around in city streets, still indicated a capacity to organise their own experience.

This was also demonstrated by children's ability to characterise the differences between the channels, for example this group from an inner-London primary school:

INTERVIEWER   What is the difference between the BBC and ITV?

BOY 1   They are both in different places and on different channels . . .

BOY 2   I know, ITV has got a lot of adverts, but the BBC hasn't.

BOY 3   I think that ITV and Channel 4 have better music and films but not that many good cartoons for children. I think CBBC have more things for children but ITV and Channel 4 do not think much about children; it is more for adults.

An 8-year-old girl from the same school explained on her questionnaire:

I watch Sky. Sky has lots of channels like Nickelodeon, Cartoon Network, TCC, Disney Channel. Sky is not like cable, because cable has a little bit more channels than Sky.

Although many children had screens in their bedrooms, the children in our study continued to enjoy communal viewing in families – as drawings in both Livingstone's and our study showed (see Figure 1).

When children view television in common domestic space, they make arrangements to claim it for their own. As Patricia Palmer (1986) pointed out, the space around the TV set can be organised by children as their own territory, marked off by cushions and blankets, and accompanied by favourite pets and toys. An aspect of children's relationships with the screen, particularly the screen-based bedroom, noted by Livingstone and Bovill, is that danger on the streets has provided children with more liberty within. This may be lamented by those of us who remember a childhood freely travelling on buses, trains and on foot, playing in open spaces and in relatively traffic-free streets. However, every adult memory of childhood has a 'golden age' perspective to it. 'Things' for contemporary children are never 'what they used to be', and the pertinent issue for our study was whether children *felt* themselves to be disadvantaged in terms of their control over their cultural environment. The evidence from these children suggests that many do not.

There are marked age differences in access to, and control over, both public and private space. Livingstone and Bovill (1999) found that it

Is there anything else you would like to say about Children's Television? Please write or draw your own ideas here in this box.

I Yolle like Demon HeaD manster and poyw rangos and Smavi ha HAHAHA HA HAHA owl sff goog

Figure 1 Boy, 6, suburban primary school, Buckinghamshire

was particularly after the age of 11 that children in Britain found the lack of things to do outside the home irksome. Seventy-three per cent of 12–14 year olds and 80 per cent of 15–17 year olds were discontented with leisure alternatives outside the home. This was in contrast to children in other European countries. British parents were particularly anxious about letting their children outside the home, compared to other European parents. Livingstone points out that, given these domestic circumstances, television continues to be a welcome source of access to a wider world of experiences – including access to the public sphere. As she put it (ch. 3, p. 5): 'television provides a breadth of gratifications for a heterogeneous audience.' Some of these gratifications are shown in the organisation of domestic life, as in the case of this 9-year-old girl, in an inner-London primary school, whose grandparents came from the Caribbean, defending the inclusion of *Sesame Street* in her children's schedule:

I think we should keep *Sesame Street* because nearly all my family watch this in the mornings. When my granny wakes up she usually cooks the breakfast, after she does that, she just sits down and watches *Sesame Street*.

Measuring consumption: the ratings

Analysis of the behaviour of viewers as consumers of television, is defined by the broadcasting industry, and media industries generally, through ratings (audience numbers), or box-office takings (cinema) or sales (books, toys, video games). In the case of TV, audience numbers (how many and what kind of people are watching which channel and when) are collected and paid for by the industry, through the Broadcasters' Audience Research Board in the UK, and through Neilsen in the USA (see chapter 1). Even the industry has sometimes queried whether they are getting value for money from this system, yet ratings not only continue to be used; they are becoming ever more dominant in the increasingly competitive world of multichannel viewing when every young viewer gained by MTV is a viewer lost to ABC; where every viewer switching to Sky 1 (as some children in our sample wanted to do) is a viewer lost to the BBC.

At the time of writing (1999/2000) the most widely watched programmes both for adults and children continue to be from network terrestrial television, but this is likely to change. In the case of children, as mentioned, programmes targeted at them may be confined to specialised channels in the multichannel near-future, rather than occupying a protected space in the main networked schedules, as provided by CBBC and CITV in the UK. There have been no protected slots for children's 'educational' programming in the networks of the USA since the 1970s, except for Saturday morning cartoon programmes. The minority public service channel, PBS, puts out the daily educational programmes, such as *Sesame Street*, *Where in the World Is Carmen Sandiego* and *Ghostwriter*, but programmes labelled 'educational', no matter how entertaining, may not be attractive to the kinds of children seeking to relax after school that we found in our study. As this 9-year-old boy in an inner-London primary school pointed out:

This [children's channel] is on after school, OK, they have had their day of learning, they want to relax and do not want any more education, they have already had a full day of learning; why would they want more?

In Britain, specialised children's programming has always been labelled as 'entertainment' and has had a protected afternoon slot on the main networks of BBC and ITV. This has helped to sustain quite large shares both of the general audience and of the child audience, for children's programmes. However, as with the growing market for computer software and CD ROMs, in a future where channels are obtained through 'choice' and subscription, it may well be that the aspirational parental desire for educational programming will supersede the old-fashioned aim of producers with a show-business background of simply providing 'fun'. Gradgrindism may be facilitated by the new technology, when parents become consumers, rather than children being viewers.

Thus, the place of the child as a member of the wider public sphere, sharing in a generalised broadcasting provision, with a mixed schedule serving both adults and children, could be reduced in the new multi-channel world – an example of children's access to adult spaces being blocked which, it could be argued, may turn out to be as problematic for children's access to the public sphere, if not more so, as the fact that children are now less likely than in the past to roam freely in the city streets.

The status and validity (or presumed lack of it) of ratings as a reliable way of understanding audience behaviour has been challenged by academics such as Ien Ang (1993) and John Hartley (1992) who take issue with the view that it is possible to define or measure audiences in any meaningful way, and that such attempts are a repressive means of social control, rather than an enlightened way of democratically con-sulting the tastes of consumers. However, whether audiences as mea-sured by ratings are 'fictive' or not, audience numbers continue to be the major determinant of whether a television programme is deemed to be 'successful' or not. Audience numbers determine to a considerable extent the BBC's accountability to the public who pays its licence fees; audience numbers, in the case of children, provide ammunition for wider moral arguments about the socialisation of the young, as, for instance, the oft-lamented fact that adult shows, such as the London-based adult soap *EastEnders*, get higher numbers of children in their audience than do children's shows.

Figures showing the high numbers of children in the adult audience, give rise to press comment. Questions are raised, such as: does this mean that childhood is at an end? There are also economic questions, such as: does this mean that there is no point in spending money on special children's drama?, which were very much in the minds of BBC executives, we believed, when they commissioned our study. As Buckingham *et al.* (1999) point out, similar questions were being asked in the 1950s, at the time of the Himmelweit study, when children were just as likely, if not more so, to prefer adult shows to children's. These questions are still being asked today, as if children watching horror genres (now *The X Files*, then *The Twilight Zone*) or drama about broken marriages, crime and illegitimacy (then *Z Cars*, now *Brookside*) were something brand new. In determining which programmes we should talk to children about, and what principles might underlie the questionnaires and tasks, we took a look at television drama ratings among child audiences for the preliminary literature review of the study (Davies and O'Malley, 1996).

Rating drama

We used the standard measure of consumption – the ratings and share analyses provided by BARB – to find out what were the most 'popular' drama programmes for children in the 5-year period prior to the study. We chose 10 sample weeks, in the years 1990 to 1995 inclusive. We also had access to privileged information, supplied by the BBC, but not able to be published because it is exclusive to the industry – the Appreciation Indices, a measure of children's 'appreciation' of particular programmes, on a scale of 1–10, as collected for the Young Viewers' Genre Reports by BARB for these 10 weeks (they did not conflict with the ratings as a measure of popularity).

In all 10 of our sample weeks, sampled from different times of the year, *Neighbours*, the Australian soap, then, and still, being shown twice a day on BBC1 at 1.30 and 5.30 p.m., was consistently the top-rated (that is, the most numerously watched) programme among 4–15 year olds, apart from a couple of occasions, in November 1994 and November 1993, when it was ousted from its number one position by *Gladiators*, the game show. As an illustration of the inroads made on viewing figures by the introduction of new channels, *Neighbours* fell from its high point of a 39.2 per cent share of the child audience in November 1992, to a much lower 26.9 per cent in November 1995. In our 10 sample weeks, the most popular of the special children's drama programmes, *Byker Grove*, had a 28 per cent share of the whole viewing audience (adults *and* children). It was for this reason that we chose *Byker Grove* as the children's drama representative in the Channel Choice exercise described in chapter 1. Both of these programmes were continuing series – 'soaps' – and they continue at the present time (1999/2000), an indication of the successfulness of the soap format in attracting and sustaining child viewers.

Several comments from children emphasised the pleasure of tuning in regularly to the familiar characters and scenarios of long-running soaps. Repetition and regularity were the key features of its appeal, for example:

I think that *Home and Away* should be on at the weekend and not every week day. *EastEnders* is a very good programme with a lot of drama in it. It should be on every night apart from the weekend . . . I think *The Bill* should be more interesting and on for an hour every night apart from the weekend because you cannot always understand it because it is not on for long enough. (Girl, 9, suburban primary school, Oxfordshire)

The realism of the soap form was also valued:

BBC does quite well on the television but it could improve. I don't like *Grange Hill*. I'd rather watch things like *EastEnders* as I find *Grange Hill* silly as most of the storylines wouldn't happen in real life but *EastEnders* is more realistic. (Girl, 11, secondary school, Co. Durham)

The ratings popularity of *children's* programmes (that is, those made by children's departments of the broadcasting organisations, and shown in the special children's schedules) is measured separately from the general programme ratings. An analysis of the Top Ten *children's* programmes in the sample weeks in our study showed that, each winter, drama was the most frequently represented genre in these Top Ten programmes, filling 4 or 5 slots – around 40 to 50 per cent – in each sample. In November 1995, for example, the Top Ten included two episodes of *Byker Grove*, BBC1; ITV's comedy drama for younger children, *Woof!*, and the BBC's Sunday 'teatime' serial, *Just William*, based on Richmal Crompton's classic children's books – all examples of the three kinds of drama, soap, series and serial, identified as intrinsic to the medium in the BBC's policy report *People and Programmes* (BBC, 1995). These three examples provide a fairly representative snapshot of the kinds of drama programmes that are persistently successful with child audiences.

Byker Grove was – and is – a realistic, contemporary 'soap', with an ensemble cast of older and younger children, set in a youth club in the north-east of England, regularly dealing with problematic issues, such as pregnancy, drug-taking and, controversially in 1996, a homosexual storyline, attracting some criticism from adults. *Woof!* was a comedy fantasy about a young schoolboy who unexpectedly kept turning into a dog, produced by Central/Carlton TV, part of the commercial ITV system. It began in 1989 and, although no longer in production, is still being shown around the world in syndication; *Just William* had the format of a 'classic' serial, a book adaptation shown on Sunday afternoons for a family audience, a scheduling format revived by the BBC, after a long interval, with *The Chronicles of Narnia*, in 1988. The *William* books were written and set in the 1920s, and, in the dramatisation, the period was recreated with authentic costume and set design, rather than being represented as a contemporary drama, as in earlier serialisations in 1962 and 1963. In this, the style of dramatic literary adaptations 'for children' showed a significant departure from earlier children's serialisations.

The self-conscious historicising of the *William* books seemed intended to have an ironic appeal to adults who might remember the books from their own childhoods, even though those of us who read the books as children in the 1950s and 1960s would not remember the 1920s. This re-presentation of *Just William* seemed another indication of increasing cautiousness on the part of the BBC, in order to attract more middle-of-the-road adult and family audiences, having lost faith in their ability to win high ratings with children only. The 1920s setting was either intended to be a parody of a world forgotten, or was genuinely intended to attract an audience in their seventies, but, either way, it could not have a direct appeal to children of William Brown's age. A further example of the BBC's nostalgic promotion of a vanished world of childhood, in which small boys wore grey-flannel shorts and blazers, was their 1998 promotional film, intended to reassure licence payers of the excellence of the service they were providing and entitled 'Future Generations' – somewhat misleadingly, given that the 6-year-old child who presented it was dressed in the fashions of forty years before. Again, reinforcing the targeting of conservative adult audiences, not children, most of the programmes mentioned were not in the vein of contemporary realism seen as valuable by the children in our study, but were primarily preschool and fantasy programmes from the past, which parents would remember from their own, or from their grown-up children's, early childhood.

In the case of *William*, the nostalgic appeal to adults of the 'heritage' approach to production, did not add to its appeal for children. The children in our study did not recognise the title as familiar. Only 37 per cent of 6 year olds and 49 per cent of 7 year olds recognised it as a 'children's drama'; 60 per cent overall recognised it as 'children's', compared to 78 per cent recognising *Grange Hill* as children's, and 88 per cent recognising the Saturday magazine show, *Live and Kicking* as children's. For children's drama to survive, ways must be found of making it identifiably 'children's' and not just something that adults will agree to subscribe to, with just sufficient child-interest included to make their subscriptions worthwhile.

One of the ways in which children's drama can sustain itself as distinct from adult drama is in competing with adult drama, and getting better ratings. During our analysis, this occasionally happened. In the sample period of our analysis between 1990 and 1995, three children's drama programmes got into the *all-programme* Top Tens, thus 'beating' adult competition. They were ITV's science fiction drama, *The Tomorrow People*, produced by Alan Horrox's company, Tetra Films, ITV's series set in a hospital, *Children's Ward* and the BBC's *Byker Grove*. *The Demon Headmaster* also achieved this in 1996/7. These figures indicated that ratings for children's drama at the time were holding their own, both in comparison with other children's genres, and, sometimes, even with the most popular adult programmes. But the types of programme that were successful in beating off adult/family competition are of importance too: the two genres of most universal appeal to children from this analysis were first, fantasy/science fiction, and, second, realistic contemporary drama, in which children's lives, and concerns, including painful subjects such as abuse, family breakdown and death, were dealt with. Both these kinds of genres were repeatedly stressed as important by the children in the study, and in this there was some agreement between them and producers.

Since then, the amount of children's drama available has fluctuated and audience shares have continued to fragment, as more channels arrived and built up their audiences. Sunday serials continue and so do the 'soaps' *Byker Grove*, and *Grange Hill*, with a certain amount of comedy drama on both ITV (such as the inspired *Welcome to 'Orty Fou'*) and BBC, such as *Microsoap*, a co-production with the Disney Channel. Short-run comedy drama, with an appeal to younger children, has become more of a regular feature than the social–realist type serial dramas of the 1980s, clearly aimed at older children, such as *Break in the Sun* and *The Cuckoo Sister*. The other popular genre is the kind of material which was once extremely controversial (Home, 1993) – stories featuring the supernatural, such as the Canadian *Goosebumps*, shown on BBC1, and home-grown dramas such as the spring 2000 *The Ghost*

Hunter, also shown on BBC1. The economic constraints resulting in these changes in generic provision were discussed in chapter 2. One of their most striking characteristics is that virtually all British-produced drama is now being made by independent production companies, and many of them are foreign co-productions. Whether this matters to children remains to be seen. There were some reservations among our sample of children about American programming – but also some envy at the profusion of choice on offer in the USA, for instance this 12-year-old girl from an outer-London secondary school:

When I went to America my uncle had about 63 channels on like 10 channels; there's Barney and cartoons and . . . on the other ones there was *Knots Landing* and really good dramas and on the others there was sports and cookery programmes.

However, this range by itself was not sufficient for one of her fellow-pupils, who pointed out that home-produced programmes had to be accountable to their audiences in ways that American imports were not:

we can't really [complain about] violence about American programmes like *The X-Files* and *The Simpsons* because we can't change that. The BBC can't write a letter saying can you quieten it down, but on stuff like *EastEnders* . . . you can make a survey and send it to *EastEnders* and they can tone it down, or make it more adventurous.

The distinctiveness of children's drama

A key question of our study, we believed – especially for our sponsors – was to try to find out what was seen as distinctive to children about children's drama, and whether, indeed, they did see any distinction between drama intended for adult or family audiences, or drama intended for children. Through these distinctions, light might be shed on how contemporary children characterised the state of childhood, as opposed to the state of adulthood, and how popular cultural products could provide vehicles for such theorising. One ingredient seen as necessary by, and for, children was comprehensibility, for example:

On page six, you have asked us to tick which programmes are specially for children. *EastEnders* can be for children of a maximum age so they could understand it. Also I would like to see more programmes or things children could understand, like more drama like *Casualty*, more of teenage drama like *Neighbours* and *Home and Away*. (Girl, 11, outer-city secondary school, Cardiff)

All the programmes mentioned by this girl are adults' not children's programmes. Because of our interest in whether children really did see any differences between programming aimed specifically at them, and other kinds of programming, one of the exercises in the questionnaire

Table 8. *Proportions (percentage) of boys, girls and all children classifying the following programmes as children's programmes*

	Percentage answering 'children's'			Percentage answering 'not children's'			Percentage answering 'not sure'		
	All	Boys	Girls	All	Boys	Girls	All	Boys	Girls
EastEnders	20	20	20	57	59	54	23	21	26
Grange Hill	76	75	77	11	13	10	13	12	13
Gladiators	64	68	61	14	13	15	22	19	25
Newsround	45	44	45	34	35	35	21	21	20
Men Behaving Badly	12	14	9	69	72	69	19	15	22
Live and Kicking	88	88	88	6	7	4	6	5	8
Just William	60	62	59	9	9	9	31	29	32

required children to identify a list of programmes (see Table 8) as either adults' or children's. Four of the programmes in Table 8 (*Grange Hill, Newsround, Live and Kicking* and *Just William*) were produced by the BBC Children's Department. *Gladiators*, also included in the list, had a children's version, aired on ITV, so it was possible that many children would classify this show as 'children's' – as they did. The rest were adult programmes. Table 8 shows how children classified these titles.

Despite ratings popularity among children, the adult soap *EastEnders* and the laddish comedy *Men Behaving Badly* were generally recognised, with convincing majorities, as 'not children's' programmes. In the case of the three regular programmes produced by the BBC Children's Department, *Grange Hill* and *Live and Kicking* were correctly identified as children's programmes by large majorities. The third was much less clearly identified. An unexpectedly high number of children – 34 per cent – identified the special, daily children's news programme, *Newsround*, as 'not a children's programme'. There was an age difference in this judgement, with 54 per cent of 12 year olds, and only 33 per cent of 6 and 7 year olds, identifying it as 'children's'. Even among the 12 year olds, a recognition factor of only 54 per cent indicated a high level of uncertainty among these regular viewers of Children's BBC.

The case of *Newsround*

Newsround is 'hammocked' within the Children's BBC schedule, with popular cartoons and comedy preceding it, and popular magazine or drama shows coming afterwards. It has an award-winning graphics style, particularly designed to be appealing to children, and focuses on items of special interest to children, such as animal stories and school issues – in other words, it is replete with children's signifiers. But even *Just William*, which received the highest number of 'Not sure' scores about whether it was drama or not – 47 per cent – reflecting the children's relative lack of familiarity with the programme, was identified more confidently as 'children's' than was *Newsround*. Younger children were particularly emphatic that *Newsround* was not for them. Nearly half of 6–8 year olds were sure that it was 'Not children's'. This is despite the producers' efforts, as noted by Buckingham (2000a, pp. 44–5), to provide educational 'thematic frames' for news stories, with plenty of background explanation and historical context, in contrast to adult news reporting, which is more likely to be 'episodic' and to assume prior knowledge.

The failure of large numbers of children in our sample to recognise the graphic signifiers and framing devices characteristic of 'children's news', suggests that news, per se, may be seen by children as an adult genre, regardless of its context within a children's schedule and its production treatment. This has implications for how children see themselves as members, or not, of the public sphere. There is evidence, as Buckingham (2000a) points out, that news is not a particularly popular genre with children, but in the qualitative data in our BBC study, a number of children discussed news as an essential part of the schedule, and several specifically mentioned *Newsround*. For instance, a 10-year-old boy in an inner-city primary school in Cardiff, said: 'I would like to see more of *Newsround* on television'; a 9-year-old boy in an Oxfordshire suburban primary school argued that: '*Newsround* is good because it tells children about the news around the world and it is not serious like the other news'; and an 8-year-old girl from the same school allied the programme with two popular drama series: 'Can we have more of *The Queen's Nose, The Ward* and *Newsround?*' On the other hand, some of the consumer comments from the free section of the questionnaire expressed distaste for news. A 9-year-old girl from a Didcot primary school argued: 'I think there should be a lot more after *Home and Away* . . . I sometimes get bored watching the news after *Home and Away.*' An 11-year-old boy from an inner-city primary school in Milton Keynes was the most succinct of our respondents: 'More drama, less news.' Thus, children in our sample characteristically expressed dislike of news, as other studies have found, but the methodology we used of making children responsible for scheduling revealed that many children, despite the questionnaire evidence that news is seen as 'not children's', believed that news *ought* to be in a children's schedule.

The variation in the classification of programmes as 'children's' or 'adults" raised questions about *how*, and on what grounds, children distinguished between one and the other. One indicator mentioned by the child above, on the subject of *Newsround*, was accessibility to children, or what one child characterised as 'non-seriousness' – *Newsround* was seen as 'not serious like other news'. This suggests that one of the functions of a children's, as distinct from an adult's, version of the news, is that, no matter how grim the events described, it should ultimately offer reassurance. Similar criteria of reassurance were produced by a group of children from a Buckinghamshire primary school discussing the difference between adults' and children's drama. The boy articulated the view (also held by producers) that when a programme is *classified* as 'children's', children watching are able to feel safe: 'in programmes like *The Demon Headmaster*, if someone says they are going to try and kill somebody you know they are just making it up'.

Another distinguishing mark of children's programmes for the children in the study was that such programmes appeared to recognise the presence of young and vulnerable people in the audience. One group of inner-London secondary school 11 and 12 year olds was very emphatic that *EastEnders* was 'not for children' on the grounds that it failed to consider these vulnerabilities:

INTERVIEWER   So shall we get rid of *EastEnders*?

ALL   Yes.

INTERVIEWER   Why?

BOY 1   It's good but it's not for children really.

INTERVIEWER   Why isn't it for children, can you say?

GIRL 1   It does have some rude language in it.

BOY 1   Younger children can't understand it.

BOY 2   The younger children, they copy things that they hear from people.

INTERVIEWER   But *EastEnders* was one of our top scoring choices.

GIRL 1   The point is, it's not for children.

BOY 1   The point is, younger children will not understand it.

Summary

The consumer child is in theory a powerful child: the model encompasses the child as a 'pesterer' of adults, the member of a family group or household who has unique influence on adult purchasing generally. The child as consumer of culture and media is also a powerful person who can be offered a range of channels and programming, assumed to be attractive to him or her, and who will then freely choose, as a matter of personal taste, what he or she will give attention to. The consumer model of the child encompasses some important assumptions about children's autonomy and competence: it assumes that children are capable of choosing for themselves what they will, and will not possess and what they do and do not like. The consumer child is not at the mercy of controlling adults (parents, teachers, clergy and so on); the child has direct access to the marketplace – the world of goods and services for sale. In the case of television programming, no mediating from adults is necessary; the child can 'buy' the channel of choice directly by pressing the remote control button. In fact, as already discussed, in a media system where parents are subscribers, initial choices as to what should be made available are made more by parents than by children.

The wider question is how free any of this choice really is; commentators such as Kline lament the fact that, instead of parents, relatives, teachers and others who know the child directly, different and distant adults, representing powerful corporate influences, are claiming the child's attention and influencing his or her behaviour. Are these more or less trustworthy for the child than the known adults? Are they more or less likely to be acting in the child's interest? Marketing adults have a vested interest in seeing the child as autonomous, and in freeing him or her from potentially interfering adult mediators. Is this what children want? The children in the study wanted the BBC, and broadcasting generally to serve their interests, in terms of preparing them to be citizens as well as consumers, and this was not seen as mediated by parents or other adults; it was a direct responsibility of the broadcasters to them. Many, particularly the older ones, saw the corporation as accountable to them, and to 'the future,' as one 13-year-old boy put it:

I think the BBC should put more realistic television programmes on, because then more children will learn what it is like growing up, and what the future is like. (Boy, 13, outer-London secondary school)

Why should anyone bother to listen to children and pay heed to what they say they want? Obviously the answer to this is partly a question of marketing prudence: there are profits to be made from children and their tastes. But, in the words of the 13 year old above, what about 'growing up' and 'the future'? What *are* growing up, and the future, like? Market research, based on what has been popular in the past, does not necessarily provide the answers to these questions. Dependent on meeting children's requirements for learning, escape, reassurance, diversity and guidance on the path to maturity, is a supply of adults who have a clear idea of what they are trying to do for children, and the enthusiasm and resources for doing it. Michael Forte, head of Children's and Young People's programming at Carlton-Central, one of the ITV companies, was asked what his conception of his audience – or 'market' – was, and his answer was revealingly personal and imprecise:

They're all different in a way. We try not to paint by numbers or to configure programmes to fit the audience. You just have to be excited by an idea really. You have to have a sense that they're going to love this; it's either going to make them laugh or excite their imagination or it's going to be a certain amount of transference. Or it's a wonderful fantasy.

Part II

The social functions of broadcasting

5 The Reithian agenda: setting good examples

Máire Messenger Davies and David Machin

Well we wanted to choose *Friends*, but we did not think it would be a good one for young children and *The X Files* is for grown ups and it may scare younger children.　　Boy, 12, secondary school, Oxfordshire

I think that *The X Files* has to go because *Live and Kicking* has got lots of programmes in it. *EastEnders* – everybody likes that, *Top of the Pops* because it has got lots of songs on it and everyone likes that and *Men Behaving Badly* because it is comedy and lots of people like that as well. *The X Files* is too scary for the little kids that are watching it.
Girl, 9, primary school, Buckinghamshire

I don't think you should get rid of *EastEnders*. It's about people, it's a drama. It's just about people and you learn things when you're older about growing up.　　Girl, 10, primary school, Milton Keynes

Anthropologists, such as Evans-Pritchard (1937) and Geertz (1973), have drawn attention to the ways in which cultures have different available representations for discussing social and cultural phenomena. These representations may often be contradictory and have no direct relationship with the actual topic of conversation, but they form a body of usable and accepted public knowledge on which to draw in discussion. One of the ways in which we approached the discussion data in the BBC study was to analyse it to see what kinds of available cultural representations about 'being a viewer', or 'being a child', or 'being a spokesperson', or 'being in charge' were used by children. In an earlier study (Machin and Carrithers, 1996), David Machin, the Research Fellow working on these analyses of the qualitative data in our BBC study, had studied the way Spanish factory workers discussed tabloid newspapers. The study found, in interviews and focus groups, that these workers drew on a range of largely contradictory folk assumptions to talk about 'sleazy' newspaper readers who were fascinated by sensationalist stories. Contradictorily, these workers also argued that newspapers are an essential form of knowledge and indicative of a discerning person, thus positioning themselves both within and outside the category

127

'newspaper readers'. Machin and Carrithers found that the speakers always aligned themselves alongside the more discerning group, whether it was the street-wise readers of sexy tabloids, or the discerning kinds of citizens who scorn them. In applying this anthropological approach to the qualitative data produced by the children in the BBC study in the discussion tasks, it was found that there seemed to be evidence that children could relate to their culture and draw on its available pool of ideas about how the world works, in ways similar to those used by adults; they seemed to be using 'thematic frames' drawn from adult discourses circulating in the public sphere in a variety of forms (see also Davies and Machin, 2000a).

In the scheduling tasks carried out in the study, requiring children to prioritise some programmes over others, the children had to articulate production values, or other kinds of social or ethical values in order to justify the inclusion or exclusion of programmes. This chapter discusses some of the values and selection criteria underlying the children's decisions in the tasks where they were required to act as channel schedulers, choosing and rejecting programmes. Despite deregulation and commercialisation, it is still the case that, in British culture, public service, Reithian values remain current, as they were at the time of the study. ITV companies, then and now, operated under the terms of the Broadcasting Act of 1990, which was intended to safeguard 'high-quality' children's programming, including a range of factual, drama and entertainment genres.

This chapter describes the exercise in which children were asked to act, not on behalf of themselves as individual consumers, but on behalf of others, as responsible decision-makers, as active members of the public sphere, in order to find out what criteria, value-systems and assumptions about audiences would be brought to bear on these decisions. Children aged between 8 and 12 (on teachers' advice, we did not carry out this exercise with children younger than 8), worked in small groups to role-play a team of children's channel 'controllers'. Their task was to select a mixed schedule of 6 or 7 programmes, from a large range of options, for a 'new children's channel'. This selection exercise was piloted in an Essex primary school in Colchester and the somewhat unexpected results of the pilot led to some changes being made to the final version for the main study. The final version of this selection task was the most-frequently used qualitative exercise for the study as a whole because it had worked so well in the pilot as a way of involving all children productively. Secondly, and more importantly, it turned out to be very revealing in terms of the way children conceptualised what the job of a channel controller in British broadcasting in the 1990s should be.

The sample and method

The main study-scheduling exercise was carried out in 4 schools: an inner-London primary school (7 on the special needs index); an inner-London secondary (7 special needs); a suburban primary in Buckinghamshire (no special needs); and an outer-city secondary school in Cardiff, which taught through the Welsh language (no special needs). In 3 other schools – an inner-city primary in Milton Keynes (6 special needs); a secondary school in Oxfordshire (1 special need); and a primary school in Didcot (1 special need) – a similar exercise was carried out drawing up a drama schedule for a *drama-only* children's channel. The rationale for the general schedule, including both drama and non-drama programmes, was to see how drama fared in comparison with other genres. The rationale for the drama-only schedule was to produce some more detailed opinions about the genre which was the primary topic of the study, and to explore children's distinctions between different categories and functions of dramatic storytelling.

The programme titles were drawn from a list of several hundred of the most familiar titles generated by four classes of children in our pilot primary school in Essex. The twenty-five most frequently mentioned titles were selected. Two other titles – the dramas *Grange Hill* and *The Biz* – were inserted by the researchers, using, as explained to the children, a 'supreme controller's' prerogative, given that the BBC wanted especially to know about drama, including children's drama. This turned out to be a wise imposition, since both *Grange Hill* and *The Biz* produced some revealing comments. Each programme title was written on a card, and each small group of child 'schedulers' had a bag of colour-coded cards with the same titles in each bag. Children were given the choice of using both adults' and children's programming. There were also some blank cards for adding programmes of their own choice, or of their own creation (1 or 2 groups did come up with ideas for their own programmes). The titles for the general schedule, and for the drama schedule, are listed in Tables 9 and 10.

The task had a two-stage structure and the second stage was a reversal of the first. In the second stage, a small group of representatives from each group, took the 6 or 8 most frequently mentioned titles from the whole-class discussion – the final schedule for the channel – and then had to whittle it down, one by one, because their channel 'was losing money'. This second-stage discussion was tape-recorded. Only children aged between 8 and 12 years old were used for these qualitative tasks, on teachers' advice – with the exception of the infants' class who discussed *Rugrats* (see chapter 9).

Table 9. *List of programmes used in the scheduling task – 'channel controllers'*

Channel	Programme	Genre
BBC2	*Fresh Prince of Bel Air*	Drama: other series/serials – non-UK
BBC1	*Rugrats*	Children's acquired animation
BBC1	*Top of the Pops*	Music programmes: contemporary
BBC1	*Live and Kicking*	Children's magazine (UK)
BBC1	*The X Files*	Drama: other series/serials – non-UK
BBC1	*Match of the Day*	Sport
ITV	*Home and Away*	Drama: long-running series – non-UK
BBC1/Nick	*Clarissa Explains it All*	Children's drama – non-UK
BBC1	*EastEnders*	Drama: long-running series – UK
BBC1	*Songs of Praise*	Religious
CH4	*Saved by the Bell*	Children's drama – non-UK
ITV	*Power Rangers*	Children's acquired animation
BBC2	*Ren and Stimpy*	Light entertainment: cartoons/animation
ITV	*The Bill*	Drama: long-running series – UK
BBC1	*Newsround*	Children's factual (UK)
BBC1	*Wildlife on One*	Documentaries and features
BBC1	*Fudge*	Children's drama – non-UK
ITV	*Man O Man*	Light entertainment: quiz shows
BBC1	*Blue Peter*	Children's factual (UK)
ITV	*Are You Afraid of the Dark?*	Children's drama – non-UK
BBC1	*Men Behaving Badly*	Light entertainment: situation comedy
BBC1	*Animal Hospital*	Documentaries and features
BBC1	*The Biz*	Children's drama (UK)
BBC1	*999*	Documentaries and features
BBC1	*Grange Hill*	Children's drama (UK)

Welsh Programmes added (from S4C): *Slot Meithrin* – Preschool; *Heno* – News programme; *Pobyl Y Cwm* – Welsh soap; *Superted* – Preschool cartoon; *Brodyr Bach* – Light Entertainment.

Asian Programmes added (from BBC2): *Chanakya* – Epic saga set in Ancient India; *Network East* – Arts and entertainment magazine; *Bollywood or Bust!* – Hindi film quiz.

Table 10. *List of programmes generated for drama scheduling task*

Channel	Programme	Genre
BBC1	*Grange Hill*	Children's drama (UK)
BBC1	*Byker Grove*	Children's drama (UK)
BBC1	*The Queen's Nose*	Children's drama (UK)
BBC1	*The Demon Headmaster*	Children's drama (UK)
BBC1	*The Genie from Down Under*	Children's drama – non-UK
BBC1	*Julia Jekyll and Harriet Hyde*	Children's drama (UK)
BBC1	*Fudge*	Children's drama – non-UK
ITV	*Power Rangers*	Children's acquired animation
ITV	*Are You Afraid of the Dark?*	Children's drama – non-UK
ITV	*The Ward*	Children's drama (UK)
ITV	*Woof!*	Children's drama (UK)
ITV	*Retrace*	Children's drama (UK)
CH4	*Hollyoaks*	Drama: long-running series – UK
CH4	*Sister Sister*	Children's drama – non-UK
BBC1	*Clarissa Explains it All*	Children's drama – non-UK
CH4	*California Dreams*	Children's drama – non-UK
BBC2	*Jackanory Gold*	Children's drama (UK)
BBC2	*Fresh Prince of Bel Air*	Drama: series/serials – non-UK
BBC2	*Star Trek: The Next Generation*	Drama: series/serials – non-UK
BBC2	*Lassie*	Children's drama – non-UK
BBC2	*Heartbreak High*	Drama: series/serials – non-UK
BBC1	*Sweet Valley High*	Children's drama – non-UK
BBC1	*The New Adventures of Superman*	Drama: series/serials – non-UK
BBC1	*Neighbours*	Drama: long-running series – non-UK
ITV	*Home and Away*	Drama: long-running series – non-UK
ITV	*The New Baywatch*	Drama: series/serials – non-UK
CH4	*Saved by the Bell*	Children's drama – non-UK
CH4	*The Waltons*	Drama: series/serials – non-UK
BBC1	*Casualty*	Drama: series/serials – UK
BBC1	*EastEnders*	Drama: long-running series – UK
BBC1	*The X Files*	Drama: series/serials – non-UK
BBC1	*Men Behaving Badly*	Light entertainment: sit./comedy
ITV	*The Bill*	Drama: long-running series – UK
ITV	*Coronation Street*	Drama: long-running series – UK
ITV	*Heartbeat*	Drama: series/serials – UK
ITV	*London's Burning*	Drama: series/serials – UK
ITV	*Soldier Soldier*	Drama: series/serials – UK
CH4	*Brookside*	Drama: long-running series – UK
CH4	*Friends*	Light entertainment: sit./comedy

Categorisation of programmes from BARB programme data, BBC Edit genres (Davies and Corbett, 1997).

In this task, unlike private comments on the questionnaire, children were operating in a semi-public sphere – the classroom – and taking on public adult roles through the drama of the exercise. Obviously, when children are required to take on roles where they are apparently speaking with other voices, questions are raised about the validity of the opinions they express. Can views voiced in a role-play exercise be accepted as reliable statements of children's own views? We believed that they could be, with certain provisos. We were interested not so much in children's own personal views for the purpose of this exercise, but more in children's perceptions of how broadcasters behaved, made decisions and came to conclusions, and, further, how children thought that broadcasters *ought* to behave. If children were speaking in uncharacteristic ways, this was, in a sense, the point of the exercise: such modes of discussion would indicate assumptions about the priorities that adult decision-makers are expected to take. The ability to predict how adults in the public sphere take decisions, and on what ideological and practical bases, is an aspect of children's theories of mind, an aspect with social and civic implications, as well as psychological ones.

An important qualification here is that, unlike some of the other exercises in which children had to pretend *to be* specific groups of adults, such as 'teachers' or 'parents', children in the scheduling exercise were not specifically told: 'you are adults'. They were simply told: 'You are in charge of a children's channel.' In this exercise, it was an adult function which they were being asked to perform, but they were not specifically being asked to take on adult 'roles'. Many of the scheduling discussions seemed to be children's own opinions, expressing what they personally would do if they had a channel to run; this was apparent, for example, from the interactions between the individuals in the groups, frequently addressing each other, or arguing with each other, by name, and referring to areas of common knowledge and interest. However, alongside these interpersonal comments, many of the perspectives they expressed seemed to have been drawn from ideas about how adults doing the same task would behave, or think. The variety, and the occasional contradictions, of these ideas indicated that children were drawing on a range of cultural representations about what it means to be 'a spokesperson', which we discuss in more detail below.

Structure of the tasks

In the small, first-stage groups, children had to arrive at agreement through negotiation and discussion; to facilitate this, each group was chaired by a 'group leader' appointed by the teacher. The discussion process in the groups, all mixed ability and mixed boys and girls, although often arousing some arguments, always ended in consensus. The children adopted a variety of strategies to reach agreement – voting, making piles of cards of different genres, taking turns for each group member to list his or her choices – and so on, under the chairship of their group leader; no advice was given on procedure, except in terms of keeping to time. Rarely was any intervention needed from adults in this first, programme-selection stage; an exception was in a drama schedule discussion when one girl got very tearful because her choice of programme had been eliminated by the group, an indication of how seriously the children took the exercise. In the second stage, a researcher was present as the children discussed the discarding of programmes, and probed for their reasons. The time limit for drawing up the schedules in the first stage was 15–20 minutes; discipline in reaching consensus was provided by the group leaders and general peer-group persuasion.

An illustration of the processes of negotiation is given by these groups of 11–12 year olds in an inner-London secondary school, reporting back to the whole class on their discussions, explaining how they reached their final selection, and how they dealt with disagreements:

BOY 1, REPRESENTING GROUP 1   We put all of them [the cards] on the table and decided which ones we definitely agreed on and then we put the rest of them away. And then we put the next lot into seven and chose from them. Then we put the rest of them away. And then we put the next lot into seven and chose from them.

GIRL 1, REPRESENTING GROUP 2   We spread them all out on the table and because we don't have six people and because I'm the group leader, I chose two and everyone else chose one. And we had some disagreements about one of them which was *Power Rangers* but we were out-voted [*Power Rangers* was left out].

BOY 2, REPRESENTING GROUP 3   We put them on the table and thought about what children were not interested in.

INTERVIEWER   Did you disagree about anything?

BOY 2   *Match of the Day*, where we [boys] all wanted it but they [girls] didn't [*Match of the Day* was in their final list].

Some children reflected on what adult schedulers might do, in contrast to what they themselves had done. These 9–11 year olds at a suburban primary school in Buckinghamshire were asked how they thought real-world schedulers arrived at their decisions:

GIRL 1   In magazines sometimes they have this poll to ask what we like and then they send them to the station and then they see what the audience like.

BOY 1   I think they think about what the people like and they should also ask things like 'is *The Biz* going out of fashion?' and see if no one wants to watch it any more.

BOY 2   I do not think they think of anyone, they put all these rubbish programmes like *Tots TV* [an ITV preschool programme, made by the makers of *Teletubbies*] . . . They are all civilised adults and they all sit around a table and choose things like *Tots TV*!

Teachers stayed in the room alongside the researchers while the whole-class groups were working, but were not otherwise involved in the tasks. They were impressed by the extent to which children stayed 'on task' and also with all the children's extensive knowledge of broadcasting. Very rarely did any child express lack of familiarity with any of the programme titles (in contrast with many of their teachers), which made all the exercises thoroughly inclusive. Despite their extensive knowledge, none of the children in the study were receiving formal media education; only two of the schools in the sample (both secondary) offered media education and this was only in the upper, exam classes, not to the lower year-groups used in the study. The children's specific expertise as broadcasting schedulers appeared to come from deductions and inferences about the media's functions, organisation and ideologies acquired outside the specific curricula of their schools, and on which they drew in these exercises.

The pilot study

The pilot study gave us the first hint of children's tendency to extreme moral seriousness in making judgements about programmes; in fact, it generated data so heavily biased towards a sense of public responsibility that the task was changed for the main study, in order to permit a greater range of expressions of likes and dislikes and other opinions, particularly about television drama – the object of the exercise – to be generated. In the pilot task, carried out in an urban primary school in Essex, the children were told that they were in a space capsule which was going to visit a civilisation – the planet 'Andromeda' – which did not have any television programmes for children. They had to choose six programmes, taken from the list in Table 9. They were told that something had gone wrong with the space capsule and videotapes had to be thrown out one by one to make the capsule lighter, until only one was left.

The following exchanges took place as a group of 9–11 year olds in the pilot school discussed whether they should throw out the programme *999* (which is a reality 'rescue' programme, similar to *Rescue 911* in the United States):

GIRL 1   *Animal Hospital* we can get rid of.

GIRL 2   *Animal Hospital* can stay.

BOY 1   Yes because that is sort of helping people learn about animals.

GIRL 2   *The Bill* should go then.

BOY 2   *The Bill*, Bye, Bye Bill.

INTERVIEWER   Why do you want *The Bill* out?

BOY 1   Because it's teaching people to sort of like – do things like commit murder. Someone might watch that and think, oh, that looks like a load of fun and go out and do it.

In these cases, the programmes were assessed almost entirely from the point of view of children learning something socially valuable, or being protected from bad examples. This was perhaps to be expected in the case of *999* or *Animal Hospital*. However, the same moralistic principles were applied to programmes where learning was a much less obviously expected outcome. After the discussion of *Animal Hospital*, the next programme to be threatened with jettisoning in the pilot group was Nickelodeon's *Clarissa Explains it All*, a popular comedy, which generated some gender differences in discussion. The processes of negotiation used to reconcile these differences in taste, with sometimes boys' and sometimes girls' choices prevailing, always tended towards consensus – to find a schedule, or a programme, that would please both groups:

BOY 1   *Clarissa*, I think.

GIRL 1   No, no. It explains about growing up and everything. How to deal with your brothers.

Once again, *Clarissa* was assessed using learning criteria. In this case, it was social skills, including the gender issue of being a girl having to deal with brothers, and for the time being *Clarissa* was kept. The children then reached the point of discussing whether or not to throw out *Man O Man* (a down-market dating show) from the schedule:

BOY 1   I don't see any point in the programme; it isn't like it's a game show as well, it's just that I don't think it is like a programme.

INTERVIEWER   Who is going to speak for the programme, who thinks it should be in?

GIRL 3   I will. I think it should be in, because it helps women make their decisions for what man they want to go out with.

INTERVIEWER   Why do you think that it is important to show another civilisation?

GIRL 3   It may show them to help them to make their decisions.

So, even *Man O Man* – the kind of public-embarrassment dating game, that has led to accusations of 'dumbing down' in British broadcasting – was justified on the grounds that it would 'help' people. Children may well not actually think in this 'Reithian' way when they watch the programmes at home; it is much more likely that they do, in fact, watch programmes like *Man O Man* for fun. What was revealing, in the context of the exercise, was that children felt that it was appropriate to be seen to use socially responsible terminology about such programmes.

Because it seemed that the 'colonial' nature of the pilot task itself, taking television programmes to a new culture, might be biasing the children towards these evangelical positions, it was decided to revise the instructions of the task for the main study. The task was redesigned in order to give children the opportunity to express likes, dislikes and more consumerist reasons for choosing programmes, which was what the BBC required from them. The first stage of the task was kept – with small groups choosing an ideal schedule of 6 or 7 programmes, this time for a children's channel. But, in the second stage, the task was given a pragmatic, real-world application, with financial rather than moral (or life-preserving) incentives to cut the number of programmes. Despite the redesign, and the pragmatic motivations required, the same socially responsible, paternalist themes continued to dominate the reasons children gave for valuing or rejecting programmes.

This group came from an Oxfordshire, outer-city primary school:

BOY 1   I think that the *Power Rangers* should go because a lot of people criticise it for the violence.

INTERVIEWER   Anyone else.

GIRL 1   *Men Behaving Badly* because it's rude.

BOY 2   (Of *The X Files*) It is not suitable for the little children because they may be scared by it.

These same children thought about the needs of the majority, rather than themselves, when choosing:

GIRL 2   *Top of the Pops* stays because everyone watches it, *Men Behaving Badly* should go.

BOY 2   Keep *EastEnders* because a lot of people watch it.

And magazine programmes were retained because they had something for everybody:

GIRL 1   *Live and Kicking* has got lots of different programmes on it so that has to stay.

GIRL 2   *Live and Kicking* has more things on it and *EastEnders* – well, I know that it is a good drama but it has not got as much in it.

A group of 11–12 year olds in a Cardiff secondary school used similar, public service, protective criteria:

GIRL 1   [Get rid of] *Ren and Stimpy* – it is a cartoon so children might think it's a cartoon it's OK, but it's quite dirty, it's crude . . .

BOY 1   *Blue Peter.*

BOY 2   Not *Blue Peter*, because people like it and people who have got problems like leprosy and disability and in a wheelchair . . .

Several voices: *Ren and Stimpy.*

BOY 3   Oh . . . Children my age think it's funny because all the other cartoons, little children find them funny, but older children don't. *Ren and Stimpy* is a really funny cartoon, but little children wouldn't find it funny . . .

BOY 2   I'd say, put *Ren and Stimpy* out.

[And they did.]

Despite children demonstrating a lack of enthusiasm for news in their questionnaire responses, when it came to constructing their own schedule for a children's channel, news had to go in, as in the case of this group from a suburban primary school in Buckinghamshire:

GIRL 1   All the good programmes should start at 6 o'clock.

BOY 1   No 7.

BOY 2   What about the news, where are you going to put the news?

BOY 1   In the middle of the night as far as I am concerned.

GIRL 2   A lot of pensioners go to bed at about 8 o'clock; when are they going to be able to watch the news?

INTERVIEWER   Do you think that the news is important?

BOY 2   The news is, yeah.

GIRL 2   It is important for people to know what is going on in the world.

BOY 3   They should add on a channel with just news on it.

BOY 2   They do but it is on satellite

Yet another example came from the Cardiff, outer-city secondary school, discussing *EastEnders* and *Top of the Pops*:

BOY 1   [*EastEnders*] It's not very suitable, it's a bit violent, a lot of aggression.

GIRL 1   A lot of the songs [in *Top of the Pops*] have got swear words in them.

BOY 1   And there's drinking on stage and alcohol and stuff;

GIRL 1   Most of them, some of them pop singers take drugs and that might influence young children.

BOY 2   The thing is, on *Top of the Pops* they just show you the music, they don't really tell you the background of the band so you're not learning – not like *Live and Kicking* when the guests come on. On *Live and Kicking* they ask them all about them.

Thus, even *Top of the Pops*, which is a BBC show-case for middle-of-the-road commercial pop music, aired at 7.30 p.m., and thus specifically not the kind of programme which shows drinking on stage, or drugs, was found wanting in comparison to the representation of pop on *Live and Kicking*, which promoted 'learning' through its interviews with band members. The desire to protect children from the bad behaviour in *EastEnders* in the middle-class Buckinghamshire school (no special needs), and to try to reconcile such protectionism with recognising the needs of a wider audience, was also shared by a group of 8–11 year olds in a much less advantaged school – an inner-London primary school at the other end of the special needs scale (seven special needs):

BOY 1   I was thinking of getting rid of *Match of the Day* because not a lot of people watch it.

BOY 2   But they do, I was thinking about *The X Files*, because there are a lot of things here for older people like secondary, but if little kids watch it they will take ideas from it.

GIRL 1   I was thinking about getting rid of *Top of the Pops*, because the little babies, like, watch it and get nightmares from it. I reckon it is quite scary for little kids.

BOY 2   OK so do you think we should lose it?

BOY 1   Well hold on, what about *EastEnders*?

BOY 3   No, no my mum likes that. I like that, I like that.

BOY 2   *EastEnders* is already on BBC1 anyway.

BOY 1   No, listen *EastEnders*, yeah, there has been a lot of violence on it, a lot of swearing as well.

Thus, the main characteristics of children's talk when they were trying to decide whether to keep or throw out programmes, were that programmes should be kept if children were able to learn something from them, usually some kind of socially and morally responsible example. This type of reasoning was used to defend even the inclusion of programmes like *Man O Man*. For children of their own age group (8–12), but not younger children, if something was unpleasant or not liked, then there was always another channel or the off switch. The parents of younger children were expected to be responsible for protecting them from harm.

These moralistic comments are representative of the way that all the groups talked about selecting programmes, whether they were inner city, outer city, suburban or rural, and irrespective of the socio-economic status of the school's intake. However, there were some limits to the extent of the mind-improving information the child-public should be asked to accept, for example, this 12-year-old boy from an outer-London secondary school:

There are so many, like, non-related documentaries at times when kids are coming home from school and they want to relax. Like stuff like a review on countries like Fiji and it's got nothing to do with our lives so we don't really care about it; it's not going to affect us. If it was something like the ozone [layer] – here's a hole and how to stop it – that's something that will affect our lives more than, you know, the life of a Fiji person. Someone in the Fiji Islands doesn't really affect us.

This could be seen as a worrying indifference to the fate of other people around the world. However, looked at within the general framework of how all the children in the study approached the task of scheduling, this comment is of a piece with the children's general discourse of requiring programmes to be socially useful. This boy is pointing out that programmes *should* 'affect us'. If he does not see programmes about Fiji as 'affecting us', this is more of a reflection on the way that other parts of the world are represented as exotic and 'other' on television, than a total indifference to the fate of Fijians on his part. Even given the apparent irrelevance of the representation of Fiji to this boy, the concern for learning and self-improvement remains.

Apart from their desire to position themselves as sensible persons, by drawing on what might be seen as contradictory standpoints, another cultural representation used by the children was that of the Fourth Estate. Children often pointed out that, if something was unacceptable or shocking, it was always possible to switch off or switch over to another channel. Here, children were suggesting that media must represent their viewers or else they will be ignored. In an increasingly market-dominated broadcasting world, such priorities are becoming paramount; even the publicly funded BBC's representation of its 'small people's' programming as an idyllic haven of childhood innocence in their 1998 promotional film about children's TV, *Future Generations* – programming made possible, as the film argued, by the BBC's 'unique form of funding' – was a calculated piece of marketing aimed at adult licence-payers, not at contemporary children. Of course, there are other representations of the media's role in public life, such as those deployed by academics. Scholars working in media studies will investigate ideological messages or semiotic codes in programmes, or the heterogeneity of audiences. But such representations do not seem to be part of the popular repertoire for talking about television programmes. Why did these children choose such persistently righteous positions?

One powerful representation of children in Western culture is that they are all the same the world over; this, as discussed, is a view held by marketers, who exploit supposedly universal qualities shrewdly. Children are often depicted as innocent and vulnerable, and they also represent the possibility of living together in harmony, free of adult prejudices and complications – part of what Paul Hazard (1947) called 'the world republic of childhood'. Childhood and children are often represented as having universal common features, as in *Blue Peter*'s travels to other countries, where local children are shown to the British audience as having much in common with the viewers at home. Childhood is thus seen as transcending adult-constructed, artificial boundaries and is presented as an example of how unified the world could be. The universality of childhood is most powerfully constructed in the international Convention on the Rights of the Child, drawn up by the United Nations in 1989 and ratified by all but two of the 191 member states, although, as discussed in chapter 3, some of its provisions are controversial. In the Convention, the pursuit of knowledge through education is seen as the right of all children so that both they and their societies can develop. It seems possible that this sense of children as 'the future', with a perceived need to be schooled and educated in order to improve the world, will be taken on by children as part of the way they, as children, need to be, and of the way that they will talk about society.

A continuing theme in children's fiction too – which includes television drama – is that children have the right to a voice. Although virtually all children's fiction is produced by adults, a key characteristic of the genre is its representation of the child's point of view, rather than that of the adults', as being central to the development of the story, resulting in narratives which are 'subversive' of adult society (Lurie, 1990). According to Bazalgette and Staples (1995), what is true of children's fiction is also true of cinema; a story being told from the child's point of view is the mark of distinction between a children's film and a 'family film'. As Carpenter (1985, p. 8) pointed out, children emerged into fiction at the end of the eighteenth century, being represented as more alive and in touch with the essence of life itself than were adult characters. British poetry of the late eighteenth century, such as Wordsworth's *Ode on the Intimations of Immortality*, popularised the notion that 'children are in a higher state of spiritual perception than adults, because of their nearness to their birth and so to a pre-existence in heaven', as Carpenter put it.

Given their supposed access to paradisal wisdom, one public role for children is to speak out on behalf of society, because adults have lost contact with essential truths. This is why animals and aliens (as in *ET*) trust children; children are presumed to have an untainted vision and the uncomplicated wisdom to see truths hidden from adults. In children's fiction, such as *Little Lord Fauntleroy* or *Pollyanna* (also available in film and television drama form), it is the adult who needs the child for moral redemption, rather than the other way around. According to this representation of the primevally wise child, one public role for children is that they must speak up for other children – as the children in our study repeatedly did.

In this regard, one important element in the children's use of morally responsible discourse was the context in which our study took place. In the environment of the classroom, taking part in an official exercise such as a research project on behalf of the BBC, many of these children must have been aware that certain forms of explanations would be more acceptable than others. They would have learned during early schooling (see, for example, Wertsch in *Voices of the Mind*, 1991), that personalised explanations are less approved by teachers, than generalised and rationalistic explanations. In fact, one 12-year-old boy in an outer-London secondary school, indicated that this was so, by offering a mischievous parody of the kinds of educational explanations that he knew were needed to justify enjoying a TV programme; he was taking part in one of the other tasks – a debate to replace children's with adult drama:

BOY 1   Oh yeah, I just forgot to say something else, you know you get a better education by watching adult stuff because, um on *The Queen's Nose* [a children's drama] they've got the vocabulary like 'oh wicked, oh no, I don't know' and on *The X Files* like, one day you learn how to pronounce cat and the next day you watch *The X Files* and know how to pronounce phenominol.

GIRL 1   Phenomenal.

BOY 1   Yeah, whatever.

So along with the classroom setting, which may have encouraged a more rationalistic form of discourse among the children in our study, whether parodied or not, a possible explanation of why the children chose to talk about television programmes in such Reithian terms is that they saw themselves as needing to make the voice of the universal child heard. In this situation, they were no longer the young children they often referred to as needing protection from harmful images and messages, but responsible spokespersons for their generation and for 'the future'.

Children were more likely to say that they just liked something because it was 'funny', or that they did not like something because it was 'boring' in the individual comments on the questionnaires in the study, which were filled in privately, and which could be seen as more 'honest' because free of peer pressure. However, the view that individual private expression is of more value – the consumerist view – is at odds with arguments about publicly agreed values for broadcasting and media generally. As Habermas' theory would suggest, public sphere values are brought about through the translation from the private to the public: hence, it is in discussion and negotiation with fellow-citizens, as simulated in the exercises carried out in our study, that social contracts begin to be drawn up. What was going on was not so much different from other 'artificial' social structures like the committee system, with its agendas, chairs and points of order, from which 'real' social and political consensus is derived.

'Private' judgemental language was certainly used in the discussions in these scheduling exercises. In these cases, the relevant outcome was that a programme being 'boring' or 'funny' eventually carried less weight than the moral and social value of programmes; through the group process of negotiation, moral and social values always prevailed. Even where children produced some fairly harsh judgements about programmes they did not like along the way, public service values were finally accepted, as in this case of a group of 12–13 year olds in an outer-London secondary school, deciding between *Byker Grove* and *EastEnders*:

GIRL 1   I think that it [*Byker*] is boring, I like *EastEnders* . . .

GIRL 2   Let us get rid of *Byker Grove*.

BOY 1   Why?

BOY 2   It is like *EastEnders*, it is just the same.

GIRL 1   But *EastEnders* has got better lines.

BOY 3   Yeah and it has got more funny things like people getting kicked in the face a lot.

GIRL 2   And shot.

GIRL 1   *Byker Grove*'s Barney is a joke.

BOY 3   In *Byker Grove* it is sad.

GIRL 1   That is because no one can understand them.

However, the single programme left at the end of this group's elimination process was the magazine programme, *Live and Kicking* – the same choice as two of the other schools who did the same scheduling exercise. Once more, the public service values of serving a wider audience, and greater diversity of content provided the criteria for choosing this, rather than the drama *EastEnders*, as Girl 2 explained:

GIRL 2   *Live and Kicking* has more things on it and *EastEnders* well, I know that it is a good drama but it has not got as much in it.

The single programmes which made the 'final cut' in the scheduling elimination exercises mostly reflected this persistent public service bias. They were: *Live and Kicking* (three times); *Rugrats* (which just beat *Live and Kicking* in the Welsh-language secondary school – partly because of the English language bias in *Live and Kicking*); and, in the case of the inner-London secondary school, *The Simpsons* – which had just been introduced on British terrestrial television towards the end of the study, and which was included in the schedule as the pupils' own choice. The reasons for choosing *The Simpsons*, included 'it's funny. . . it's hilarious', but they also, typically, included: 'It reflects some things from life.'

In the drama-scheduling exercises, the last programmes to survive were: *The Queen's Nose* (Milton Keynes inner-city primary school) – reasons being 'It's for girls and boys. Kids like wishing for things', in an Oxfordshire primary school, *EastEnders* was preferred to *The Queen's Nose* because '*The Queen's Nose* is just imagination – it is not so good as *EastEnders*'; and *The X Files* (Oxfordshire secondary school) was preferred to the younger children's comedy drama, *Fudge*. As the 12-year-old spokesperson (a boy) put it: 'The *X Files* stays because 3 year olds should be outside making mud pies and stuff.' Once again, despite the sardonic tone, the concern for public issues such as the educational and social well-being of 3 year olds is paramount in this comment.

Summary

Two broad themes arose from the analysis of this qualitative data: first, the somewhat unexpected finding that children consistently used socially responsible, public service criteria of 'education', 'helping', 'learning' and 'good/bad examples' to defend their choices, despite the tasks being redesigned to permit them to express more consumerist criteria, such as 'fun', or 'making money', or enjoyment – what the BBC, as providers, were looking for. This bias towards Reithian values suggested to us, when we looked more closely at the transcripts, that the children's way of talking about their programmes was drawing on adult cultural representations, both about television and about childhood itself, circulating in the culture at large, in ways similar to adult discourses (Bellah *et al.* 1985; Machin and Carrithers, 1996).

The children knew that their discussions were located within the current media context of increasing globalisation and commercial independent production – especially as they knew they were taking part in a study to, as many assumed, 'help the BBC to make better programmes'. They were clearly aware of issues such as the decline of public service ideals, deregulation, criticism of the BBC, and the growth of an entertainment-based consumerism in the way that broadcasting is organised, and the processes of discussion led to a position in which most groups seemed to feel the need to resist these developments. As the quotes at the head of the chapter illustrate, some of the children's discourse reflected the words of the first Director General of the BBC, Lord Reith, in his 1924 broadcast, in which he talked about broadcasting as 'disseminating the best in human knowledge' and stressed the broadcasters' responsibility to avoid harmful material (Reith, 1924). Although many children showed a sophisticated awareness of global commercial developments, such as Rupert Murdoch's bid to monopolise televised sport and movies, the most marked characteristic of their discussions was idealistic, an idealism which could not entirely be shifted by the commercial imperative to entertain.

Other data from the study showed a more 'consumerist' than 'citizenship' perspective, and what might be described as a more typically childlike desire for entertainment, as in the qualitative comments in the questionnaire. Children's discourses thus varied depending on the perceived requirements of the task. This is not an invalidating 'experimenter effect', but evidence of children's ability to move between different modes of discussion, depending on the circumstances and the audience. It provides evidence of children's capacity to act as citizens-in-the-making, capable of operating sensibly and purposefully in the public sphere, while at the same time displaying some of the more conventional 'pester power' characteristics of the child-as-consumer model, or the child-as-cheeky-rebel model. The other familiar model of public discourse – the child-as-vulnerable-victim, with its reverse side of the coin, the child-as-demonic-tearaway – did not appear at all in the conduct of the children as they carried out the scheduling exercises. Individuals did not get bullied, or excluded or teased about their choices and tastes at any stage in the process, in any of the schools. This is certainly a tribute to the schools and to the children concerned, but it could also indicate an effect of the task itself: structured processes which allow negotiation and debate, requiring responsible decisions to be reached, all under the leadership of children themselves, can help to inculcate citizenship behaviours. The vulnerable-victim model was one which these children themselves held about younger children, and this will be discussed further in chapter 6. But the overall data from the study suggest that all these models of childhood are not mutually exclusive in any individual child or groups of children, though one sort of discourse could prevail more than another depending on demographic variables, such as gender balance in the group, or the context in which the exercise took place.

As James and Prout (1997) have pointed out, whenever children's interests in social and political arrangements are talked about, children themselves are rarely consulted. Oswell (1998) has drawn attention to how discussions on regulation of the Internet for children in the late 1990s took place without any reference to actual children. Kitzinger (1990) looked at the way representations of child abuse in media lacked a sense of the child's experience but instead used idealised concepts of childhood – toys, hobbies, traits – to move emphasis away from the person as victim, to focus on innocence, and to stress a sense of the need for adult protection. Those who professionally study children empirically, such as developmental and educational psychologists, often show little interest in children's media and culture, and the representation of children in culture, except as a source of possible harmful 'effects'. Thus, again, such empirical work as there is with children, denies children themselves a voice in these matters.

The data from this particular task suggest that children feel a strong sense of social and moral responsibility when it comes to making judgements about broadcasting provision. Like adults, they use representations available in the culture, along with ideas drawn from their own experience, to navigate a sense of who they, their peers and their siblings, including 'little kids', are, and where they fit into the society around them. Despite the supposedly corrupting effects of television assumed by many adults, these children in middle-childhood were capable of being highly responsible and socially minded when discussing the impact of the medium on their own and other children's lives. All of this has relevance to the topic of the next chapter: the question of the taboo.

6   Censorship

If you ban it they'll be complaining it's not on.
> Girl, 10, inner-city primary school, Cardiff

I do not like *Grange Hill* because it has swearing and children of my age are not meant to. The things that they do are not realistic and nobody would dare to do the things that they do.
> Girl, 10, primary school, Oxfordshire

I think there should be more programmes for little children. Bad things should not be put on at 8 o'clock because I will see it.
> Girl, 9, suburban primary school, Didcot, Oxfordshire

That could, like, change the way they . . . look at things; when you see people playing football, [like] that song football coming home or something, you see like a mental foul in it, they [children] go outside and [they] go: 'it was in a film; let's see if I can do it' . . . and they probably go and hack someone.
> Boy, 12, outer-London secondary school

The history of children's relationship with media is, in many respects, the history of much larger historical attempts to control the media generally. The desire to protect children from harmful effects from published material, whether in print or in other forms, is the great central battlefield (and one of the few such battlefields) in which children have a prominent place in the public sphere. Children are the main targets of censorship and regulation of media material in contemporary society, hence film and video classifications, from U to PG, to 12, 15 and 18, the 9 p.m. watershed in the UK, the introduction of the parental-control V Chip in the USA, and restrictive legislation limiting the availability of videos such as the amendment requiring more stringent classification of videos in the Broadcasting Act of 1994. This chapter discusses issues of censorship and regulation, and this is contextualised by comments from children on the same topics.[1]

---

[1] Method: this is, first, through direct first-hand comments, in the free comment section of the questionnaire, and, second, in tasks which specifically required them to act in the role of regulators. One task was a debate to ban the children's programme, *The Demon*

Historical control of children's information

Protecting children as a pretext for the control of information generally has occurred regardless of medium, technology or genre. The process is not only about the attempts of ruling classes to limit the access to knowledge of the lesser orders of society (see, for instance, Barker and Petley, 1997); it is also a historical process enabling standards of cultural value to be established on the basis of upgrading what was popular in the past, rather than seriously critically appreciating what is enjoyed by the contemporary populace. This contemporary 'mass' judgement cannot be validated by scholars, until the medium has begun to be *un*popular, at which point its cultural value is rediscovered and canonised by people who disregarded it in its heyday. McLuhan (1964) quoted in Starker (1991, p. 3) described this process thus: 'Each new technology creates an environment that is regarded as corrupt and degrading. Yet the new one turns its predecessor into an art-form.'

As each new technology causes more alarm among the guardians of public information, so the preceding technology's value as cultural capital is elevated. Neil Postman (1982) valorises printing as necessary for a civilised culture, but Sir William Berkeley writing in 1671 did not agree with him:

I thank God there are no free schools or printing . . . for learning has brought disobedience and heresy and sects into the world and printing has divulged them and libels against the best Government. God keep us from both. (Sir William Berkeley, Governor of Virginia, 1671, quoted in Starker, 1991, p. 39)

No other medium, however, has been vilified as much as television, the most domestically pervasive medium, and hence the most available to growing children. Film, the most similar form to TV in terms of being both visual and oral, has had its social and moral critics – but, following the McLuhan progression, film has been recognised as art, and film studies as a form of high academic endeavour, whereas television studies (as, to some extent, in the case of this book) still have to be justified as a form of useful sociological and political comment. Television is also (particularly in the USA) a public health problem, sometimes seen as a mainlining injection of antisocial values into the home – a 'plug-in drug' in Marie Winn's telling phrase – against which children need to be

Headmaster; the other required them to discuss the differences between adult material and children's material in a debate about replacing two children's dramas – the realistic school serial/soap *Grange Hill*, and the fantasy drama The *Queen's Nose* – with two adult dramas which came from similar genres – *EastEnders* and *The X Files*. The censorship debate was carried out in two schools – an inner-city primary in Cardiff and a village primary school in Buckinghamshire. The replacement schedule was discussed in an inner-city secondary school in Middlesbrough and an outer-London secondary school.

defended and immunised. Starker (1991 p. 136) quotes a number of examples of attacks on the medium, including that of Edward Podolsky, Senate Subcommittee on Juvenile Delinquency, 1954: 'Seeing constant brutality, viciousness and unsocial acts, results in hardness, intense selfishness . . . on the native temperament of the child.'

Britain, too, has had its fair share of public moralists on this subject, as in this example from the *Sun* newspaper (7 June 1996, p. 6) in an editorial on children's television: 'by destroying children's innocence we are destroying society', it claimed. Many more examples can be found by opening newspapers at random in any week. The concern is always either about imitation – or social modelling – and following on from this, about corruption of innocence, including a corruption of the child's capacity to learn.

Attempts to control access to information are, ostensibly, in order to protect groups vulnerable to harmful effects; actually, as Barker and Petley (1997) suggest, they are to control access to information from those who might seek to destabilise existing power structures. Habermas's case for the existence of a public sphere depends on the success of public opinion in evading the attempts of governments to limit the flow of information about their activities, and in bringing the influence of citizens to bear on political decision-making. Children are not the same as adult electors; they are, by definition, non-citizens with no electoral or public sphere role, they are not consulted in political public opinion polls, and, traditionally, they have had no structural means of destabilising power structures – apart from direct public action, for example the schoolchildren of South Africa in the 1960s, protesting about the imposition of teaching of Afrikaans in schools. In such cases, they are easily, and brutally, overpowered. The relative civic, as well as physical, powerlessness of children has not stopped the efforts of adult society to control their access to media from being both strenuous and strident. This has especially been so in the past decade, when there have been a number of highly publicised cases of child delinquency in the UK, in which film and video have been named as culprits in a flurry of 'moral panic'. The history of these incidents has provided a great deal of comment among media studies researchers, some of it only tangentially related to the needs and interests of children.

Springhall (1998, p. 5) argues that the phenomenon of 'moral panic' over media is very little to do with children directly, but serves social and political functions. It is: 'a periodic tendency towards the identification and scapegoating of "folk devils" . . . whose activities were regarded by hegemonic groups as indicative of imminent social breakdown. Panics served as ideological safety valves whose effect was to restore social equilibrium.' Through children and young people's presumed technical and cultural competence in new media (a reinvention of the Romantic idea of childhood as a state of access to superior wisdom) the construct of 'the young' (as distinct from actual children) can be seen as particularly threatening to adult society, and a challenge to existing power relations. As Springhall (1998 p. 7) puts it, 'Media panics can help to re-establish a generational status quo.' Springhall is not uncritical about the concept of 'moral panic', with its 'patronising' overtones of an impressionable public, unthinkingly swayed by demagogic propaganda in the press. He draws attention to the way in which 'moral panic' is used as a 'deflating phrase' to 'condescend to excitements among the general populace'. He points out (1998, p. 8) the risks of academic complacency on this topic: 'The academic message is a reassuring one; "do not worry, we have been here before, your concerns are an ersatz compound manufactured by the media, a few odd bishops, strident voices from the left and the right, moralists and nostalgists of all kinds".'

Books such as Starker's, and the Barker and Petley collection, *Ill Effects* (1997), discussed in more detail below, offer us plenty of examples of censorship of what we would now find harmless material, thus enabling modern readers to feel a sense of amused superiority. Who would now want to be aligned with Sir William Berkeley? Young people know that our society now permits much more explicit scenes of sexuality and violence to be represented and witnessed by audiences, including youthful ones, than was the case with their parents' generation. Should they infer from this that the modernist progressive developments of seventeenth- and eighteenth-century Enlightenment and the liberalisation of public debate are continuing, as each new taboo in representation is removed? Or do they see these developments differently?

Several of our producer and regulator interviewees commented on how 'the envelope had been pushed' in children's, as well as adults', drama, during the period in which they had been working in the industry, for instance, Stephen Whittle (interviewed for the Broadcasting Standards Commission study in spring, 1997) of the Broadcasting Standards Commission, formerly a producer with the BBC:

The things that happened in *Grange Hill* in 1978 . . . look comparatively innocent. More recently, [there was] a family . . . in trouble with money lenders and the money lenders came and smashed the flat, which was pretty tough for a child audience, I would have thought.

Many of our child commentators agreed with him about the 'toughness', although they continued to stress the moral purpose of children's drama as distinct from adult drama, for instance, the 12-year-old spokesperson for this Middlesbrough group discussing the replacement of children's with adults' programmes:

CHILD   Everyone in our group said it [the schedule] should stay as it is, except for one person who said that *EastEnders* should come on at children's time and *X Files* should come on later . . . We think *Grange Hill* introduces the big school to children and teaches them right and wrong.

INTERVIEWER   Does that not happen in *EastEnders* or *The X Files*?

CHILD   No.

It is debatable whether the idea of progress, at least in terms of the destruction of all representational taboos, *is* accepted by children and young people in a postmodern era, when absolute cultural standards, whether aesthetic, moral or political, can no longer be generally agreed and passed on to them in ways which are both authoritative and personally supportive. It is possible that the commercial spectacles of late twentieth-century Hollywood are seen, not as evidence of a desirable liberalisation, but as socially regressive. The comments at the head of this chapter asking that 'Bad things should not be put on at 8 o'clock because I will see it', suggest that children have ambivalent feelings about unrestricted access to 'bad things'. The question is: how should adult society respond to those feelings?

Children protecting 'other' children

One way is to suggest that children are not being wholly honest when they express a desire for protection, because many children relish horror films and want to see adult videos. Given children's contradictory statements, perhaps we should accept as more true the child's opinion favouring greater liberalisation, and which, conveniently, most supports adult desires for freedom from censorship. In this context, in his article on 'electronic child abuse' in *Ill Effects* (1997, p. 38), David Buckingham comments on the phenomenon of 'displacement', in which people express concern about media effects, but only on other people, not on themselves. He describes a 'kind of infinite regression' in which all children, no matter how young, will agree that 'television violence can cause violence in real life' in people younger/more vulnerable than themselves. But, says Buckingham, they will insist that '*we* aren't influenced by what we watch: it's only little kids who copy what they see'. The phenomenon of displacement occurred repeatedly in our study too – and, of course, was made more likely by children being specifically asked to take roles in which they were schedulers, regulators and adult authority figures.

This group of 10–12-year-old children, from a village primary school in Buckinghamshire, illustrate how effectively they were able to carry out 'displacement', depending on the roles they were enacting (they were debating a ban on *The Demon Headmaster*). The results of the feedback session from the first, whole-class stage of the debate were as follows.

The first group, representing children, aged 4–8, voted for a ban, because:

It's hard to follow; they [small children] want *Mickey Mouse, Winnie the Pooh*. If it is not banned, it [*The Demon Headmaster*] should be classified as PG.

The second group, representing children 9–14 – their own age group, did not want a ban because:

We think it should be put on later between half seven, quarter to eight when the little kids go to bed. We think it should be on for 9–14 year olds because we know it is not true.

The third group, 'parents', were ambivalent and thought they would probably ban it because:

It is up to the parents to tell their children to watch it or not . . . children will be put off from doing their school work and some might think their headmaster might try and hypnotise them. You could put it on later when the little children can't watch it.

The teachers' group expressed concern about the image of school, but still voted against a ban:

If children see it they may get the wrong impression about school. Young children might get nightmares. People who don't like it don't have to watch it.

The group representing producers made a similar point: 'if they don't like it they should just turn the TV off'. They also had a reassuring message for parents, pointing out that the special effects could be misleading: 'It's not as scary as parents think it is, it's because of the music.'

In taking the parts of these different interest groups, these children provided convincing representations of the discourse they thought was likely to be used by such groups; those representing the industry, for instance, characteristically defended themselves by arguing that parents should not rush to judgement, and, if they did not like something, they could turn it off. However, the final, consensual decision argued against a ban. The exercise permitted children to show multiple intellectual perspectives on these issues. As a result of debate and discussion, each of these groups – despite showing awareness of potential harmful effects – eventually came up with convincing reasons for voting against a total ban. Very much as a real committee would do, they arrived at compromises, such as later scheduling, warning labels and a recognition of the responsibilities of parents. These multiple perspectives show a more complex perception of issues of regulation and protection on the part of these children than simple psychological 'displacement'.

The study also provided evidence that the displacement regression was not 'infinite.' In the first place, there were age differences. Older children resisted being placed in the category of little children, younger children did not. The youngest children in the study – 5 to 7 year olds – referred to *themselves* as little children, demanding appropriate services and programming for 'babies'. In the second place, particularly in the individual comments, there were some robust demands for the control of certain kinds of offensive material which were being made on the writer's own behalf – not on behalf of others. Such material included 'kissing'; ' "rude" behaviour and language'; 'swearing'; 'violence' and 'fighting'. Girls, particularly, objected to violence, reflecting a gender difference in attitudes which is found in adult commentaries on the subject too, for instance these comments from the free section of the questionnaire:

I like Children's BBC, I think there should be more of it and not as many films. I think there should not be as many death programmes and I do not think they should have programmes like *The Bill* and *Casualty*. (Girl, 9, suburban primary school, Oxfordshire)

There is too much fighting in cartoons. There are too many baby films, there should be more films for children of our age. (Girl, 11, inner-city primary school, Milton Keynes)

I think children's programmes should be more exciting and dramatic but should not show bad language or fighting. (Girl, 12, outer-London primary school)

A demand for protection could also coexist with a desire not to be treated as 'babyish' and for more grown-up material for children – which, in the case of this boy, clearly did not mean more representations of sexuality, which he found 'rude':

They should stop making rude channels after nine. They should make it 12 o'clock or something. (Boy, 11, inner-London primary school)

Equally diverse demands were expressed by this 10-year-old girl from an inner-city primary school in Cardiff, who was more offended by the kissing on the early evening *Neighbours* than she was by the scary effects of the post-watershed *The X Files*:

I would like to say that on children's programmes like *Neighbours* they are very rude and they kiss a lot. I like programmes that are exciting and funny, really funny. Some of the cartoons are really BORING, they go on and on and on just like *Ace Ventura Pet Detective*. *EastEnders* is really good and I would like it if they showed it more often. *The X Files* is also very good and I think that it should come on more often and earlier.

Generally, children aged 8–12, increasingly dissociated themselves from the 'little children' category, and it was only children who did this who showed evidence of 'displacement'. The most striking example of this was in the questionnaire statement: 'Cartoons are only for little children' (see chapter 7, Table 12) in which the majority of 5 and 6 year olds agreed with the statement, but, from 7 upwards, an increasing majority disagreed with it. The quotation above from a 9-year-old girl in Oxfordshire is a rare, but not unique, example of a child openly admitting that she, not others, needed protection: this child did *not* see herself as wiser and more immune to effects than others, but specifically asked that 'bad things' should not be put on when she would see them.

Ill effects and protecting children

In the mid to late 1990s, the debate about media effects on children was brought painfully up to date by a particularly terrible incident in Liverpool in 1993 – the abduction, torture and murder of 2-year-old James Bulger, by two 10 year olds, Jon Venables and Robert Thompson. One of the first academic comments on it came from child psychologist Elizabeth Newson. She was asked to produce a discussion paper by Liverpool MP David Alton, who was proposing an amendment to the Criminal Justice Act to tighten British Board of Film Classification requirements of video material, partly prompted by this murder case. Newson's paper, 'Video violence and the protection of children' (reprinted in the journal of the British Psychological Society, *The Psychologist*, in June 1994) discussed the extreme savagery of the James Bulger murder, and raised the question of what could have prompted it (Newson, 1994, p. 273):

What then can be seen as the 'different' factor that has entered the lives of countless children and adolescents in recent years? This has to be recognized as the easy availability to children of gross images of violence on video . . . It now seems that professionals in child health and psychology underestimated the degree of brutality and sustained sadism that film makers were capable of inventing . . . let alone the special effects technologies which would support such images; and we certainly underestimated how easy would be children's access to them.

Newson's paper, signed by thirty-six other health and education professionals concerned with children, was publicly circulated by Alton, with obvious political intent, which resulted in a storm of press comment, including a sensational headline: 'U Turn over Video Nasties: 'Naive' experts admit link with real life violence', in the *London Evening Standard*, which shocked Newson. As she said, in an article headed

'Ordeal by media' in *The Psychologist* (June 1994, p. 276), 'Almost all the papers copied the inaccuracies of the Evening Standard: the U turn (when only about three of us had ever spoken publicly about the topic before).' Among the large postbag she received as a result of this publicity, was a short paper signed by twenty-two media academics, 'rubbishing me for knowing nothing about the media; oddly, this paper quoted simplistic statements that I had already rejected as too simplistic, and dealt only with adults not children'.

These twenty-two media academics formed the basis of the group who produced, in 1997, a collection of essays, entitled *Ill Effects* (Barker and Petley, 1997), to combat the views expressed in the Newson Report. This book constitutes one of the most useful collections of media commentaries on the question of violence, censorship and regulation to be produced. It challenged the empirical validity of Newson's report. In the words of one of its editors, Martin Barker (p. 1), the Newson Report 'had not a single fact to its name, good or bad. It was a thin tissue of claims whose only virtue was that they were what every politician and newspaper wanted to hear.'

Barker and his co-editor, Julian Petley, like Newson, also complained of 'ordeal by media' – in their case, of being ignored (p. 3). 'When Elizabeth Newson issued her report, the press, radio and television, were lining up to cover it. When we tried to state the opposite case, no one wanted to hear.' Barker and Petley (1997, p. 3) blame this lack of attention on 'a real problem with the state of our press in Britain today . . . The idea of the press as a critical forum, asking awkward questions of those in power (other than about their private lives), seems increasingly bizarre.' They blame the attention given to the Newson Report on the efforts of a group 'lurking' in the background of Alton's amendment – the Movement for Christian Democracy, which had 'a quite specific moral agenda which, in its own words, used the Bill as a means of "coming of age politically"'. Like Newson, too, Julian Petley (1997, p. 2) experienced emotional disturbance: 'What I read [about the academic U turn over video nasties] both calmed and worried me.'

Before reviewing some of the issues raised by this debate, in the context of what children in the study said about it, I want to acknowledge a sense of inadequacy at the intractability and painfulness of the issues and feelings it raises. Anybody, whether academic, journalist or member of the public, who ventures into this area (as I have done on a number of occasions, sometimes on the same platform as the protagonists mentioned above) has to recognise that they are entering into a minefield, and I believe it is important when entering such an exposed position to be honest about one's own views. As a media academic, I sympathise with the position of Barker and Petley (eight years before *Ill Effects*, I wrote a book called *Television is Good for Your Kids* making many of the same points); as a psychologist, I sympathise with the position of Elizabeth Newson and her professional concern to understand 'the long drawn-out and merciless' attack on James Bulger, committed by two children, who in her professional view, were not 'freaks' nor psychopaths, with 'little evidence of extremes of abuse or neglect' in their (admittedly unhappy) home backgrounds. Her conclusion that 'perhaps we should consider future Roberts and Jons and how far society should accept some responsibility for children who, at least in some sense, are its victims themselves' is the kind of humane, and reasoned contribution to an emotive debate that the psychological profession needs to make.

No expressions of sympathy by strangers are in any way adequate to the parents and family of the victim, but they should be made. As a parent, I also sympathise with parents who worry about their children being upset by bloodthirsty videos, and who are concerned at the dominance of a macho commercial cinema culture aimed at a target audience of young men aged 14–24. However, I also sympathise with the children who find a fascination with the representation of unimaginable horrors. As a child I used to like gory stories; as an adult, I am notoriously squeamish and the object of amusement and irritation to my own (now grown-up) children, but, as such, I am obviously an exhibit for the defence. Reading accounts of martyrdom in Butler's *Lives of the Saints* (a Catholic upbringing provides all kinds of opportunities in this regard) has not turned me into a killer, although it has probably encouraged tendencies towards being oppositional. Now, I cannot watch violence on the screen. I do not like being frightened – perhaps because I once had a terrifying fear reaction, after a serious operation, in which I thought I would die. I do like science fiction, special effects and all, but (and this is no offence to the many nice horror fans I know) I think the horror genre (at least in its contemporary cinematic manifestations) is ludicrous, with no mitigating narrative interest to justify the grossness of some of its effects. I am a trade unionist, with left-of-centre views, and I retain my membership of the Labour Party, mainly out of loyalty to those who went before me, including my Labour councillor father. I am a wife of 30 years and a mother of 4 grown-up children, 2 male, 2 female. All those who comment on the media have a similar list of personal feelings, tastes, experiences and ideological positions, and it is useful for other participants in the debate to know what they are when asked to contribute to it.

I have given a brief outline of the two academic positions on either side of the debate about the Newson Report as an illustrative point: to show that, when it comes to academic controversies about *children's* relationship with media, the issues – whether intellectual, political, emotional or all three – are almost invariably expressed in terms of how *adults* think and feel. These feelings may relate to the shortcomings of the British press, or the sinister 'lurkings' of Christian Democracy, or the brutality and sadism of film-makers, or the lack of respect accorded to our own intellectual disciplines. What all sides of the argument have in common is that the pretext for the discussion – children and their specific problems – is sometimes forgotten in the cut and thrust of academic critiques of other people's intellectual disciplines. As Petley (Barker and Petley, 1997, p. 2) put it, when he became 'worried' about the *Evening Standard*'s headline: 'those who'd performed the alleged U turn were not media academics but were in fact a group of psychologists, psychiatrists and paediatricians none of whom had any particular expertise in the media'.

The fact that these people might have had some expertise on the subject of children was apparently of no significance. Similarly, Newson could have saved herself some of her 'ordeal by media' if she had taken the trouble to review some of the research, and critiques of research on the subject of children and media, which had been circulating in the British public sphere for several years prior to this event, for instance, the considerable coverage given to children and media in the period leading up to the 1990 Broadcasting Act.

Other responses followed, particularly from media academics; indeed, quite an academic industry has grown up around the reporting of this particular case and the issues raised by it. One of the first contributors to the industry was David Buckingham, in 1996, with *Moving Images*, based on research commissioned by the Broadcasting Standards Commission in Britain to investigate children's emotional responses to film and television, especially 'what they find frightening, moving or upsetting'. Barker's and Petley's *Ill Effects*, prompted by the 1994 Newson Report, and including further comment by Buckingham among others (all male, with two exceptions), was eventually published in 1997. In 1998, historian John Springhall's *Youth, Popular Culture and Moral Panics* began with an account of the 'sensational reporting' of the Bulger case, and John Major's comments as UK Prime Minister about the 'relentless diet of violence' and its 'serious effects on the young'. Also in 1998 came *Children, Media, Violence*, an international collection of essays published by UNESCO, edited by two women – Ulla Carlsson and Celia von Feilitzen of the Nordic Information Center for Media and Communication Research, and its Clearing House on Children and

Violence on the Screen. The essays in this collection accept as axiomatic that adult society should be concerned about children and their relationship with images of people being 'shot, knifed, blown up or raped before their bare eyes' (Thomas Hammerberg, p. 21). The diverse international contributors all argued, from differing research perspectives, that research on violence on screen is necessary, that children are vulnerable to it, and that national and international regulation was necessary to protect children from it.

Petley's view that psychologists, psychiatrists and paediatricians should not have been asked to comment on possible media influences in the Bulger case, because they 'had no particular expertise in the media', is an example of what Springhall (1998) draws attention to – the way in which 'moral panic' is used as a 'deflating phrase' to 'condescend to excitements' among the general populace. To Springhall's 'ersatz compound manufactured by the media . . . [of] bishops . . . moralists and nostalgists of all kind', we can now add 'psychiatrists, psychologists and paediatricians'. There is an unfortunate and perhaps unintended sense that experts whose expertise does not include media analysis have no right to talk about the media – as if medical experts and psychologists were outside the public sphere constituted by media and other discourses. If non-media experts have no right to comment on the media, then the question is raised as to whom precisely the mass media serve. There is a construction of non-media experts as the kinds of gullible consumers that children, and the lower classes, are usually seen as being, and hence not to be trusted in any public debate. Newson was clearly being used by politicians, and others with their own agenda, such as the Christian Democracy movement, but this did not invalidate her expertise, nor her right to express her opinions. What the press make of those opinions – what they make of anyone's opinions – is another issue, and this, of course, is a subject of legitimate concern to media academics.

Thinking about children

In a section headed 'Thinking about children', Barker and Petley (1997, p. 5) complain that 'the incantation of phrases about the need to protect children . . . is the flipside of worries about dangerous classes'. In other words, once again, we are not 'thinking about children', children are being used as a pretext to move on to think about something more academically interesting – social class. More will be said about the unhelpfulness of equating children with any one social class in chapter 7. In the meantime, while acknowledging the concerns about evidence, and the abuses of the press, described by Barker and Petley, in the context of media regulation, it is still important to recognise that some of the things Newson said in her report about protecting children needed to be said, because they came from an expertise that media scholars do not have. Newson is an expert on psychopathic children, who have no sense of responsibility or of the 'relevance of moral issues'. Her expertise enabled her to make the statement (Newson, 1994, p. 273) that 'the processes of "desensitization" and "flooding" are well known methods for modification of behaviour by reducing the impact of the original accompanying emotion' – a statement that media academics do not have the necessary training or experience either to make, or to rebut. In the case of children, Newson (*ibid.*, p. 273) argued, the problem of their inexperience and lack of knowledge compounds the problems of exposure to disturbing material, whether vicarious or not: 'The *child* viewer receives distorted images of emotions that he has not yet experienced so must accept – especially dangerous where love, sex and violence are equated . . . Victims must be portrayed as somewhat subhuman so that they need not be pitied.'

None of the contributors to *Ill Effects* have any stated expertise in the techniques of behaviour modification, or in child psychiatry, and if one group of academics are to be criticised for entering into an area in which they are not qualified, then so can the other. However, academic name-calling seems to me to be a singularly unhelpful response to a tragic and sensitive situation – which still continues, since Jon Venables and Robert Thompson are about to become adults, and their sentences are being reviewed, and, once again, debated in an atmosphere of moral panic (spring, 2000).

'Art is never without consequences'

Newson and her colleagues may well have been wrong in their assumption that exposure to gratuitous vicarious screen brutality was an influence in this particular case; if it had been, one would have expected it to be mentioned by the defence in court. Nevertheless, Newson and her colleagues were clearly not wrong to engage in 'thinking about children'. Given her expertise, she was not wrong to raise issues that might affect the ways in which children learn to behave, which include cultural representations of behaviour. Nor was she standing outside a tradition of cultural analysis of the purpose and seriousness of art. Bertolt Brecht in 1940 in an essay on 'unprofessional acting' (Willett, 1964, p. 151) wrote how, against his better judgement, he enjoyed the British film, *Gunga Din* in which the 'magnificent age-old culture' of

Indians was stereotypically distorted to show the British as 'good chaps' and the Indians as primitive and wicked:

Obviously artistic appreciation of this sort is not without effects . . . Art is never without consequences and that says something for it . . . It matters how love, marriage, work and death are treated on the stage . . . In this exceedingly serious sphere the stage is virtually functioning as a fashion show, parading . . . the latest ways of behaving.

Brecht (Willett, 1964, p. 152) goes on to point out the effectiveness of dramatic performance in teaching behaviour:

human education proceeds along highly theatrical lines. In a quite theatrical manner, the child is taught to behave; logical arguments only come later . . . the theatre is, so to speak, the most human and universal art of all, the one most commonly practised, i.e. not only on the stage but in everyday life.

Brecht was not a psychologist or psychiatrist, but it is legitimate for those who are, to put his assumptions to the test. Consultants on mental pathology have a responsibility to examine phenomena which might affect the cultural climate in which parents and other caretakers of children, including those who produce cultural representations, are operating. To analyse all possible means for the prevention of damage to children, which means examining all possible sources of influence in such damage, is the job of psychologists and paediatricians. In a case as appalling as the Bulger case, the public is entitled to expect that no potential source of influence on the perpetrators should be ruled out; this is what we expect from people who are trained and publicly resourced to understand pathology. To imply that such people have no right to comment on one of the worst cases of harm to a child, by children, ever reported, in the name of freedom of speech, is at odds with a case – so eloquently argued in *Ill Effects* – which opposes censorship. It is also not in the interests of the children on trial. Petley expresses justifiable concern at the witch hunting press comments surrounding the case and it is precisely in such circumstances, that children need to be defended by authoritative professionals. Children accused of crimes need specialists, like Newson, who are used to working with children in trouble and their families, and who can support them in court and during their sentences. Media academics are not those professionals.

The question for media academics is not a negative one, but a positive one. What *do* cultural representations teach children? What are the representations of dismembered bodies sprayed against walls in a video game like *Doom* intended to convey to children, and are they different from the bodiless heads bloodily flourished in the Tim Burton movie *Sleepy Hollow* (1999)? Adults, with the civilising function they take on when bringing children into the world, need to have some idea what they want cultural representations to teach children, and to make arrangements for ensuring that such representations are made available – whether they embody egalitarian attitudes to race and gender, or Marxist economics, or simply the, for some, liberating idea that life can be fun sometimes. Whether children take the meanings from these representations that adults intend cannot, of course, be guaranteed, but this does not obviate the responsibility, and need, of adult caretakers to offer information and entertainment to their young.

This question of 'what to tell the children' is the more pressing, the more we accept that childhood is a social construction, and not just a natural, biological state. If children are not born 'wicked', or 'good', but have to learn to be so, then cultural representations, whether family traditions, or stories told on television, or games in the playground, must, as Brecht argued, be influential in showing children how to behave. Indeed, it could be argued that the purpose of cultural representations, particularly dramatic ones, is precisely this: to give help to the adults who have direct responsibility for passing on social practices and values (such as parents) by showing children forms of behaviour which they cannot easily be taught through the routines of everyday upbringing. All cultural representations for children are a form of hypothesising – 'what if?' Extreme and exotic forms of torture (as distinct from everyday childish aggression) come into this category for most children. If children learn how to torture, it is reasonable to suppose that they may have acquired this knowledge from some cultural source. To acknowledge the possibility of such cultural influences is not necessarily to seek to ban, but to seek to explain, and, especially, to help.

Media scholars know, too, that it is through discourse, the mediated organisation of experience, that we construct our identities, and learn to do so in childhood. Spoken language is mastered very young – most of it by the age of four. Certain forms of linguistic discourse are very powerful for children – cruel jokes, grim tales and fantasy play among them. In a chapter about the 'demonic' representation of childhood popular at the end of the twentieth century, in contrast to the innocent images favoured by the Victorians, the only individual female contributor to *Ill Effects*, Patricia Holland, points out that contemporary cultural representations of children/childhood say much about adults' anxieties about how to manage, control and ensure the survival of, their young. Holland (1997, p. 53) discusses the dangerousness of the concept of play, as echoed in the title of the film *Child's Play*, and points out:

The horror comes when play merges into reality. In this discourse it is also the margin between the experience of being a child and that of being an adult which is at stake. Robert Thompson and Jon Venables acted out those confusions in their most horrific form when they murdered James Bulger.

A further strand in the anxieties about children of the second half of the twentieth century, as Holland suggests in her account of the 'demonic child', has been the increasing rarity, expense and luxury of children, the more prosperous a society becomes. Even the 'normal' event of the arrival of a child can seem a threatening prospect, given the child-unfriendliness of a post-industrial society, in which work continues 24 hours a day, and child-rearing is characterised socially and economically as an inconvenient and undesirable interruption to the accumulation of status, power, capital and consumer goods. Anxieties aroused in prospective parents by the threat of economic and professional disadvantage are further fuelled by press discussions of *in vitro* fertilisation, surrogacy and genetic manipulation of embryos. Images of childhood, and children, have become the focus of adult worry on a major scale. There has been the appearance of the 'accessory child' in advertising, the child with 'pester power' in the discourses of consumption, the uncontrolled 'under-class' child in discourses about class and education, and, in cinema, the child with special, sometimes demonic, powers, for instance *The Sixth Sense* (1999). The exposure of systematic, long-standing and unreported child abuse in institutions which were meant to be taking care of vulnerable children, as in the case of the forty North Wales children's homes, which were the subject of the Waterhouse Inquiry, 2000, contributes to a sense that adult society in Britain and other developed countries has become almost incapable of taking proper care of children at any stage of their existence, from the womb onwards. Blaming the media for this state of affairs is seductive. However, just because the media cannot be simplistically blamed for major social trends and changes, this does not mean that media do not contribute to such changes at all, nor that they do not have effects on individual children.

Reading horror

As teachers of media and culture, we have to accept the power of media influences on children, and, as discussed above, on adults – indeed, as a teacher and a writer, I would be sorry if this were not so. My own research suggests that the media literacy strategies of teaching children the difference between real and fantasy, and what is acted and what is documentary, designed to 'protect' children from harmful effects (see Brown 1991) are misconceived. Dorr *et al.* in 1980 came to a similar conclusion in their research on advertising. Understanding the modality constructions of a text will not necessarily change social or emotional attitudes, because this does not destroy the imaginative power of a narrative, or the ability of children to identify with it. On the contrary, as in Brecht's appreciation of *Gunga Din*, modal and aesthetic features can add to the audience's appreciation of it. Scary stories are pleasurable, not just *despite* the artifice of special effects, but because of it – as one of the most illuminating essays in *Ill Effects* points out.

The forbidden in media will always be sought out by children, but part of the pleasure of this is doing so within a framework of adult control, as Mark Kermode describes in an account of his experience of being a fan of horror movies, in *Ill Effects* (1997, p. 57). The 'electrifying atmosphere, the sense of watching something that was forbidden, secretive, taboo' through his devotion to horror films as a child gave him 'something that was uniquely *mine*, something that existed outside the domain of my parents' control and authority'. Kermode (*ibid.*, p. 61) argues that horror audiences need to understand the directors' intentions in order to appreciate the genre appropriately. Only privileged readers, 'the horror fans', are capable of doing this:

The bizarre physical mutations of *Videodrome*, the body 'shunting' of *Society*, the skin-flailing tortures of *Hellraiser* – none of these on-screen wonders are intended to be read as depictions of 'real' physical possibilities . . . The horror fan understands this, and is thus not only able, but positively compelled, to 'read' rather than merely 'watch' such movies. The novice, however, sees only the dismembered bodies, hears only the screams and groans, reacts only with revulsion and contempt.

Kermode's account of fanhood (1997, p. 59) reveals a sense of cultural elitism based on the uniqueness of his, and his fellow fans' tastes: 'I was made profoundly aware of the absolute divide between horror fans and everybody else in the world.' This seems to have led to what anti-elitists might consider a harmful 'effect' – a scorn for other kinds of children who did not want to obsessively discuss in detail with him the horror films they had seen, but preferred to 'talk about football and girls'. Kermode is actually supporting Newson here, in arguing that 'novices' cannot automatically appreciate the genre; they need to learn how to do so. Newson argued that, in evaluating effects of all kinds – positive, negative, emotional, aesthetic, intellectual – we have to take developmental factors into account: children need to *learn* to make sense of stories. Hence, young children may not necessarily see the moral that Martin Barker saw in *Child's Play III*; indeed, not even his colleague David Buckingham, in the same volume, did. Barker argues (Barker and Petley, 1997, pp. 18–19): '*Child's Play III* is . . . one of a thousand films which show a sort of rite of passage of adolescence . . .

This is a very *moral* tale.' Buckingham (1997, pp. 39–40) says: 'To defend media violence on . . . claims about "artistic quality" is almost guaranteed to produce incredulity, particularly in the context of a film like *Child's Play III* . . . [it] was described by many of the children in this research as a comedy (in my view quite accurately).' If two sophisticated media experts can disagree about the moral seriousness of a film, it is difficult to be sure that children will always pick up the intended moral messages underlying violent and anti-social representations.

The other problematic aspect of graphic visual representations of extreme violence, whether 'playful' or not, is the strength of persistence of images in memory, compared to words and narrative. Memory may remove the narrative context of a filmed event, but will retain images of 'skin-flailing tortures' for many months, even years, during which the image may be recalled, divorced from the 'moral' context of the story. Such de-contextualised memories ('flashbacks') can be very disturbing. Buckingham notes this phenomenon in his book on citizenship (Buckingham, 2000a, pp. 173–4) when he comments on 'the relative importance of the visual aspects as compared with the verbal ones' in young people's discussion of news footage. To his surprise, they remembered brief scenes of children rioting and dancing on cars, and forgot the political discussions that surrounded them.

If, as Kermode argues, one needs to learn how to read horror films appropriately, the issue when it comes to provision for children is: how can we be sure that they *are* reading things appropriately, without 'contempt and revulsion' or other disturbing reactions? And if they do have disturbing reactions, to the extent of nightmares, flashbacks, or anti-social behaviour, what should adults do? Both Buckingham and Barker point out the difference between being taught how to be terrifying and how to be terrified; in one case, the problem is one of behavioural imitation, the other case shows a necessary recognition of what *should* be feared. Newson, too (1994, p. 273), acknowledges the psychological safety-valve of nightmares: 'a relatively healthy reaction, denoting the child's continuing sensitivity to such images'. Nevertheless, it would be naive to ignore the link between fear and aggression; frightened children (and frightened adults) are capable of doing very violent things, and fantasy fear and fantasy aggression are closely linked in narrative, as Bettelheim is not the only writer on children's culture to point out. The central question of media effects is whether these implied moralistic lessons are actually derived by children from the scary tales they profess to enjoy. The data from our study suggest that, for many of the children we were talking to in the research, moral lessons can be learned from violent representations, with some provisos.

Enthusiasm for horror

Many children in the study expressed enthusiasm for the horror genre and enjoyment in scary programmes, while also acknowledging the negative aspects of their effects, for example, these 10–11 year olds from a primary school in Oxfordshire:

BOY 1   I like watching *The X Files*, it makes me jump all the time and makes me feel ill and sick.

GIRL 1   I know a book called *Trick or Treat*, it is horror and I think that it would make a good TV programme.

Some of the questionnaire comments made similar points:

I do not really like watching children's television. I like watching blood thirsty and action packed films on Sky. . . I would like more action packed stories to be on the television. (Girl, 10, suburban primary school, Oxfordshire)

I would like you to put on more cartoons about witches and monsters. And call it the spooky channel. (Girl, 8, village primary school, Co. Durham)

I would like a bit more teenage programmes for children my age because some cartoons are a bit babyish. Some of my friends like horror films and so do I. We like mystery stories as well. (Girl, 8, outer-London primary school)

The wishes of these children are certainly being met, to some extent, in recent seasons of children's drama on British television. Between 1996 and 2000 there were the three series of *The Demon Headmaster* (in which, befitting a true children's narrative, the demonic influence was adult, and in which the children were the heroes), the supernatural/horror-like *Goosebumps* series (shown on the BBC) and the comedy series *The Worst Witch* (ITV co-production with Canadian television); in the 1999/2000 season there were *The Magician's House* and *The Ghost Hunter* on BBC1. In the UK, as in the United States, *Buffy the Vampire Slayer* is a hit with young people, though it is not a children's programme. Programmes for children featuring magic and the occult used to be controversial, as Anna Home pointed out in her history of children's television (Home, 1993), but producers' reservations about these elements now seem to have been overcome. Indeed, stories featuring supernatural events – J. K. Rowling's extraordinarily successful Harry Potter books being another recent phenomenon – are almost the only kinds of dramatic stories currently widely available and popular for children and young people, and we may speculate about what this says about the current relationship between the young and those in charge of them. One feature of such stories is that they can facilitate a sense of power in child protagonists, and they offer more adventurous narrative possibilities to authors. The Harry Potter books are an ingenious updating of the 1950s boarding-school story – 'Jennings' with spells. Given the constraints on contemporary children's lives, realistic drama can no longer show children having adventures on their own in cities and countryside, as in the days of *Running Scared*, or, further back, of *Swallows and Amazons*, nor do realistic boarding-school stories permit the majority of state-school-educated, ordinary children to be protagonists. Magic powers can enable young child protagonists of all classes to have control, and to extend the possibilities of adventure.

In discussing such science fiction-based drama series as *The Demon Headmaster* (BBC1) and the adult *The X Files*, the children in the study dissected the concept of 'scariness' at length, both from their own points of view, and from their imaginative projections of what other children might feel, for example:

It's too scary for sevens and under, although [some people said] it shouldn't really be banned because older children like a bit of a thrill. A lot of children might get scared of coming to school. Special effects might be too much for them to handle. (Group spokesperson, boy, 10, Cardiff primary school, proposing reasons for banning *The Demon Headmaster*)

A 12-year-old girl in an outer-London secondary school argued that, even for her age, some gruesome and explicit representations were too much to take. She also pointed out that her 7-year-old cousin seemed to be less squeamish:

I am not being mean or anything but I was watching this programme, I was staying home, I was sick and lying down in bed and there's this really horrible I mean gruesome . . . and I thought, OK little kids could be watching this and it's really horrible, it's like this man nude running across a field. . . . My cousin, he's only seven and he watches all late films, my uncle doesn't mind . . . he just sits up and stays up and he's not scared or anything, he just goes 'oh look at this bit, this man's just about to get stabbed and all his guts and everything'. (Girl, 12, outer-London secondary school)

As Buckingham argues in *Moving Images* (1996) we can never be sure what children are going to be disturbed by, and children in our study seemed to have a working developmental theory that younger children were protected from the full impact of 'gruesome' representations by their immaturity, and inability to comprehend. If children were disturbed, though, the child commentators of the study did not want adults to ignore the problem:

I don't think the BBC have any problem about showing things too early. It's people like Sky and cable who are making all these gruesome and bloody films and putting them on at 4 or 6 . . . The BBC don't have any problem about making it too violent at a certain time, you can turn on at 10 o'clock and still find something that is, you know, OK. (Boy, 12, outer-London secondary school)

Parents' role

Parents are increasingly seen as the main arbiters of children's media consumption, and the privatisation of children's culture is giving them more control over what their children do and play with. Adult caretakers have control by default, for example, letting children have a TV in their bedrooms, and leaving them to get on with it; or by design, that is, by making sure that children have access to a range of parentally sanctioned cultural products. This is a vital component in the circulation of the values of the bourgeois public sphere, and in the establishment of cultural standards of taste. Certain kinds of cultural consumption for children are sanctioned by middle-class parents, and other kinds are not. Sanctioned consumption will include classic literature, music, theatre, the arts, museums and some approved film and video products. Certain kinds of popular culture may also be permissible if, for example, the parent has discovered a particular popular form to be culturally interesting, as did Mark Kermode (1997) in the case of horror movies; in such cases the children may be encouraged to watch *Alien* and *Nightmare on Elm Street*, even though they might prefer to watch *Blue Peter*.

Middle-class parents may be libertarian when it comes to freedom of speech in the bourgeois public sphere, but they may be less so in their attitudes to the cultural materials which their own children consume. Their children may be stopped from reading Enid Blyton, or from owning Care Bears, or watching soap operas. Middle-class parents may limit their children's exposure to cultural products which might expose them to undesirable socially stereotyped attitudes, as did one adamant opponent of censorship of my acquaintance who was horrified when I said I did not mind my children reading *Little Black Sambo*. I pointed out: you've read it, and I've read it, why shouldn't they? But this parent was not convinced. Middle-class parents move house to make sure their children can get into 'good' schools, where sanctioned forms of cultural consumption will be provided, or they sacrifice their surplus capital and, perhaps, their left-liberal 'principles', to send their children to private schools. This increases their children's already considerable access to cultural capital and ensures that the middle-class cultural values of the home are perpetuated and reproduced. Middle-class cultural values, whatever they happen to be, work through the processes of parenting, and parental pressure on schools and the education system, to perpetuate themselves effectively. Broadcasting may have had élitist origins, but the constituency to which modern children's and family television is accountable, is much broader than the middle class, and this is one reason for defending it.

Working-class parents, stereotypically demonised as feckless, also have concerns about their children, but they have to rely more on the state to help them cope, in all departments of life, including media provision and regulation. Livingstone and Bovill's (1999) data indicated that parents did want the state to regulate for children, especially as children got older. 'Once people reached their early teens many parents consider it impracticable to attempt restrictions on media use in the home.' Hence, they argue (p. 2) parents want to 'rely on the good judgement of broadcasters and media regulators'. In their study, 82 per cent of parents thought the watershed was a good idea, and 25 per cent wanted it to be extended to 10 p.m., not 9 p.m.

Conclusions

As historians of childhood point out, and Livingstone's discovery of a 'bedroom culture' indicates, the recent history of Western childhood has been one of increasing privatisation, leading to a state of affairs in industrialised countries in which parents are seen as almost the sole arbiters of what should happen to children, with teachers in school, acting *in loco parentis*, and increasingly seen, not as professionals with their own expertise on children, but as accountable to 'parental choice'. Children do not relate much to adult society in other ways. One of the few areas where they are offered access to a wider public sphere of adult debate and activity is broadcasting.

One negative consequence of the late twentieth-century privatisation of childhood, with parents and families deemed to be solely responsible for the behaviour of children, and children almost entirely invisible in public spaces, is that adults generally have ceased to believe that socialisation of the young is a general, collective responsibility. Again, broadcasting is one of the few remaining areas in which society, collectively, accepts that the responsibility for, and to, children, has to be shared. The reluctance of adults in public places to take responsibility for other people's children has relevance for the case of the murder of 2-year-old James Bulger, whose abduction from a busy public place by two 10 year olds was not prevented by any of the numerous adult witnesses to it.

This case illustrates the necessity of distinguishing arguments about the behaviour of children, including their media consumption, from discussions about freedom of information for adults. When the two issues are conflated, illiberal positions result; the desire to protect children leads to calls for infringement of the liberties of the free speech of the press and the media, for example, the 1994 Video Recordings

Act, and the troubling case discussed by Hartley (1998), where a Visual Arts student in Australia was prosecuted for taking photographs of her own naked young sons. However, if the debate focuses exclusively on adult rights to freedom of expression, then the central issue of children's vulnerability and lack of empowerment in an adult world – whether as victims or as perpetrators of crime – may be overlooked.

Children in the study did not want this to happen and had a variety of recommendations for adult intervention, as in these comments from 10–11 year olds in the debate about banning *The Demon Headmaster*:

It is up to the parents to tell their children to watch it or not . . . children will be put off from doing their school work and some might think their headmaster might try and hypnotise them. You could put it on later when the little children can't watch it.

Some children are too young to watch it. It shouldn't be banned – It is up to us to stop our children from watching it – if we don't want our children to watch it we should turn over the channel. (Group representing parents, Buckinghamshire village primary school)

The group representing regulators in the same school argued:

It should be banned because of the hypnotising which is not good for the younger children.

It should be put on for the older children at a different time so the parents would be at home.

It should be banned for the 4–8 year olds because they wouldn't know it wasn't real.

And the sound effects would scare younger children.

It is worth comparing their comments with comments from the producers of *Grange Hill*, Leigh Jackson and Steven Andrew, who often ran into trouble with parents and teachers. They were asked, if children were totally free of regulation, what they would watch, and they proposed a model of the child audience which sounded rather different from the one embodied by our child regulators:

STEVEN ANDREW   They would watch everything at the edge of the scale, I think, boys would. Everything they are not allowed to watch, because children are hungry to find out the next stage . . . Most kids would tap into things they are not allowed to tap into, that and cartoons.

LEIGH JACKSON   I wonder how many parents strictly reinforce children not watching television after 9.30 p.m. at a certain age, because I know with my children I didn't and I just wonder if there is a whole generation that has grown up which actually don't have those sort of taboos and let children watch things.

Patricia Holland, in *Ill Effects* (1997, p. 55), describes media regulation in terms very similar to those used by some of our child regulators in the study: as a necessary safeguard for guaranteeing children's political representation in the public sphere:

One of the reactionary effects of a resistance to the regulation of television, video and cinema is . . . a privatisation of childhood . . . regulation is one of the ways in which society as a whole can take responsibility for its children . . . Without such regulatory structures, ordinary, everyday children will have even less opportunity to speak for themselves.

Children in the study agreed with her, as with this group from an inner-city primary school in Cardiff, representing public service broadcasting:

We decided that it shouldn't be banned but maybe it should have a small warning at the start such as that 'this programme might not be suitable for very young children'.
Reasons were: firstly there were some parts that small children might find frightening, but the programme was not very scary all the way through.
Our second reason is that it's quite a good programme and more people enjoy it than don't. We think it would be fine if it came on at a later time – about 6 or 7.
If parents aren't happy with the programme they don't have to let their children watch it.

The kinds of regulations proposed by these commentators do not necessarily infringe the liberty of adults to access different kinds of material. The age classification system for film and video regulation, like the 9 p.m. watershed, does not ban; it merely delays. We lack evidence that long-lasting harm is done by keeping children waiting until their early teens before they can see graphic horror movies or explicit representations of sex and violence. If they were allowed to see them more freely in early childhood, some of the forbidden pleasures of the taboo, as thrilled to by Mark Kermode (1997), would disappear. It is also important in this debate not to equate children with adult groups, including the lower-orders, to whom, as in Springhall's book and also in *Ill Effects*, they are so often compared. Children are people who are not yet adults, however adulthood is defined, and they are found in every social class.

Another tempering proviso to the view that children's voices should be heard, that children's rights of access to taboo material should be upheld, and that it is unjust to deny even pre-pubertal children the civic empowerment of freedom to any kind of information at all, without limits, is that such a view is an idealised model of a very wise, and almost certainly non-existent, child. In some respects, as noted, the media-competent, Web-surfing super-kid seems to be a reinvention of Wordsworth's Romantic infant, 'trailing clouds of glory' from a heavenly pre-existence, and carrying superior wisdom which becomes lost in 'the light of common day' as he grows up. The view of the morally competent, empowered child, while upholding the dignity of children as potential citizens, also has a negative side for them, in that it can be used to treat children as legally responsible adults in criminal cases. This is one of the reasons why the killers of James Bulger were tried in an adult court (a procedure which the European Court of Human Rights ruled in 1999 was unjust) and is one of the more unpleasant aspects of the kind of witch-hunting press coverage which labelled these children as monsters and freaks.

There is no question that the children in the BBC study exhibited wisdom, maturity and pragmatic and democratic debating skills. Some of them used these qualities to recognise that not only younger children, but also on occasion themselves, needed to be supervised, protected and, where necessary, kept in check, by adult society, in the form of a range of regulatory procedures – both private ('change the channel') and public ('put it on later'). The burden of Neil Postman's (1982) argument about the cultural construction of childhood is that through its progressive organisation of graded literacy skills, it is a process based – necessarily and ideally – on delay. If we want to change our cultural construction of childhood, from being a process based on delay to one based on haste, scholars of childhood, including experts in child health and development, need to advance some moral and intellectual justifications for doing so, supported by evidence that such haste is in the interests of the welfare and survival of children.

There are plenty of *commercial* and capitalistic justifications for a childhood based on haste: the sooner children can be encouraged to consume adult products, the more profitable the cosmetics, fashion, music and entertainment industries will be. But what are the educational, intellectual or – to use Martin Barker's italicised word about *Child's Play III* – *moral* justifications for hastening the cultural arrival of adulthood? In dealing with the young, who are legally, as well as (in their early years) physically, entirely dependent on adults, those of us adults who are in a position to influence cultural debates and public policies, have to offer some justification for the ways in which we construct the childhoods on offer for our children. Pragmatic, commercial, new-Romantic and adult-oriented ('freedom of expression', 'artistic quality') justifications may not be sufficient for *them*.

7 Aspects of identity

I think it comes from England, because they speak our language.
Girl, 9, inner-city primary school, Milton Keynes

Livingstone and Bovill (1999, p. 55) point out: 'not only are children and young people in many ways distinct from adults, they are also a diverse population – varying according to gender, age, social class, lifestyle, etc. and so are not readily reduced to simple categories'. Livingstone's and Bovill's comment reflects the paradox that the social subgroup 'children' is a homogeneous one with fewness of years of life as their common distinguishing factor; but they are also a microcosm of the whole population in their demographic diversity. This makes confident generalisations about them difficult, and without very carefully selected and scrutinised data, unwise. Our sample was not a scientifically representative one, but with 1,332 children in seventeen different schools in England and Wales, with nearly equal numbers of boys (631) and girls (645), and a reasonable spread of social advantage and disadvantage (as measured by the schools' statistics), it was comparable to Livingstone and Bovill's and was certainly much more representative than much research on children and media. More details of the sample are given in the Introduction and in Appendix 1.

Social science research generally takes the view that demographic factors function as independent variables, that is they make a difference to what people do. This is a view also held by scholars from other traditions. Whether one is a cognitive scientist or a feminist literary critic, one accepts that being male or female is likely to make a difference to how people behave and think; that socio-economic class makes a difference; and that ethnicity makes a difference. Different combinations of factors, for example, being of Afro-Caribbean origin, male and middle class, can produce different responses from someone who is of Afro-Caribbean origin, female and working class – these combinations of influences are statistically known as interactions. Whether these differences are performative and derived from social and ideological

171

constructions imposed on us, perhaps in childhood, perhaps later (a cultural studies position), or whether these differences are a combination of inherited genetic factors, interacting with identifiable and measurable social experiences, particularly in early childhood, which are predictable (a developmental psychological position), the differences are observable, and we all assume that they matter. Who we feel ourselves to be contributes greatly to our sense of well-being, and we want these identities to be recognised and appreciated by others. Popular media and storytelling both reflect and shape identities, especially in childhood – one of the reasons people worry so much about their content and effects – and the children's responses to drama, and other programmes, in this study, revealed a number of aspects of identity.

In dealing with questions of identity, it could be argued that elusive concepts such as subjectivity and gender roles cannot be effectively captured through ticking boxes in a questionnaire, and then counting the ticks. However, there is a sense in which this numerical approach is a valuable technique for questions of identity – it acknowledges equality. Depersonalised, numerical quantitative data give each individual equal value. In this study, as in any study using quantitative data, this equality was expressed in equivalent numerical weighting for every child's responses. As the numbers of children in particular categories, such as age groups, or types of school, making particular responses added up, so patterns based on age, or school-type, or gender, emerged, which helped to indicate what these different individuals had in common. Numerical data are not an easy read for the kinds of people usually interested in television drama, including producers (despite the broadcasting industry's obsession with ratings), whereas comments from individual children are. This is why the bulk of the data reported in this book uses the children's words. However, some numerical data have been included here, first, because these data help to support verbal comments (comments which carry their own problems of reliability and validity, as discussed) and, second, because it is only through the numerical data that every single individual child in the study can be represented – a democratic imperative.

Where children made individual verbal comments, as in the qualitative data, the equality conferred by numbers becomes harder to guarantee; obviously some children were more eloquent, more knowledgeable, more talkative, wittier, faster writers and better spellers, than others. Hence, those whose words are quoted in this book are privileged; they were selected to speak for the whole, but they cannot be seen as wholly typical. No individual comment ever can, and, indeed, some comments were genuinely quite unique. With this proviso in mind, we have done our best at every stage of the presentation of this research, to make sure that all the qualitative comments selected were selected fairly (i.e. a sub-sample selected randomly from the whole sample) and that those quoted came from all the schools in the study, from children of different ages (where these were identified) and from both boys and girls. This is particularly necessary when children are talking about aspects of their own identity, the aspects of themselves that concern them most deeply. This chapter deals, briefly, with four such aspects: age, gender, class and cultural identity as determined by locality and ethnicity.

Age

Developmental psychology, particularly cognitive psychology, has especially stressed biological age and stage of development as primary factors determining the intellectual performance and competence of growing children. Although the hostile charge of biological determinism is sometimes levelled at developmental psychologists (for example, Bazalgette and Buckingham, 1995, p. 4; Cassell and Jenkins, 1998, p. 5), it is in many ways unjustified. It is now over twenty-five years since the developmental psychologist Martin Richards pointed out, in his book on the integration of infants into a social world (1974), that child development must be seen in a wider social, historical and cultural context, than simply as the growth of a baby within its family. Richards went on to produce more influential work on the cultural and social determinants of development (for example, Richards and Light, 1986), but one problem with developmental psychology (as with Richards' work) is that it has always focused most on very early childhood and infancy, and thus has had little to say about children and culture. Infancy is a period of life when people have limited direct interactions with the public sphere. Nor do they have the communicative skills in order to be able to tell us what these interactions mean to them. Studies of the very young and their culture have to be mediated via the babies' families, and focus, for instance on child-rearing practices (see, for example, Woollett and White, 1992).

Developmental paediatricians further emphasise the *physical* processes of growth and maturation in explaining and accounting for children's behaviour. Such physical factors as nutrition are not of central interest to social and cultural theorists. Physical processes are, however, recognised as crucial by health and welfare workers in accounting for behavioural and cognitive variation in children, increasingly so, the further 'down' the social scale they are. Class inequality generally is most reliably reflected not in different kinds of cultural behaviour, but in higher rates of mortality, disability, failure to thrive and illness among the poor. These inequalities have been increasing in the UK and in the USA during the past two decades. Children's media usage thus takes place in a complex social context in which health (related to income), age, and family circumstances, including the child's position in the family, are the major determinants of differences between children of different social classes. Media consumption is, interestingly, one area where evidence of inequalities is rarer. Media usage is one of the levelling factors in children's lives, reducing differences between middle- and working-class children, as Livingstone and Bovill's study suggests – and this has been one of the contributing factors to moral panic about media, their 'levelling down' (never 'up') effect.

Age and cultural childhood studies

Although definitions of children as an age group continue to be central in debates within broadcasting, age as an adequate way of defining childhood generally has many shortcomings, as childhood theorists have pointed out. 'Although the expectations and competencies of age may be thought to be generationally specific, at any point in time they turn out to be individually and momentarily negotiable' say James, Jenks and Prout (1998, p. 59) in a chapter on the shifting boundaries of the 'temporality' of childhood. Bazalgette and Buckingham (1995, p. 4) also criticise developmental psychology for a too-rigid 'cognitivist' categor- isation of children by age and stage: 'the psychological focus on develop- ment and more specifically on cognitive development – has almost inevitably led to an emphasis on children's inadequacies as compared with adults'. Such a 'deficit model' of children's differences is not inevitable; there is no logical reason why perceived differences in the way children talk about culture and the way adults do, should make children appear at a disadvantage – quite the contrary, in the case of many of the children quoted in this study.

Age: quantitative findings

The distribution of children across age groups in our sample is given below. The primary target age range was 6–12, but a few 5 year olds were found in the 6-year age group, and, similarly, a few 13 year olds were included in the 12-year age group, because they happened to be in the same school classes.

Age

5	6	7	8	9	10	11	12	13
10	119	193	194	235	193	267	110	8

57 children did not give their age.

Our study accepted the category of children as a group of people defined by age, partly because this is how children are categorised in both schools, the institutions within which we accessed children, and by broadcasters – the group on whose behalf we were conducting the research. The decision to select a particular age group for study was thus a pragmatic decision, but also one with implications for the theorisation of childhood as a category, and children's own role in contributing to this theorisation. Children between 6 and 12 were chosen because younger than this meant a totally different methodology and hence less viable comparisons between different ages of children. This age group is also the main target group for children's programmes. Most of the Year Seven (12- to 13-year-old) children in the study were in secondary schools, and, in this sense, belonged to a socially older group, which was also useful from the point of view of mapping changes in children's attitudes as they grew up and changed their circumstances.

The 6–12 age range is of further interest in that it includes the period – around 7 to 8 – when developmental shifts in understanding, reasoning and linguistic skills seem to occur (see chapter 3) leading to increased ability to make sense of and enjoy cultural products, and to make moral and other value judgements. It also leads to the linguistic and – at the upper end of the range – the literary ability to express ideas reasonably competently. This last was particularly important for the qualitative discussion tasks.

A central question of the study, both for the BBC (we believed) and also for us as academic researchers, was whether children preferred adult programming to children's, and why; and a number of questions in the questionnaire asked what children thought about age appropriateness in programming. Table 11 emphasises the importance of 'for my age' as an essential programme quality for the children in the study.

There was uncertainty in around a fifth of the sample (least among nine year olds), but, nevertheless, the proposition 'I want more programmes for children my age' received the highest 'True' vote of all the questions on the questionnaire – 70 per cent of the whole sample, with 74 per cent of 9–12 year olds agreeing. Allied with the next highest majority vote – the 68 per cent of the whole sample who believed that 'children need their own programmes' – this finding indicated a strong sense of ownership among children about television programmes – an

Table 11. *The proportions (percentage) of children in each age group agreeing/disagreeing with the statement: 'I want more programmes for children my age'*

Age (years)	True	Not true	Not sure
5	70	10	20
6	68	18	14
7	65	15	20
8	64	14	22
9	75	15	11
10	73	10	17
11	73	6	21
12	75	6	19
13	50	0	50

ownership based on 'age', whatever this construct was taken to mean by different individuals. The children obviously believed that they were entitled to their 'own' material, and that this material should reflect them and their lives: a reality which included a representation of children at the same stage of life as they were. 'My age' was clearly a meaningful aspect of identity for these children, and one of the most important ways in which they defined their tastes. What 'my age' meant to each of these children, was, of course, as James and Prout remind us, negotiable.

Age in the qualitative data

Repeatedly 'age' was used as a justification for choices in drawing up schedules, for instance these exchanges between 8–10 year olds from an inner-London primary school.

INTERVIEWER   And how did you decide?

GIRL   We tried to think of the age of the children. *Live and Kicking* was our age and *999* and *The X Files* was for older people and children.

or:

BOY   *Clarissa Explains It All.*

INTERVIEWER   Why did you choose that one?

BOY   Because it is a programme for teenagers and parents.

Children obviously do accept the rigid age categories through which they have to live their lives in a Western European industrialised society – school grades; time-of-day routines, such as early bedtime for 'little kids', and later slots for 'adult' programmes which their parents are likely to enjoy. But, for these children, age was also a psychological category – an explanatory label to account for ways in which (as they clearly had noticed) children of different ages differed from each other.

One of the tasks was a debate in which children were asked to discuss replacing two children's programmes with two adult programmes. In this task, children were required to take on different roles in their groups: one group represented children aged 4–8; another, children in their own age group (9–14); a third group represented teachers; a fourth, parents; a fifth, children's TV producers; and a sixth, adult producers. In discussing the thinking of children younger than themselves, these groups produced a number of theoretical propositions about how younger children would behave, as with these 12 year olds in a secondary school in Middlesbrough, in the north-east of England, discussing the meaning of magic:

GIRL 1 [defending keeping *The Queen's Nose* in the schedule]: *The Queen's Nose* has got magic in it.

INTERVIEWER And is that good?

GIRL 1 Some people don't think it is very good, because small children think there is magic everywhere.

INTERVIEWER These are the small children: do you think there is magic everywhere? [addressing a group representing 4–8 year olds].

GROUP LEADER No.

INTERVIEWER Would you if you were four?

GROUP LEADER Yes.

Some children also defined age as a social category, constructed through life-changes such as going to secondary school. In this case special children's programmes could be useful in helping younger children to know what was in store for them; another Middlesbrough 12 year old pointed out:

Grange Hill has problems when you get older in secondary school and children watch them happen, so it can prepare them.

Occasionally the task developed into conversations between children in which they followed their own speculations about the fluidity of age categories, as with these two 12-year-old Middlesbrough girls, discussing *The Queen's Nose* and the relationship between age and programme-tastes:

GIRL 3 Well it is just like really for everybody, isn't it, Emily?

GIRL 4 Anybody who wants to watch it – our age really. As I said, my mum likes to watch it and she is 33 and she likes it.

GIRL 3 I mean little kids can watch it because of the magic and wishing and stuff. It is quite funny, they are always arguing like me and my brothers.

This girl also reflected on the pleasures of being able to watch a long-running programme (*Grange Hill*) which her mother had also watched. She showed an awareness of both the temporality of childhood with its aspects of continuity across generations, and the intertextuality of popular soap series and their interchangeable performers. In the context of the debate to replace *Grange Hill* with *EastEnders*, Girl 3 referred to watching reruns of *Grange Hill* showing at the time, and to actors such as Todd Carty, who played a mischievous 11 year old, Tucker Jenkins, in the first series of *Grange Hill*, in 1977 and is now playing the thirty-something, reformed drug-addict, Mark Fowler in *EastEnders*:

GIRL 3   It [*Grange Hill*] has got all the stars in it . . . all the characters from other films, that is how they started off. You can think like 'ooh! my mum used to watch this when she was little' and you have always wanted to know what has been on the telly before and now it has come back . . . You see stars in it now and you think back and you wonder what they were doing when they were not as old, and you find out what they were doing when they were young.

These comments expressed this girl's sense of being part of a continuum over time, both in her family, through her mother, and through her mother's experience of watching the same children's programmes as the child watched, and through the programmes themselves, and their stars. 'Finding out what stars were doing when they were young' seems linked, for her, with her own need to remember, and to look forward in her own life – a pleasure which video has captured for children and their families at the end of the twentieth century.

Gender

Crucial to debates about identity formation is the role of children's culture – playthings, stories, films, television programmes and commercials selling them all – in promoting gender roles. Differences in clothes, toys, birth congratulation cards – blue and tough for boys, pink and frilly for girls – signal these expectations from the moment of birth. A powerful conglomeration of cultural devices – advertisements and marketing (Kline, 1993; Klein, 2000); narratives and toys (Seiter, 1993); fairy tales (Zipes, 1986; Lurie, 1990; Warner, 1994) and, most recently, computer games (Cassell and Jenkins, 1998), both determine, and reinforce, gender role expectations. In Western culture, a constant stream of mass media products, from Barbie to Lara Croft to Mortal Kombat, to Disney's Pocahontas and her marketing spin-offs, combine to define and impose cultural expectations of gender roles, resulting in much social and scholarly concern. Kline (1993, p. 249), in an analysis of gender constructions in advertising to children, argues that current sensitivities to gender in the population generally are not reflected in marketing practices: 'Despite the theories about the need for non-sexist socialisation, the pragmatics of marketing lead advertisers to rely on children's strictly gendered notions of peer play: "Boys prefer invincible action figures . . . Girls prefer cuddly creatures, action figures or incline to romanticism." '

Imposed gender roles are not accepted unquestioningly by children. Many parents know the impossibility of trying to force tomboyish daughters into pretty dresses, and the pointlessness of trying to insist that the 7-year-old boys at their son's birthday party should not fight. It is not proven that children accept and perform the roles offered to them unquestioningly and plenty of evidence that they negotiate and resist them. If they negotiate, the question arises as to what are the means, whether psychological, social or cultural, which help them to do so. In Brecht's words (Willett, 1964), what is the 'theatrical manner, [in which] the child is taught to behave'? This research raised the question of the extent to which television storytelling contributes to these processes.

Lurie (1990) has pointed out that one of the primary functions of children's fiction is subversion. The most durable and popular stories are those in which the prevailing social attitudes of adult society are challenged, and she stresses particularly the ways in which children's fiction extended the possibilities of girls' social roles. Talking of *Little Women*, by Louisa May Alcott, published in 1868 (most recently filmed in 1994), she writes (p. 13): 'For at least five generations of American girls, Jo was a rebel and an ideal and Louisa May Alcott's understanding of their own impatience with contemporary models of female behavior . . . nothing less than miraculous.' Lurie describes how, during the second half of the twentieth century, 'the limits of socially acceptable behavior for girls were steadily pushed back' as books featuring feisty female protagonists were published, initially condemned and then turned into classics, for example, Louise Fitzhugh's 1964 *Harriet the Spy* (also recently filmed, in 1996, with Michelle Trachtenberg as Harriet).

The ways in which these stories have been rediscovered and recast many decades later by contemporary film-makers, suggest that the pathways of identity formation, via culture, are not simple or direct, nor are they only contemporaneous with the publication of the text. It is not only children's texts which are defined by use – just as Janice Radway (1984) has pointed out women's subversive uses of stereotypical romance literature, similarly, Ellen Seiter (1993) has discussed girls' appropriation of (to some critics) 'insipid' toys such as Strawberry

Shortcake and My Little Pony, to stake out their own imaginative, female territory. As Lurie acknowledges, *Little Women* would not be seen by girls of the 1990s as a particularly liberating text. However, the film project was brought to screen by the determination of a young female actor, Winona Ryder, as co-producer, and the radical Australian director, Gillian Armstrong, who made her name with a female *Bildungsroman*, *My Brilliant Career* in 1979. The combination of feminist director, and actors known for independence in their private lives, as well as for the groundbreaking nature of some of their roles, such as Susan Sarandon (*Thelma and Louise*) as Marmee, and Winona Ryder (*Heathers*) as Jo, produced a reconfiguration and updating of *Little Women*'s feminist themes, restoring some of Alcott's original radical feminist message. The filming and updating of 'classics' is thus not just a way of enforcing traditional bourgeois values from the past; on the contrary, it is one of the ways in which popular media, such as film and broadcasting, can continue to fulfil their 'subversive' functions for young audiences.

Broadcasting, and to some extent 'family films' such as *Little Women*, are unlike toys, clothes and magazines, in that they cannot be commercially successful unless they reach a 'mass' audience, which must include both males and females. Children's programming, struggling to maximise ratings in every way it can, needs particularly to find storytelling formats which can attract both boy and girl audiences. This is an economic imperative, if not a social and moral one, and it has been an imperative for the last twenty years in the UK. Stories which do well in the ratings, like *The Demon Headmaster*, have an androgynous quality; they have both female and male central protagonists, and villains, and permit all the child characters to have narrative functions, whether in terms of action, comic relief or problem-solving. In a piece of BBC in-house research prior to the programme's transmission (reported in Davies and O'Malley, 1996), its producer and director, Richard Callanan and Roger Singleton Turner, interviewed 55 children aged from 9–12 and found that only 2 of them thought it was 'for boys only' or 'girls only' (1 for each). Fifty-three of the 55 identified it as being 'for both sexes' – which the producers felt was a considerable achievement, validated by the programme's eventual 70 per cent audience share of the 9–12 age group.

In one of the schools in our study, a Cardiff inner-city primary, the following discussion took place between a boy and two girls over the representation of gender in this programme, with each child showing a recognition of gender issues as a necessary tool (no doubt learned from adult examples, since 'sexist' is not a term invented by children) for interpreting dramatic narratives. However, they also recognised that narratives had their own constraints which had to be recognised, such as the necessity of having a central villain. The discussion comes from the group feedback sessions in the whole-class discussion of the task, and this group were representing '9–14 year old children':

GIRL 1   It shouldn't be banned because it's not violent. It's a very interesting programme for children from 9–14.

INTERVIEWER   Why is it interesting? [inaudible murmurs] . . .

BOY 1   It's a bit sexist. It's got a Demon Headmaster, why not have a Demon Headmistress instead?

INTERVIEWER   Were there any scary female characters?

BOY 1   There was Rose and Eve – in the current series . . .

GIRL 2   Can I just say that he made the point that it was sexist because the Demon Headmaster is a man. But if there is only going to be one main villain then either way it's going to be sexist.

Sandra Hastie, from the USA, produced one of the first realistic children's dramas in the UK to have a strong central female protagonist, and to treat controversial themes, such as parental child sex abuse – Thames/Carlton's *Press Gang* (ITV, 1985–1992). It starred Julia Sawalha (Saffy in *Absolutely Fabulous*, Lydia in the BBC's 1995 *Pride and Prejudice*) as a modern Jo March, the editor of a young people's newspaper. Like Lurie, Hastie (interviewed for the BBC study in spring, 1996) saw as a central ingredient of its success, a spirit of independent eccentricity – a subversion of standard broadcasting values:

Press Gang had amazing potential – a good mix of young people . . . Working in this country . . . is [getting] much more like the US [When] I came here 12 years ago there was a kind of eccentricity about children's programmes in this country . . . [people's] shoulders weren't looked over by their bosses because children's programmes weren't taken as seriously as prime time . . . [we were] doing it the way we wanted to do it, a bit indulgent, not to satisfy advertisers.

The central character in *Press Gang*, in her determination not to be sidetracked from her professional ambitions by boyfriends, family or friendship, and, in her occasionally ruthless pursuit of stories, regardless of ethical considerations or personal soft-heartedness, was similar to adult female characters in films of the time, such as *Working Girl* (1988), *Baby Boom* (1987) or *Three Men and a Baby* (1987) – conflicted between emotions and work. However, in the case of Lynda in *Press Gang* (unlike even her hard-boiled Hollywood precursor, Rosalind Russell's Hildy Johnson, in *His Girl Friday*, 1939), there were no Hollywood solutions to her conflicts in the form of the happy, wedded-couple ending; here, the cautiousness of children's series drama in avoiding sexual pairings,

Table 12. *Proportions (percentage) of boys, girls and all children combined agreeing with the following statements*

	percentage answering 'True'			percentage answering 'Not true'			percentage answering 'Not sure'		
	All	boys	girls	All	boys	girls	All	boys	girls
There are too many programmes for little children	40	42	38	40	39	40	20	19	22
I like watching programmes with teenagers in them	60	56	64	18	21	14	22	23	23
Cartoons are only for little children	27	29	25	63	61	66	9	10	9
I want more programmes for children my age	70	70	71	12	14	10	18	15	20
The stories on children's TV are babyish	30	34	27	45	41	49	25	25	24

which not only produce narrative closure, but which can also put off younger viewers and occasionally parents, made the story much less soft-centred than an adult version would have been. *Press Gang* is still talked about by producers as one of the crowning achievements of British children's drama, yet, like other such achievements, it is very difficult to find a copy of it.

Gender differences in the study

In the quantitative data the general similarity of view between boys and girls was one feature of the questionnaire findings which must have given some reassurance to the study's sponsors. Most of the questionnaire responses did not show very marked differences between girls and boys. On issues to do with, for instance, the social role of television drama – something children stressed in their discussions – equal numbers of boys and girls agreed that television helped them, but helped other children more. There were other issues on which the gender differences were greater. Table 12 has the same set of opinion-statements about children's and adults' programmes discussed above in terms of age, here broken down by gender.

The proposition that 'There are too many programmes for little children' had nearly equal numbers of boys and girls answering both 'true' (40 per cent) and 'not true' (40 per cent) and 20 per cent were 'not sure' – an example of how gender, in this case, was a much weaker predictor of differences than age. The slightly different wording in a similar question – 'the stories on children's TV are babyish' – with a specific emphasis on 'stories', produced more disagreement, with 34 per cent of boys agreeing, and only 27 per cent of girls. The majority of the sample *dis*agreed that stories on children's TV were babyish, with girls (49 per cent) significantly more likely to disagree than boys (41 per cent). Although both sexes gave strong majority votes to the proposition 'I like watching programmes with teenagers in them', girls were significantly more likely to agree with this. Thus, girls were both more likely not to see stories aimed at children as 'babyish', and much more likely to like programmes about teenagers – people older than themselves. The common denominator here was likely to be girls' preference for stories about relationships, a finding noted generally in studies of children's culture, and one which permits a degree of fluidity and permeability in roles in girls' tastes greater than that permitted to boys (see Durkin, 1985). However, Cassell (1998, p. 301) has argued that these differences in taste are not inevitable; in designing computer games for girls, which she suggests are also enjoyable for boys, she emphasises the importance of narrative and in doing so underlines some of the main findings to emerge from the study described in this book, in which the discussion of dramatic narrative generated a variety of reflections on identity and social responsibilities. Cassell argues: 'The ideal playing field for the construction of self is storytelling and other kinds of narrative activity.'

Children's comments about gender: qualitative data

In their own comments, children frequently showed awareness of gender as an issue of identity politics. Television programmes – like the dating show, *Man O Man* – could be used by boys and girls to raise gender issues among themselves in ways that would have been more difficult without a text to stimulate debate. In debates about getting rid of programmes, familiar assumptions about gender appropriateness appeared, and were then challenged, as for instance this group of 8–11 year olds in Milton Keynes:

BOY 1   We might get rid of *Pirates*, if girls watched it they might get frightened.
[Chorus of noises.]

BOY 2   They play *Power Rangers* on their little brothers.
[They voted to get rid of it.]

Next they debated getting rid of the adult drama, *Soldier Soldier* (BBC1).

BOY 2   Who votes for *Soldier Soldier?*

GIRL 1   I think we should get rid of it. Most kids don't know about things like that.

BOY 3   It's about war. Most kids don't know about war . . .

GIRL 2   Because I'm not too keen on *Soldier Soldier*, it's just about fighting, and I'm a girl and I'm not into that stuff.

GIRL 1   It's alright for me but I don't think little children will like it that much.

INTERVIEWER   What do the boys think?

BOY 2   Some boys would like it.

BOY 1   Boys that want to be good, and that, and want to do all different things – they wouldn't like it.

Again, traditional views about what boys and girls are supposed to like – boys like war, and girls do not – were used by the children to align themselves with a particular position on gender identity. Girl 2 openly admits that not being 'into that stuff' is because 'I'm a girl.' The boys seemed to be resisting the position that just because they were boys, they should like it. They agreed that 'some boys would like it', but not the kind of boys 'that want to be good, and that'. Which kind of boys they thought they themselves were, was not clear; they seemed to want to be seen on both sides of the divide, rather as Machin and Carrithers' Spanish factory workers wanted to align themselves, simultaneously, both with working-class rude common sense, and more refined middle-class discrimination, in their comments on newspapers (Machin and Carrithers, 1996 – see chapter 5).

A group of children in an Oxfordshire primary school, discussing their drama-only schedule, decided to get rid of *Sister, Sister*, not necessarily on gender grounds – though these were raised – but on quality grounds:

INTERVIEWER   It seems to be *Sister, Sister*, why?

GIRL 1   Well it has got bits in it that are good and bits in it that are bad but most of it is bad.

BOY 1   It is a bit of a girlie thing.

The girl did not come back to challenge this judgement and *Sister, Sister* was dropped – it seemed that, to her, the show's 'badness' was not necessarily because it was 'girlie', but because it just was not a very entertaining programme. Later, this group had a general discussion about what makes a 'good programme', and their remarks could almost have been written by a psychologist seeking to demonstrate classic gender differences in narrative tastes:

BOY 2   Lots of violence.

BOY 3   Action packed and bloodthirsty.

GIRL 1   Problems and how the characters work through them . . .

INTERVIEWER   Who is your favourite character in *EastEnders*?

GIRL 2   Joe, because he is a bit nutty.

GIRL 1   Grant and Phil because they are a bit rough, they can be nice but they are alcoholics and things like that.

The task-negotiating structures meant that conflicts over whether a particular slot in the schedule should include a 'girl's programme' or a 'boy's programme' in the end had to be resolved consensually – and there was a variety of strategies for doing this, often by choosing a non-favourite programme that both sexes could agree on. This was a type of scheduling strategy also attempted by adult producers, such as Peter Tabern (interviewed for the BBC study in spring, 1996), of the independent production company, Childsplay, who produced the adventure comedy series for BBC1, *Pirates*, although he admitted that he was surprised by its success: 'What is strange is that [*Pirates*] has a girl as a central character but it appeals quite strongly to boys, which is unusual. It does appeal very much to nine year old boys. Lots of girls like the books.'

What was strange to him, seemed less strange to our child negotiators, who usually ended up choosing a programme as their final survivor, which had something for everyone, as this 9-year-old boy, from an inner-London primary school, explained about the group's final choice of *Live and Kicking*, the Saturday morning magazine show:

I think *Live and Kicking* because it's mixed and it has got things for everybody of all ages. It has chats for older people, competitions for our age (that's if you like competitions) and cartoons and there is fiction and stuff like that and non-fiction for people who like that. It also has *Rugrats* for babies so it is fair for everyone.

Class

Say you are a poor family and you have just got a TV and a phone and that and you do not use it very much because you are very poor and you turn to *Live and Kicking* and you have not got many toys because you may want to win some toys. You cannot win anything on *Top of the Pops*. (Boy, 11, inner-London primary school)

In the UK, class has traditionally been seen as a key variable in determining how children react to cultural experiences. For example, Buckingham *et al.* (1999, p. 36) describe debates within the BBC during the 1960s and 1970s about the kinds of behavioural models that should be offered on children's television, and they comment disapprovingly: 'Whatever its desire to represent previously unscreened aspects of popular experience, it [the BBC's Children's Department] remained attached to a core of values in which middle-class attitudes and universal moral principles had come to be seen as one and the same thing.' The authors quote Edward Barnes, head of the children's department in 1982, as saying that 'our children must not be the proles of tomorrow': 'Thus', comment Buckingham et al. (1999, p. 37) with a suggestion of scepticism, 'public service television could deliver children from an Orwellian future and draw them away from the wastelands of popular taste into a different and richer cultural life'.

The view that class and children are coterminous when it comes to judgements on popular culture was articulated particularly explicitly by Julian Petley (1997, p. 87) in Ill Effects, on 'the media and violence debate' (see chapter 6). Petley argues: 'Lurking behind these fears about the corruption of innocent minds, one finds time and again, implicit or explicit, a potent strain of class dislike and fear. The . . . spectre of the working class in general . . . the underclass . . . the lumpenproletariat.' According to this view, the desire to control and regulate children's media consumption comes from an élitist tendency, particularly strong in British society, as Petley observes, to suppress the tastes and voices of the working class, and furthermore, that the working class can be equated with children. Just as the workers are patronised and deemed to be incapable of making discriminating judgements about controversial material, such as violent representations of 'thugs' and 'spivs', so children are similarly 'protected' by a 'discourse of rescue' (Buckingham et al., 1999) from seeing such representations.

Although this is a persuasive argument, which works in the interest of taking seriously the tastes and intelligence of the working class, it is less helpful for children. The conflation of the working class and children, as groups equally discriminated against by middle-class broadcasters, ignores the point, highlighted by Livingstone and Bovill's data, as well as ours, that the category 'child' crosses other demographic categories, including class. There is an implicit assumption in class-based critiques of media, based on adult cultural differences, that working-class children will enjoy different kinds of cultural experience to middle-class children because of the (adult-defined) differences in their backgrounds. This is not a logical assumption, because it fails to take account of the common denominator of 'being a child' – a state of being which has a strong determining effect on children's sense of identity and media choices, not least because, for all children, it is an oppositional category to 'adult', however 'adult' is defined.

The concept of 'the world republic of childhood' (Paul Hazard, 1947), is problematic, because of the necessary recognition that the experience of being a child will vary in significant ways depending on cultural and geographical circumstances (one of the most important of which is poverty). Nevertheless, being a child is of central demographic importance in deciding what kind of a person you are seen to be, both by yourself and by others, and in determining what social arrangements should be made for you by governments and their institutions. If children are to be seen as a separate demographic category, to be recognised independently in the public sphere, for example in social statistics (see Qvortrup, 1997), and if this perception is an issue of rights – the rights of children to be recognised as a group with their own policy interests independent of those of adults – then it is against these rights to conflate all children's interests with those of only one social class. Equalising the life-chances of all children born, a desirable goal proclaimed in 1999 in the UK by Prime Minister Tony Blair, means recognising that 'childhood' is a discrete and recognisable demographic category based on age, crossing all the other categories, such as class, parenthood, race, religion, gender or sexual identity, any or all of which can act to reduce, or promote, children's chances of equality as they grow up. To use the language of statistics: the state of childhood is the single dependent variable on which the different independent variables of social and cultural status act.

Children, class and media tastes

While there are large class differences in some forms of media access, to do with differences in family income, wide differences in *taste* are not generally found in studies of children's media habits. Livingstone and Bovill (1999), found marked class disparities in children's access to new media such as PCs and the Internet (46 per cent of middle-class children had a multi-media computer, compared with only 19 per cent of working-class children), but very few class differences in children's viewing behaviour and tastes. For instance, the popularity of soap opera ranged from 26 per cent of AB children, through 25 per cent of C1 and C2s to 27 per cent of DE children (class distinctions: AB top (professional), DE bottom (unskilled working), used by advertisers and marketers). Cartoons were more popular (19 per cent) in DE homes than in AB homes (11 per cent) – possibly reflecting parental interdiction. But other more down-market genres such as chat shows were mentioned by only 1 per cent of AB children, with C1, C2 and DE children not mentioning them at all, while sport was more popular in AB homes (15

Table 13. *Selected 'True' scores according to special needs coding (SN) compared with overall scores from main sample (All)*

	0 SN	1 SN	2 SN	3 SN	4/5 SN	6 SN	7 SN	All true	Significance (chi square)
Programmes for children are best	40.5	32.9	38.5	35.6	48.2	39.4	42.8	38.5	p = 0.161
Too many programmes for little children	44.2	48.2	40.1	28.4	38.6	36.3	37.2	39.9	0.001
I like stories a long time ago	41.8	40.1	45.0	45.6	27.7	57.2	66.0	47.4	0.0000
Children need their own programmes	74.1	66.2	63.2	63.1	63.9	69.8	72.0	67.8	0.188
I want more stories from books	34.7	44.8	44.8	39.6	43.9	58.2	66.4	47.9	0.0000

per cent) than in DE homes (12 per cent). Buckingham *et al.* (1999) also found what they described as a 'distinctiveness' in children's television tastes, in which class preferences were not particularly predictable.

In our BBC study, a quantitative analysis of children's responses according to the 'special needs index', based on the schools' own statistical information about the proportions of children having free meals, in public housing, and who needed special teaching or help with English (see Appendix 1), yielded some unexpected findings with regard to class, particularly in children's tastes for TV drama genres, as Table 13 indicates.

The statements 'Too many programmes for little children' and 'Children need their own programmes' did not produce significant variations across the special needs groups, which suggests that the groups were reasonably comparable; they did not differ on every dimension. But high special needs groups were significantly more likely to *dis*agree that there were 'too many programmes for little children', in other words, the children in the schools with the highest indicators of disadvantage were more likely to favour special programmes for children.

An unexpected finding was the variation in tastes for different genres according to special needs status. Children from high special needs schools were very significantly more likely to want more stories from books, and more stories set in the past. They also showed higher scores in favour of science fiction and the view that 'made up stories are better', although these differences were not statistically significant. The call from these more disadvantaged children for 'more stories from books' and stories set 'a long time ago' was not what might have been expected from a class-based prediction, since literary-based dramatisations, and historical costume dramas (as Caughie, 1991, pointed out) have been categorised as élitist, and can be seen as an imposition by paternalist broadcasters of conservative values on people to whom such values are alien. One possible explanation for these children's responses was that this was an effect of the schools themselves; they may have been the kinds of schools which stressed heavily the importance of literature, and of history, for their less-than-advantaged intakes. If they were, the children in the schools were clearly demonstrating a receptiveness to this influence in their questionnaire answers.

One of the schools in the highest special needs group did the 'drama scheduling' task, in which children had to construct a Children's Channel of all drama programmes, and then, in the second stage, to discard their choices as they 'lost money'. The children's discussions shed more light on the finding that children in less advantaged schools were more likely to want élite forms of drama. The final choice in this group's drama schedule, after everything else was thrown out, was the BBC1 fantasy drama, *The Queen's Nose*, a serial, which got high ratings in the 1996/7 and 1998/9 seasons, and which, as described above, 'beat' the popular adult soap, *EastEnders* to the final survivor position in the schedule. *The Queen's Nose*, although full of entertaining special effects and farcical comedy, in some ways seemed a throwback to an earlier era in which heroines of children's dramas were well-bred young girls, with aristocratically eccentric families, a milieu very remote from the environment of the children in this school. Yet these children responded to it with familiarity and affection, as they explained why it had been their final choice:

INTERVIEWER   How is it different from a story like *The Demon Headmaster* or *EastEnders*?

GIRL 1   It's more funnier.

GIRL 2   She has a 50 pence and she gets it from her Uncle Ginger and she thinks her Uncle Ginger's really nice and he's trying to save the world.

GIRL 1   It's more exciting, and everyone's saving their 50 p coins now . . . She always wishes things for things that'll happen to you.

GIRL 3   She's not really a normal person, she wears all straggly clothes and things.

INTERVIEWER   What channel is it on?

CHORUS   BBC.

INTERVIEWER   Do you know what country it comes from?

GIRL 2   I think it comes from England because they speak our language.

GIRL 1   And they're in the BBC and the BBC is in London. So they're in London.

The ingredients that made *The Queen's Nose* popular for these children in many respects confirmed producers' analyses of the universal ingredients of 'a good story': 'kids like wishes' (fantasy); the mixture of the fantastic and the ordinary ('she always wishes for things that'll happen to you'); 'exciting'; 'more funnier' (the importance of humour); and a hint of idealism – Uncle Ginger 'trying to save the world'. *The Queen's Nose* also did what good stories often do – it had entered the playground culture: 'Everyone's saving their 50p coins now.' Fantasy, and being a bit 'hippieish', for these children, was not a disqualification – on the contrary. It was not only working-class children in the English Midlands who appreciated the programme either. An 8-year-old girl in an inner-London primary school wrote on her questionnaire:

I like to watch Asian cartoons and Asian films, Pakistani ones. I want to watch *The Queen's Nose*, different episodes not the same again and again.

Where children such as these have access to few other public cultural resources apart from their schools (which looked to us, as visitors, like culturally rich environments, both visually and socially), genres such as fantasy, and specialised children's storytelling, may have more importance for them than for other children with access to a wider variety of cultural experiences. The finding of the questionnaire, that groups in high special need schools, had a significantly greater taste for stories set in the past and stories based on books is also supported by the finding that it was children with less access to new technology who most valued the drama *Byker Grove* (see chapter 2).

The case for specialised children's programming made by the originators of *Sesame Street* is that it is the most disadvantaged children who are most reliant on television (Palmer, 1988). Although increasing numbers of children in our society have access to satellite/cable and computers, the UK is still a society in which 1 in 4 children live below the poverty line, and in which access to different forms of popular entertainment, once available to the poor (such as going to live football matches), is increasingly confined to the affluent. One of the remits of public service broadcasting is to compensate for this state of affairs by offering to culturally deprived children the same cultural variety on offer to the children whose parents can buy them access to high-, low- and middle-brow culture in whatever forms they choose. For the most disadvantaged children in the sample, the finding that traditional forms of children's dramatic storytelling were favoured, was unusually strong. In a market-driven broadcasting and media world, making expensive drama programmes based on literary classics for poor children will not be an attractive option for the industry, and the industry may find support among critics who believe that providing such programmes for working-class children is patronising and élitist. The needs and wants of less-advantaged children are unlikely to sustain the production of expensive classic stories in the contracted public sphere of deregulated media, in which the consumer, not the culturally questing child, is paramount.

Ethnic and local identity

Boyden, in James and Prout (1997, p. 192), attributes constructions of childishness designed to protect children to having a troubling political agenda:

the norms and values upon which the ideal of a safe, happy and protected childhood are built are culturally and historically bound to the social preoccupa-tions and priorities of the capitalist countries of Europe and the United States . . . The expansion of capitalism . . . has given the greatest impetus to contemporary images of the ideal childhood.

The discourse of cultural relativism in such analyses of family life had not filtered down into the kinds of discourses used by the children in the study. The idea of a 'safe, happy and protected' childhood as a central aspiration (if not always a reality) of families with children, underpinned many of the reasonings offered by children to justify choices or rejections of programming in the tasks. For example, two 9 year olds in an inner-London primary school, discussing what to cut from, or keep in, their schedule, gave revealing pictures of apparently 'safe' and 'happy' family lives:

GIRL   I think we should keep *Sesame Street* because nearly all my family watch this in the mornings. When my granny wakes up she usually cooks the breakfast, after she does that she just sits down and watches *Sesame Street* and starts laughing all the time, so she enjoys it and so does my granddad.

BOY   I do not think that we should lose *Top of the Pops* because my youngest baby in our family, Barvinder, every time she watches *Top of the Pops* she dances to it and she really likes it and my uncle tapes it because he knows his baby likes it.

The contrast between the negative interpretation of family values put forward by Boyden and the references to enjoyment, laughter, liking, dancing, cooking and sharing as ingredients of family life, offered by the two 9 year olds, may partly be attributed to the fact that these two children came from ethnic minority groups. Some of the children's comments in the discussion task revealed family styles and values which are different from those of many families in the USA and Western Europe, for instance, another 10-year-old girl from the same school, also defending *Sesame Street*:

You know *Sesame Street*, there are adults in it, my granny is poor and did not get a good education so she watches this because she learns from it. My granny is from a different country, St Lucia and she got pregnant and did not get a good education, so when she watches this she learns more from this than *Live and Kicking*.

Boyden's comments fail to acknowledge that within Western cultures at the end of the twentieth and the beginning of the twenty-first century are some traditions of family life which do not stem from European and American Protestantism or from the needs of capitalist modernity. The family values of many children in the UK (like those quoted above) stem from Eastern religions, such as Islam, or from the extended-family solidarity of the Caribbean. Other network traditions, such as those of Irish Catholicism, or Judaism, or close-knit industrial working-class communities, such as ex-mining villages, are also still strong in many parts of the country. Children in the different regions of England and Wales in our study gave no indication of believing that being 'safe, happy and protected' was a top-down by-product of Western capitalism. They talked about home, siblings, parents and friends as if the need to maintain good relations with them was a bottom-up process – a routine requirement of their own everyday experience, and a basic moral imperative, determined and negotiated by the participants themselves.

London vs. the rest

One of the major problems of media research, and the media themselves, is a considerable London bias in much of the published work on children and media in the UK, along with the American bias in work published internationally. Such a bias would be a problem in any kind of study, but in studies about culture and children's responses to culture, it is an invalidating factor. What London children think and do culturally is unlikely to be mirrored elsewhere in the UK, because London is culturally unique, with only New York globally rivalling it for cultural activity: it has more arts and entertainment venues than most of the rest of the country put together, and the majority of Britain's media and cultural industries are concentrated there. London is also heavily over-represented on television as a location for dramas and news stories. This was one reason why we wanted to visit cities outside London for our study, and also to visit suburbs and villages with non-metropolitan cultural arrangements – in other words, places with no theatres, museums or cinemas, and few clubs, concert halls or other places of public entertainment. Broadcasting is a mass medium; public service broadcasting is required by law to serve the whole country, not just parts of it. The majority of the members of a mass audience, in numerical terms, do not live in London, or in any capital city.

A central issue in the debate about the disappearance of childhood is the extent to which children have become as sophisticated as adults in their media tastes, and hence no longer need special children's provision; the boundaries between childhood and adulthood 'have come down'. If this were the case, it was likely that such an effect was more likely to be found in London than elsewhere in the country. One of the tasks in the study was designed specifically to test children's attitudes about the desirability of getting rid of children's programmes and replacing them with adult dramas, to satisfy more sophisticated tastes among children. Two schools discussed the replacement of *Grange Hill*, the school serial on BBC1, and *The Queen's Nose*, the fantasy drama, with, respectively, *EastEnders*, the adult soap, and *The X Files*, the US-produced adult science fiction series. One of these schools was a secondary school in Middlesbrough, in the north-east of England, an industrial and shipping town (three special needs), the other was a secondary school in Harrow, in outer West London (five special needs). In both schools, the children were aged 12 to 13, so many would have entered puberty, all had made the social transition from primary to secondary (high) school, and all had therefore reached a position where aspects of their identity included aspirations to adulthood, and a likely desire to leave cultural products labelled as 'children's' behind. This age group is an important market for teen magazines, for the fashion and cosmetic industries and for the music industry; furthermore, they were entering an age band – 13 to 19 – which is notoriously difficult to attract as a television audience (Home, 1993).

The comparison between the way the two schools performed this task produced some differences, which could be attributable to the difference between metropolitan children, part of a constantly shifting urban scene, well endowed with every kind of entertainment possibility, and equally urban, but provincial children, with a greater degree of demographic stability and for whom media leisure opportunities would be more limited than in London. The children in the London school were the only ones in the sample to be dismissive of the idea that children 'need' or are 'entitled to' their own programmes. In other parts of the country, strong defences were found for children as a special case – if not on the speaker's own behalf, then on behalf of 'little kids'. Not even this 'displacement' effect was found in the London pre-teens (the London primary-school children were different). In this task, the different groups during the first whole-class stage of the debate had to represent different interest groups: children aged 4–8; children aged 9–14 (their own age group); parents; teachers; producers of children's programmes; producers of adult programmes. In the second stage, the small group of representatives from each of these groups changed role, and had to act as a committee of regulators, arbitrating on the arguments for the proposed change.

Particularly striking was the view from the 'teachers' in the London group, speaking 'in role', and taking an authoritative tone, to argue that adult programmes were *not* something that children should be protected from, because – again – they offered superior educational value:

TEACHERS' SPOKESPERSON We are the teachers. My first idea is that adult programmes are more real and interesting. My second one is that children need to learn more about older life than what they see on children's TV. My third one is that adult programmes show more than what children's programmes would, and my fourth one is that you get better vocabulary listening to adult rather than children's programmes.

INTERVIEWER Are you supporting the motion that the BBC should stop spending money on children's programmes?

TEACHERS' SPOKESPERSON Yes.

The next London group were less obviously 'in role':

BOY 1 My name is C. and I am representing adult programme producers . . . We don't like *Grange Hill* a lot because it is like too boring really . . . We don't want to see a lot of *The Queen's Nose*.

BOY 2 Because it's got too many hairs [laughter].

These remarks illustrated the tendency of the London children to be more cynical about children's programmes, and for some of them to take the exercise less seriously. The next spokesperson, a 12-year-old boy, was ostensibly speaking for 'children's producers', but persistently used the term 'we' to mean himself and other members of the child audience:

All the decent adult programmes are on way too late so we are stuck with all these stupid programmes which aren't really funny . . . There are too many stupid documentaries which no one cares about. It has nothing to do with anything so what is the point in learning about something that we can't learn from and doesn't affect our life.

The group representing children between 9 and 14 years, in other words speaking for their own age group, produced an impassioned plea for replacing 'immature' children's programmes with 'more exciting adult ones' with an eloquence which stirred the class:

The Queen's Nose is just about a girl with a magic fifty pence piece which grants her three wishes. It would be nice if it was true but we are old enough to understand that it was fiction. *X Files* is also fiction but coming back to what I said before, it's more exciting. On the other hand it wouldn't be fair on infants because they might not understand the programmes and *X Files* would be a bit scary for them. We decided that they should be replaced by *EastEnders* and *X Files* [applause].

The London group representing children aged 4–8 years used age-appropriateness as their primary regulatory category; they felt that *Grange Hill* should remain 'because it is based on children around your age and it is to do with high school'. They decided to retain *The Queen's Nose* because 'we think younger children would enjoy it' and they thought that little children would be scared by *The X Files* – 'it is meant for older children of thirteen and over'. They and the group representing parents, faithfully trying to protect their young from being upset, were the only two groups out of the seven to want to preserve the status quo. The same views, with a majority in favour of replacing the children's dramas with adult dramas, were expressed in the small group discussion afterwards.

In the Middlesbrough school, the decisions were very different; all except the group representing 9–14 year olds agreed that things should stay as they were, with children's drama in the early afternoon schedule, and adult drama waiting until later in the evening. The adults' groups – parents, teachers and producers – argued:

BOY   Everyone in our group said it should stay as it is, except for one person who said that *EastEnders* should come on at children's time and *X Files* should come on later . . . *Grange Hill* is more about normal life.

INTERVIEWER   What about your dissenter? What were his/her reasons?

BOY   Because *EastEnders* is all right it is not that bad, but *X Files* gives children nightmares.

INTERVIEWER   He accepted the majority verdict?

BOY   Yes.

The protectiveness of this group towards 'little kids', and the fact that it did not consider itself to have outgrown these children's programmes, contrasted with the London children's discussion. Their final four reasons for preserving the status quo were:

1 It is not fair on the little kids as they won't have much to watch.
2 They would lose their enjoyment.
3 It would be selfish, because older children can watch the adult programmes *as well*.
4 The majority of our group said that our age group enjoy watching the programmes too.

It is not possible to generalise about regional differences from only two small groups of children. Nevertheless, this contrast does point to an issue that has to be borne in mind when considering the appropriateness of media material for children generally: the majority of media workers and media decision-makers in the UK are based in London (as are an increasing number of international media companies). The majority of children are not. In this sense, a London bias may be even more excluding to children in the whole of the country than an international bias and an increase in imported programmes. One advantage of American programmes, particularly for British children for whom accent and speech in spoken English are so crucial in establishing social distinctions, is that the Hollywood American accent, although symbolising to adults the global hegemony of media-conglomerates like Time-Warner/AOL, is classless. Although characters like Clarissa, or Sabrina the teenage witch, are obviously very affluent, they are not seen as 'upper class' or 'posh' or 'a load of Geordies'.

Wales and the Welsh language

In Wales the question of local identity is bound up, not only with an increasing Welsh nationalism (the Nationalist Party, Plaid Cymru, are the second largest party in the new Welsh Assembly), but also with the Welsh language. In Wales, S4C, the Welsh-language channel, has a privileged place in the media landscape, receiving nearly £75 million of public funding to support its services, although its share of the general Welsh audience is less than 10 per cent and is around 20 per cent of the Welsh-speaking audience (*source*: S4C Annual Report, 1998). Around 20 per cent of the population are native Welsh speakers, and many more learn Welsh in school. The children quoted here attended a secondary school in which all lessons were conducted in Welsh, and they were fluently bilingual. Some Welsh-language programmes were included in the schedule choices for Welsh schools, and this group's discussion of whether to include the S4C preschool programme, *Slot Meithrin* (Infants' Slot) or not, revealed issues of cultural and linguistic identity which were more immediate for them, than for children with English backgrounds. They explained their choice for the final six programmes for their children's schedule:

Firstly we chose *Slot Meithrin* because it's an early learning for young children and helps them to learn Welsh. We chose *Live and Kicking* because it has lots of music, stars and cartoons. *Blue Peter* is good because it has lots of things to make and the appeals help people across the world. *Home and Away* is a soap for the older children, and so is *EastEnders*. *Top of the Pops* is a programme about music and has the latest songs in the charts.

When it came to the point of throwing programmes out of their schedule, they agonised over *Slot Meithrin*:

BOY 1   *Top of the Pops* maybe?

GIRL 1   *Ren and Stimpy.*

BOY 2   I think it would be *Slot Meithrin*. Because if this is a channel across Britain, lots of the children aren't going to understand Welsh.

After animated discussion about discarding *Ren and Stimpy*, *Home and Away* and *Top of the Pops*, the group eventually agreed that *Slot Meithrin* should go:

GIRL 2   Not everyone speaks Welsh and even the Welsh children, not a lot of them will watch *Slot Meithrin*. I'm not sure how many of them watch Welsh television.

BOY 3   The popularity of Welsh, is like even if the families are Welsh, . . . [unfinished sentence]

INTERVIEWER   Suppose I'm the supreme channel controller and I say your channel should represent different language groups in the country, what would you say?

GIRL 1   I would say get rid of *Top of the Pops* first.

BOY 1   I agree with what you're saying but a lot of people don't . . . I don't read many Welsh books either.

GIRL 2   I think the same really, you should represent as you said, different countries, but it doesn't really matter if one Welsh programme goes . . .

BOY 3   We've got to have these English programmes; even though I wouldn't watch *Slot Meithrin*, some people would.

They then went on to argue for eliminating *EastEnders*, partly because it was seen as 'aggressive' and a bad example, but also for reasons of identity:

GIRL 2   A lot of Welsh people don't like a London accent, they don't understand it.

BOY 2   I don't agree with that at all; a lot of my family do live in London now and I think that's a bit prejudiced in a way, just because we're Welsh doesn't mean we don't like the English and just because other people are English, it doesn't mean they don't like Welsh.

Here, again, was the Reithian language of balance and tolerance, attempting to see the other cultural group's (the hegemonic oppressor's in the case of the English) point of view. As discussed in chapter 5, it was difficult to believe that children were as reasonable as this in all circumstances; the stance was more likely to have been adopted for the purposes of the exercise, which offered the opportunity to show their knowledge of the rules of rational, liberal discourse, as applied to media regulation. Eventually, it was not *EastEnders'* London and English qualities which led to its being discarded, it was, characteristically, its unsuitability for 'little kids'.

BOY 3   Yeah, I know what you think, I have nothing against London people, but it is a bit too old for people, it should be on later.

Americanisation

The issue of local and national identity raises the wider issue of the globalisation, specifically the Americanisation, of broadcasting, and children's comments on these trends often demonstrated a sophisticated awareness of the structural factors contributing to changes in household viewing habits. As one 12-year-old boy, in one of the most deprived areas of the study, in Milton Keynes, quoted in chapter 4, pointed out: 'Well, Sky Sports have taken all the football and other sports. The same thing happens with the children's channel, Sky have taken them too, which is unfair to people like me who do not have Sky.' In general, however, whether a programme was American or not did not count against it very much in the decision-making processes used in the scheduling exercises. *Clarissa Explains it All* was disparaged by one girl in the pilot study, because Clarissa was American – which served as an explanation for behaviour in the programme which violated the primary requirement of realism for this group. Of all the final choices in the scheduling exercises, carried out in 8 schools, only 2 of the last survivors in the programme-discarding stage were American: *The Simpsons* (in an inner-city secondary school in London) and *Rugrats* (in the Welsh-language secondary school in Cardiff). The choice of *Rugrats*, interestingly, was made instead of the most popular final choice for the English schools – *Live and Kicking*. This Saturday-morning magazine programme was seen in Cardiff as 'too English', and *Rugrats* was thus chosen as preferable by Welsh children.

American television and its programmes were seen as a cornucopia of plenty by the children in the study who discussed them, but this did not necessarily arouse envy, as in the case of these children in Milton Keynes:

GIRL 1   I went to the USA and Nickelodeon studios and I saw a stage all like a house, with lots of windows . . . American programmes are better because they've got more things in them.

BOY 1   They've got more drama.

GIRL 1   They've got more real things in.

The interviewer asked what would be better for a Children's Channel, American or English programmes, and there was a chorus of 'American', 'English' in which it was impossible to distinguish which was dominant, until one boy said 'Both'. The conversation, which had begun with the group discussing why they had kept *The Queen's Nose* – a quintessentially English programme – as their final choice in their drama schedule, ended with one girl talking about the profusion of 'choice' in the USA:

GIRL 1 When I went to the USA, I was in a villa and they had 200 channels.

BOY 1 Eeurgh.

Conclusion

Broadcasting, as it has traditionally been organised, has been a unifying experience for children in the UK, which, of course, is grounds for objection to it – homogeneity of broadcasting output fails to take proper account of local, ethnic and cultural differences in the audience. In the study, there were few differences attributable to class or region in response to programmes in which class could have been a divisive issue, such as *Grange Hill*, the soap about a London comprehensive school. The strongest class-based finding – one of the strongest findings of the whole study – was counter-intuitive: the finding that children from the least-advantaged areas were much more likely than others to want traditional literary and historical forms of drama – a statistical finding which was supported by the qualitative data too.

As the above brief sample of data and comments from children of different backgrounds and status indicates, children's regional, ethnic and gender identities did influence their points of view to some extent. In the case of the Welsh children, it decisively influenced their final decision to jettison *EastEnders* on the grounds of both its Englishness and its 'unsuitability' for 'little kids', and, in the case of the inner-London secondary-school children, there was some evidence of a more metropolitan sophistication than was found in other children of the same age. These London secondary-school children included a high proportion of students with an Asian, that is, Indian or Pakistani, background, and a group of programmes aimed at Asian audiences was included in the list for their schedule. Unlike the Welsh-language speakers, they did not discuss these programmes at all – they were discarded at an early stage – being Londoners and wanting to appear more adult and 'cool', in their judgements, seemed to be a more decisive factor than any other identity factor, but, again, it is important to beware of generalising from only one group of children. With regard to gender, the finding that boys defended violent-action programmes and girls liked them less, is hardly news; however, what the exercises in this research added to this well-established knowledge of gender-based tastes was the demonstrated ability for boys and girls to debate their differences good-humouredly, and to reach a reasonable consensus in which neither group felt overpowered.

Popular children's television almost uniquely provides a topic of discussion which, in this study, could be shared by each child of the 1,300+ taking part in the study; no individual in any school had to be excluded because of lack of familiarity or competence – an important and empowering feature, for children, of being in a television audience. All were able to be 'experts' in this exercise, and it was obvious from listening to these discussions that children's broadcasting, and broadcasting generally, have so far created a public space in the UK in which children can imagine that they are active participants. The voices heard in this research, from different parts of England and Wales, town and country, were distinctive and diverse; they reflected strong individual opinion, but they also reflected collective perceptions of cultural identity, based on how boys and girls felt about themselves, about each other, about the English, the Americans, the 'littl'uns', and adults, all generated through discussions about their familiar broadcast media. It is difficult to sum them up with any kind of composite image of 'today's children', but the demon child and the couch potato, of tabloid mythology, are two ingredients missing from these conversations. The nearest we got to the demonic (that is, the even mildly naughty) was the occasional cheeky joke about hairs in *The Queen's Nose*, and there was no sense that these children's viewing of television was passive and potato-like.

In every age, behind public representations of childhood, stand actual children, looking and sounding rather different from the official public versions. Behind Millais' Victorian, velvet-suited, angelic Bubbles, lay child prostitutes, chimney sweeps and dead babies. Behind our contemporary model of the sophisticated twenty-first century, bedroom-based child, living in an isolated nuclear household, *au fait* with adult sexual behaviour through his (and it usually is his) mastery of new technology on the Web and learning cruelty from watching horror videos, was a variety of actual 9 and 10 year olds, whose Jamaican-born Grannies cook breakfast while watching *Sesame Street*, whose baby cousins called Barvinder like to dance to pop music, who 'like violence' but think it is 'not for girls', or who *are* girls wanting 'more bloodthirsty programmes', who speak Welsh, but defend the rights of the English, whose identities are changing as they grow from the still-remembered and protected state of 'little kids' to the more enviable state of the teenager, and who appear to be capable of negotiating all these identities in self-aware ways with their peers. These particular children, wherever they lived, and whatever they watched on television, had many contradictory ideas about broadcasting and culture, but they mostly seemed to be clear about who they were.

Part III

The art of television

8 Media literacy and the understanding of narrative

Máire Messenger Davies and David Machin

Never, ever in a programme do you see the bad guy win.
                                    Boy, 11, rural primary school, Co. Durham

BOY 1   I'd like to see a programme where the bad guy wins; just once.

GIRL 1   Never ever in a programme do you see the bad guy win . . .

GIRL 2   The programme would have to go on for ever and ever until the good guy eventually wins.

BOY 2   There should be a programme that wants to go on, that had to go on and they had loads of ideas for it, but the bad guy would have to win, and then you'd have to have another series and the bad guy would come back.
                                    8–11 year olds, rural primary school, Co. Durham

GIRL 1   *EastEnders* get boring, it has been on for 11 years.

BOY 1   No, let me get it straight, you want to end this right, how are you going to end it?

GIRL 1   Easy, they all die (laughter) . . .

GIRL 2   *The Biz* had quite a lot of series – the same thing sort of happens, like one person gets frustrated about something.

INTERVIEWER   Is that good or bad?

ALL   Bad.   8–11 year olds, inner-London primary school

In 1948, Bertolt Brecht asked rhetorically about: 'the theatre's influence on the formation of taste. How does one express oneself beautifully? What is the best way of grouping? What is beauty anyway?' (translated in Willett, 1964, p. 151). After several decades in which absolute standards of excellence in performance are seen as impossible to agree on, at least by postmodern critics, and in which the term 'beauty' has vanished altogether from critical discourse, we now have to be aware, even more than did Brecht, that taste is not an absolute value, but is relative and ideologically constructed. As Bourdieu (1984, p. 1) pointed out: 'Whereas the ideology of charisma regards taste in legitimate culture as a gift of nature, scientific observation shows that cultural

203

needs are the product of upbringing and education . . . closely linked to educational level . . . and secondarily to social origin.'

'Scientific observation' is another value which has fallen to relativist ways of thinking. However, empirical evidence from child development and educational research did permit Bourdieu to point out that people (children) have to learn how to interpret works of art, through acquiring 'cultural competence'. Implicitly, there are no absolute aesthetic values with which we are born; we are trained to value some objects, styles, structures and combinations, above others, and, as he goes on to discuss (p. 2) in his book, *Distinction*, such values are closely related to social class: 'A work of art has meaning and interest only for someone who possesses the cultural competence, that is, the code into which it is encoded.'

The appreciation of the meaning and interest of a 'work of art' thus encompasses a recognition of the codes within which the particular work is constructed, including its generic and media-specific aspects, as well as a recognition of wider ideological and political implications, including the whole idea of 'art' as a commodity, and the way in which cultural values are established and prioritised. This encompasses a very great deal for children to comprehend. Do they do so? This chapter examines children's responses to two specific programmes through tasks which required them to demonstrate an appreciation of aspects of narrative, production values, reality, fantasy, performance, ideology and, implicitly, 'taste'.

With dramatic storytelling, particularly for children, considerations wider than aesthetic values of beauty and taste also arise: as discussed at various points in this book so far, stories for children are expected to be 'useful' for them. One of these 'uses' is supposedly to educate them in the established codes and values of their society, whether to reinforce or to subvert. Another use, as Bruno Bettelheim argued of fairy tales, is to help children come to terms with psychic inner conflicts and the struggles of development. Yet another 'use', related to Bettelheim's, is educational. For progressive educationists the value of cultural experience is child-centred and essential to person-formation; art and literature are ways of promoting optimum intellectual and creative development.

In *Potent Fictions* (1996, p. 11), a collection of essays by media educators about their work with primary school children, Mary Hilton points out the 'large emotional and imaginative investment made by children in narratives and cultural material invented for them'. Hilton's analysis of how children use popular media parallels the processes which were going on among the children taking part in this study. Her work and the work of the educators in her volume raise the question of where and how children learn about the codes and conventions of art and culture. Do Bourdieu's codes have to be taught in school, or do children infer them through the everyday cultural experiences which they have outside school, including television and film? And, if the learning of cultural codes is associated with school, to what extent can the entertainment value of art – the pleasure associated with it – be fully acknowledged? Brecht, an author more usually associated with an emphasis on the ideological usefulness of dramatic performance than with its entertainment value, stressed above all, the importance of pleasure in 'A short organum for the theatre' (1948, translated in Willett, 1964, pp. 152, 180):

Theatre consists in this: in making live representations of reported or invented happenings between human beings and doing so with a view to entertainment . . . Even when people speak of higher and lower degrees of pleasure, art stares impassively back at them; for it wishes to fly high and low and to be left in peace, so long as it can give pleasure to people.

For progressive educators, too (Hilton, 1996, p. 42), pleasure is part of the pedagogic value of children's relationship with storytelling:

if we wish to connect children with literature . . . the ends will have served out their wonderful, predictable measure of pleasure. But children, like adults, want to sustain that pleasure, to return again and again to the dilatory space in the grand narrative as *agents and authors* of their own satisfaction.

Pleasure as an ingredient of media consumption is clearly not something that has to be sold to children by educators and critics. They watch television voluntarily, and they do it because they like it. However, as Hilton and her fellow-educators argue, pleasure depends on critical appreciation too; even in pleasure, there are 'higher' and 'lower' forms. The task for children in interpreting the works of art offered to them via popular media, and, in developing into critical adult consumers and wielders of 'taste', is challengingly multifaceted: they must learn the conventions and codes; they must respond emotionally; they must derive pleasure; they must be aware of ideological implications; they must, in short, to use Raymond Williams' term, learn to negotiate in a whole variety of ways with the messages offered to them by their electronic storytellers, as they sit curled up on the sofa, after a hard day at school, sucking in what many commentators on children's culture would describe only as a 'plug-in drug' (Winn, 1985).

Winn characterised television/film/video watching as the absorption of a drug which requires no mental activity of any kind, and a large number of cultural commentators in the tabloid press continue to agree with her. For example, Peter Hitchens in the *Daily Express* (7 November 1997, p. 10), suggested that children liked contemporary children's programmes 'because they require no effort, no imagination and no knowledge' and claimed that children 'haven't the slightest desire to be informed or made responsible'. This chapter provides evidence which casts doubt on these arguments. It is obvious from the children's comments discussed in this book so far that, whatever television does to children, it does not switch off their critical faculties. A key question is: how do children acquire the cultural competence to interpret the codes, whether ideological, aesthetic, or both combined (and, indeed, are they separable?) of film and television? Some of the answers to this question are described in chapter 3, on childhood, in which studies carried out by psychologists into children's 'modality' competence are discussed. However, psychologists are primarily concerned with cognitive competence and social behaviour. Brecht, Bourdieu and Hilton are after something more intangible and contentious – cultural competence, and through this, not only personal fulfilment and enlightenment, but greater political awareness.

Neil Postman (1982) argued that no particular cultural competence is necessary to understand the medium of television, and many people, like Winn and Hitchens, agree with him. If this is true, then it is equally true of other everyday cultural phenomena – the most obvious being language acquisition in children. All human beings acquire the ability to learn and to creatively utilise language in unforeseen combinations in the first three years of life, when they are physically immature and only primitively socialised in every other way. Because even less intelligent and lower-class toddlers can do it, language acquisition can be described as a banal accomplishment, yet it would be difficult to deny its cultural importance. It is precisely because it is a universal phenomenon, on the one hand, and, given the many thousands of languages and dialects in the world, very locally specific, on the other, that language acquisition is an object of intense academic debate. The argument between Noam Chomsky (language is 'hard-wired' in the human brain) and B. F. Skinner (language is learned behaviour) in the 1950s is with us still, and it applies to the learning of the codes and conventions of visual and audio-visual messages too (see, for example, Messaris, 1994).

Even if we agree with Postman that modern audio-visual storytelling is technically banal and easily comprehensible to children and adults alike, we still have to accept that the banal, as with the grammar of everyday human speech, is constructed within 'cultural codes' – and these codes have to be inferred by, if not directly taught to, the developing consciousness. The very concept of the 'banal' implies a set of conventions which are generally accepted and thoroughly ingrained in people's ways of thinking – in other words, learned. If they are learned apparently easily, or at least, without formal, systematic, institutionalised instruction, as with language, this raises important questions about the human brain, nervous system and cognitive functioning. What does this linguistic facility tell us about how the human brain is organised? Why is it easier, for instance, to learn language than to learn mathematics? Why can several languages be easily learned in childhood, but not in adulthood? And why do people the world over respond to audio-visual and visual storytelling in such overwhelming numbers?

Because of television's reputation as banal, 'dumb' and inimical to higher forms of culture, the words used in the title of Part III of this book, 'art' and 'television', are two concepts rarely yoked together. Nevertheless, even for the hard-line champions of the dumbing-down effects of popular audio-visual culture, it has to be acknowledged that the making of television programmes requires skills and talents traditionally associated with other sorts of production which *are* classified as 'arts': writing; design; music; performance; direction; camerawork; editing; and the combination of all of these. Children increasingly learn how to deploy such arts in school as part of media studies and other lessons – they are also continually exposed to professional versions of these arts as regular viewers.

Children's television producers are among the first teachers to children of such arts. However, some of the producer/directors interviewed for this study were reluctant to admit to being 'artists' and preferred to describe themselves as 'just telling the story' without undue artifice. Some seemed to feel it necessary to disguise to children the artistry of what they were doing. For instance, Marilyn Fox (interviewed for the BBC study in spring, 1996), director/producer of *Earthfasts* (BBC, 1996), based on William Mayne's novel about a boy whose best friend dies, and who has a number of supernatural experiences associated with this death, described how she and the production team had gone to considerable efforts to create a look for the series which represented the sombreness of the theme:

MF   The whole texture of the piece had to be earth, coming out of the earth, going back to it, the colours of the houses, the costume, no red in it, everything had to look like dust to dust and ashes to ashes, which in Yorkshire you can completely believe.

INTERVIEWER   Is that within your control?

MF   Absolutely, designers will ask you what sort of thing you're looking for and go away and interpret that, but at the end of the day it's your decision.

However, when asked if children noticed the care that directors and design teams take to find the right look, Marilyn Fox answered: 'I think if they notice, we have failed. Imagery should go right in and be part of the texture of what you feel.'

Other producers explicitly acknowledged that choice of camera angle, close-up, framing and *mise en scène*, plus aspects of casting and performance, had semiotic and ideological power, whether this was seen as intentional, or simply inevitable as part of the constraints of a busy production schedule, but were not always convinced that the audience was aware of it. Roger Singleton Turner (interviewed for the BBC study in spring, 1996), director of *The Demon Headmaster*, explained some of the techniques he used in the series to make it accessible and meaningful for children: 'In *The Demon Headmaster* I was consciously putting the camera at the height of the child . . . then you get the child's perspective almost literally.' Singleton Turner described procedures which he believed were narratively effective for child audiences in his production of *The Demon Headmaster*, including point of view, use of zooms and pans, the importance of casting, and finding children whose faces were sufficiently expressive to convey plot development in close-up. He also admitted to using 'the arty shot of the week' from time to time, and acknowledged that he made conscious reference to other sorts of image, as in a 'homage' to *Psycho* in the use of music in a threatening shot of the Demon Head about to discover one of the child heroes.

Whether producers admit it or not, it is through their means that children are introduced to elements of, and references to, audio-visual culture, including implicit components of it, of which they may not be, as yet, consciously aware. Using techniques such as low camera angle, and references to other directors, the creativity of children's programme-makers gives their audience lessons in the art, craft, techniques and persuasive power of audio-visual culture. These lessons begin very young, with preschool programming, and are, of course, informal, though for some children, they may be reinforced (or negated) through media studies lessons in school.

Most young children do not have media studies in school, and so the techniques used in television storytelling have to be inferred by child viewers for themselves, as in the following example from a study I carried out with children aged 6–12 in Philadelphia in the USA; this comment (Davies, 1997, p. 122) came from a child who had not had media education in her school, talking about a British drama she had never seen before, *The Sand Fairy*, an adaptation of a book she had not read, E. Nesbit's *Five Children and It*:

Some music makes it suspenseful and it tells you when something exciting is going to happen . . . this music is like hurrying and trying to get where they are going and they are trying to find things. It also helps you to get a feel of what's going on. (Girl, 11, Philadelphia)

Singleton Turner's observations indicate that the construction of a narrative sequence in a children's drama, requires on the part of the audience an appreciation of narrative likelihood, of meaning as carried in changes of shot and close-ups, and an appreciation of background aesthetic features such as music, and set design, as well as the ability to read intertextual references – a set of skills sometimes grouped under the heading 'media literacy'. However, as Buckingham (1993), following Bourdieu, has pointed out, 'literacy' for consumers of mass culture, requires social and ideological judgements which go beyond an awareness of technique – judgements which are not usually demanded of literary studies by school children.

An example of such wider inferences comes from the same American children in the Philadelphia study, compared with British children, also discussing *The Sand Fairy/Five Children and It*. The castle used in *Five Children and It* was a real castle, and the episode was filmed on location. However, the American children were firmly convinced it was 'fake'. One fifth-grader (Davies, 1997, p. 120) argued that it was 'all a set': 'They're just trying to express to you that this film is supposed to be set in a castle, but you know it really isn't.' A first-grade boy explained: 'The castle is not made out of bricks. It would cost too much money.' The British children, who lived in Co. Durham (with remains of Roman and medieval buildings all over their locality) responded differently:

INTERVIEWER   If I told you that the castle wasn't true, it was just in a studio, they put pretend bricks up and the windows weren't real? Would you believe it?

ALL No, no, no.

INTERVIEWER What made it look real?

SEVERAL COMMENTS   The knights, the clothes, there were no pictures on the walls, the stairs.

The North American children ignored the various cues for authenticity mentioned by the British children; for them, the overriding cultural expectation was that castles are built in studios – 'Universal Studios', as one boy suggested – or possibly, Disneyland. For British children, castles used in location shooting for period drama are 'encoded' as authentic – an example of Bourdieu's 'cultural training'.

Dramatic realism

The children of the Durham school, like others in the BBC study, were not only 'trained' in the authenticity of medieval castles on television; they were also trained in the traditions of British television, including commercial television, in which the values of both authenticity and of 'heritage' are deeply embedded. Caughie (1991, p. 23) drew attention to the twin traditions of realism – 'immediacy' and heritage – 'prestige' – from the beginnings of drama on British TV: 'The effect of immediacy, of a directness which signifies authenticity, is one of the characteristics which gives British television drama its specific form – still at the beginning of the 90s, distinguishing it from cinema or from the American telefilm.' Early transmissions on television (which had to be produced live) were invariably classics, or adaptations of theatrical successes, thus not only demonstrating 'immediacy', but also borrowing the cultural legitimacy of the theatre. Caughie (1991, p. 28) argued that: 'Drama then had double benefits for the BBC, bringing prestige and quality, as well as entertainment, to the institution of public service broadcasting and offering special occasions to the public it served.' Caughie thus highlights two key aspects of TV aesthetics: – immediacy (realism/authenticity) and 'prestige' (quality, high culture, respectability), both essential parts of British TV drama tradition.

Realism was a value invoked in a variety of ways by children in the study. One 12-year-old boy in a rural secondary school in Co. Durham, rather irritably dismissed *Neighbours*, because of its distance from 'truth':

I quite like the dramas . . . But I really don't like *Neighbours* because it is nowhere near the truth and there is no way that that number of things could happen to them.

A wide range of children in the study saw realism as a necessary component of serial drama based on children and young people's lives, such as *Grange Hill* and *Byker Grove*, and, for one boy in the north-east (where *Byker Grove* is set), the programme's lack of realism was a reason for throwing it out of his schedule:

INTERVIEWER   Why *Byker Grove*?

BOY 1   I don't think it is realistic . . . The things that happen in *Byker Grove* just wouldn't happen. *Byker Grove* is just a load of Geordies going to a youth club.

Here, realism is seen as lacking because of children's own superior insight into how 'Geordies' were likely to behave. In an Oxfordshire primary school, a group of 10–11 year olds focused on production technique as a barrier to realism – again leading them to decide that a programme using this kind of artifice should be discarded:

ALL   *Fudge* [should go].

INTERVIEWER   Why?

GIRL 1   Because the boys talk to the camera all the time.

GIRL 2   Well it is just stupid and they do things that nobody would ever do . . . the older boy is always talking to the camera and Fudge is just stupid.

The interviewer then proposed that, if it was realism they were after, they should consider the realistic soaps:

INTERVIEWER   Are there not programmes like *Grange Hill*, *Byker Grove* or more realistic drama included in that list; what about *Grange Hill*?

GIRL 1   No, because they do things in school that nobody is supposed to do in school really.

GIRL 2   You find situations in *EastEnders* that are more easy to relate to, they are more interesting, you want to see the next one to know what is happening.

This group differed from some others in proposing realism as a prime value in opposition to the kinds of morally good examples seen as necessary in other groups' discussions of realistic drama. The didactic purpose of dramatic art was a topic of discussion with both producers and children, producers being ambivalent about this aspect, while defending the necessity of realism as serving a form of dramatic truth, especially when dealing with painful, and potentially taboo subjects. Producers of the realistic soaps argued for the cathartic function of drama and insisted that 'emotional themes' in children's storytelling could be as dark and painful and as rooted in human vices as in adult drama, as in this comment from Matthew Robinson (interviewed for the BBC study in spring, 1996), of Zenith North Productions, producers of *Byker Grove*: 'I try to plumb the seven deadly sins or the ten commandments. It is about people's emotional journey, how they change, from one set of circumstances. You take a human being and you take them all the way down the line.'

These producers thus often positioned themselves as arbiters of what children 'need' in potential opposition to parents, who have often objected to storylines about, for example, teenage pregnancy, drugs or, famously, as in the case of *Byker Grove* in 1995, homosexuality. The value of 'realism', the 'need' to be truthful to children's own experience of life, was seen as a justification for overriding the wishes of (some) parents – a Fourth Estate role, articulated in the international Convention on the Rights of the Child. This independence of parental wishes is mildly controversial in the UK, but would be politically sensitive in more censorious cultures, as in some parts of the USA, an issue of some concern given the increasing number of North American co-productions in British children's drama.

In discussing whether to replace the realistic school soap *Grange Hill* with the gritty adult soap *EastEnders*, and the children's fantasy drama, *The Queen's Nose* with the adult fantasy *The X Files*, realism was again proposed by a group of Middlesbrough secondary-school children as a prime value, this time in the fantasy programme, *The Queen's Nose*. In this series, a young girl, aged 12, has a magic 50 pence piece which grants wishes when the Queen's nose on the coin is rubbed. The girl, Harmony, has an eccentric, squabbling family, including a spoilt, selfish older sister and a flighty granny who constantly quarrels with her son-in-law, Harmony's father:

GIRL 1   We watch it because it is quite realistic, funny.

INTERVIEWER   When you say realistic, what do you mean?

GIRL 1   Like life.

BOY 1   I think it was good like, realistic.

GIRL 2   But a girl making a wish with a 50 pence piece – I wouldn't call that realistic.

BOY 2   My auntie – her mother hates my auntie's husband, ever since they got married, so in some ways it can be realistic.

Realism is encoded in the settings, costume and language of dramas with contemporary settings. Harmony's twentieth-century family, their behaviour, their dramatic context and the way they looked, signified 'real', despite having a magic coin in their possession. Programmes with historical settings have different signifiers for authenticity, or otherwise.

The Prince and the Pauper: heritage drama

Because of the importance of the costume drama in British television's cultural traditions, and also for its international marketability, we wanted to include a sample of the genre in our study. *The Prince and the Pauper*, based on Mark Twain's fantasy story about Prince Edward, later King Edward VI, the 14-year-old son of Henry VIII, who changed places with a poor boy who looked exactly like him, was in production in the summer of 1997, the second year of the study. The research team took advantage of an opportunity to visit the location where it was being shot, a set of 'Tudor London', and next to it a set of a 'country village', ostensibly in Kent, especially constructed for the series in the grounds of a Sussex country house. This was an interesting historical moment for British television drama itself, as it turned out; it was the last location set to be built by the set department of BBC Bristol. In future, set-building would not be carried out in-house, it would be contracted out – another aspect of Britain's 'heritage' to disappear, but in this case, with little public protest. The skilled craftsman who explained this, one of those who had helped to re-create Tudor London, was about to be made redundant and was hoping to take a job as a driver.

Ironically, *The Prince and the Pauper*, by Mark Twain, first published in the United States in 1882, is not obviously an ideal choice for pure heritage drama; it is 'a . . . fantasy with a republican edge' in Peter Hunt's words (Hunt, 1994, p. 85). Like *Little Lord Fauntleroy*, by Frances Hodgson Burnett, another American children's book 'with a republican edge', published in 1886, it is a book that permits contemporary adapters to have their republican cake and eat it too. Both stories have glamorous settings in the stately homes of England, and both have the device of the child outsider (New Yorker Cedric Errol in the case of Fauntleroy, pauper Tom Canty in Twain's novel) taking the reader/viewer voyeuristically inside these splendid environments, while at the same time offering a sharp, naive critique of the autocratic behaviour of kings and dukes (the technique also used, with somewhat different 'Kings' and 'Dukes', by Twain in *Huckleberry Finn*). Appositely, the same production team who were working on *The Prince and the Pauper*, were also responsible for an award-winning TV adaptation of *Little Lord Fauntleroy*, starring George Baker for the BBC in 1994.

Republican sub-texts notwithstanding, costume drama made by the BBC carries other connotations and expectations, including (relatively) lavish spectacle, and an awareness of the fact that the descendants of the royal family, represented in a drama about the Tudors, are still on the throne of Britain, and have featured in a number of real-life dramatic storylines of their own, of which most British children are aware. Thus, further ideological themes are likely to be inferred from any representation of the life of King Henry VIII and his successor, the young Prince/King Edward VI, as the producers were also aware. The book has been televised in the UK twice before, the last time twenty years ago. As such, the new production could be seen as an example of conservatism, of returning to what Buckingham *et al.* (1999) disapprovingly call 'The Great Tradition' of British children's television. 'The Great Tradition', the title of F. R. Leavis's classic critique of the English novel, was a term used by Jay Blumler in his 1992 report about the future of British children's television to establish a set of canonical values in children's television which should be preserved. Yet another 'great tradition' was invoked in the 1996 production of *The Prince and the Pauper*, with conscious allusion made to an earlier prestigious BBC series, *The Six Wives of Henry VIII* (1970) starring Keith Michell. Michell was cast as the dying king again – this time without the necessity for ageing makeup.

Buckingham *et al.* (1999, p. 49) disapprove of Blumler's 'great tradition' mode of characterising children's culture as 'the cornerstone of public service, an embodiment of "quality" and of a distinctively British cultural identity'. However, whenever a historical classic is reinterpreted, as much can be revealed about contemporary ideological preoccupations as about the actual history represented in the story, as Julian Fellowes (interviewed for the BBC study in summer, 1996), the producer, was well aware:

I suppose that . . . now we have a rather different attitude to politics and royalty . . . that does allow one to examine the predicament of the prince, and particularly the pauper who is living the life of the prince, in a different way . . . twenty years ago that wouldn't have been the case . . . There are characters in it who do not end happily. There's a burning at the stake . . . and that is really the shock to Edward, that this is being done in his name. This is what finally turns him and converts him.

Fellowes' hope that children would recognise the historical lessons of this sequence, and their relevance to contemporary questions about royalty and the uses and abuses of power, suggests that reinterpretations of classic literary texts are not just a way of playing safe with heritage, middle-class broadcasting. They can also be vehicles for re-examining these texts and their meanings, in the light of contemporary preoccupations. For example, Fellowes defended the representation of the scene showing non-conformists being burnt at the stake (or at least the flames about to be lit) as being a morally educational necessity, a lesson in cultural relativism and tolerance, which would not have been acceptable in a children's drama twenty years ago; he hoped it would have a permanent effect on young audiences:

Ours is not the only generation that have done brutal things and it is possible for things to be done in the name of the things one believes in, that are unacceptable . . . Nothing would give me more pleasure than if someone were to say to me when they were an old man, I remember the moment I got into history was when I saw the burning scene in *The Prince and the Pauper*.

For Fellowes, an experienced producer of period drama, including *Fauntleroy*, and also an actor, authenticity was not opposed to prestige, but an integral ingredient of it, especially in historical drama. He argued the necessity of being faithful, as far as possible, to the known ideological and moral values of the period, and not imposing what he described as contemporary 'political correctness' on characters in the past. In making this point, Fellowes gave a revealing insight into the different ways in which he thought British and American producers approached the task of updating classics and making them acceptable to contemporary audiences. Comparing his own television production of *Fauntleroy*, and the 1980 Hollywood film, he pointed out that, in both cases, the representations of the original author were altered. But Fellowes believed his own approach to adaptation was more authentic, in terms of the historical credibility of the character and the requirements of the period, particularly because it did not underestimate the intelligence of the audience:

I think when you're doing period stuff, you mustn't be afraid of it, you mustn't make it so that Jane Seymour is the only one wearing trousers, and gloves and working as a journalist because it means that within four minutes the audience knows that this is rubbish . . . It's like *Little Lord Fauntleroy* – the difficult character for a modern audience is the mother – why does she go along with it? [her son being taken away to live with his grandfather, an English Duke] . . .When the Americans did a version of it they made her very independent, taking in washing and running an industry which of course was absolute rubbish. But of course, you *are* playing to modern audiences, so . . . my Mrs. Errol [agrees, but] lays down her conditions and says well this is fine and . . . I insist on these, and these are not negotiable . . . I felt we carried the audience with that, simply by making her get behind the wheel of the choice.

In our study, a group of 12–13 year olds (the oldest group in the study) were asked to evaluate *The Prince and the Pauper*. It was transmitted towards the end of the study, and they were asked to watch the programme week by week, and to make notes of their reactions to it – a task more obviously linked to work the children were doing in school (studying the Tudors in their history classes), than were the other discussion tasks in the research project. In a discussion at the end of the transmission of the series, these school students recognised many of the elements that the production team hoped for – authenticity, production values, contemporary parallels and historical lessons – in their observations, but felt that some essential ingredients were missing:

GIRL 1 We liked the costumes and everybody acted really good, especially Henry VIII who we liked. The scenes that we especially remembered were Henry dying and the last scene, where they did not believe it was really Edward . . . we thought there should have been a bit more action, a sword fight or something like that.

The following boy recognised, as Fellowes had done, the importance of intertextual supporting material for historical, costumed shows such as this and had proposals for different kinds of scheduling:

BOY 1 We thought that the show should be twice a week but shorter and we also thought that there should be more publishing between the films . . . it fitted into our history lesson and what we are doing on Henry VIII . . . We also thought that the purpose of this show was to learn about history and for people to watch the BBC . . . the whole thing must have been quite expensive, with the costumes, scenery and the buildings.

This boy astutely recognised the value of historical drama as a national and international showcase for the production values of British film and television, especially those of the BBC. Julian Fellowes believes that this kind of creative attention to design, casting, costume and attention to detail, is part of why the BBC has a valued international reputation for 'quality', which then becomes a self-fulfilling prophecy for BBC productions:

I think the great power of the BBC is that people like to work for the BBC. For instance, in this, we were able to attract a calibre of performers for quite small parts, which if it was not a BBC children's drama, we would probably not be able to attract. Locations are happier for us to use them because it's the BBC. We've got a wonderful director of photography who is absolutely top standard; the chance of getting him to do a funny little children's drama for an unknown company is very slight, but [he will] because it's a BBC drama.

It can be galling for producers and executives in the British commercial system for costume drama to be consistently equated with the BBC, as it certainly is in the USA, where many people believed that London Weekend's *Upstairs Downstairs*, shown on PBS' Masterpiece Theatre, had been produced by the BBC, when so many classic adaptations have, in fact, come from ITV. In 1998–9 alone, ITV produced (along with US co-producers) adaptations of *Tess of the D'Urbervilles*; *Oliver Twist* and *The Turn of the Screw*. However, the fact remains that most children's/family classic adaptations and costume drama are now the province of the BBC's limited Sunday 'teatime' slot, and the classic drama serial as a staple ingredient of weekday schedules has gone. Painstaking, expensive, adaptations of children's books for one-off screenings at special times of year, such as Christmas, like Carlton/Central's award-winning *Goodnight Mr. Tom* (1998) starring John Thaw, offer some outlet for prestige productions, but productions screened once or twice a year are not going to provide the regular 'training' in codes, narratives and aesthetics, which Bourdieu talked about. Nor can they raise for children, on a regular basis, the kinds of political and ideological questions discussed by Fellowes (interviewed for the BBC study in summer, 1996), Blumler (1992) and Buckingham *et al.* (1999). As this 11-year-old girl illustrated, drama needs to have more regular slots to satisfy tastes for different kinds of genre:

I think CBBC is a really good idea. It has plenty of drama, but too much *Blue Peter* . . . It should not be on three times a week . . . When CBBC tries to put on comedy programmes, I do not think they're funny at all. Also *Julia Jekyll and Harriet Hyde* is a bit rubbish! There should be more funny programmes that actually are funny.

Art and life, 'reality and fantasy'

The task in the study which provided a particularly focused opportunity for children's critical judgements to be explored was a task given to a whole school group of 5–11 year olds in Co. Durham. This task was to explore the use of fantasy, and its relationship with reality in a BBC drama programme which had been exceptionally popular with the child audience in 1996 – so popular that its 60 per cent share put it into the top ten of all programmes watched by children, including adult programmes, a rare ratings feat for a children's show. The popularity and public debate surrounding this programme meant that it turned up a number of times in the research, eliciting a variety of different kinds of discussion and criteria for evaluation as drama. *The Demon Headmaster* was also a book adaptation, but, as Anna Home (interviewed for the BBC study in 1996), Head of Children's Programming at the BBC at the time, admitted, not a classic: 'it's good children's literature, not great children's literature'. The first series of the programme was based on *The Demon Headmaster* and *The Prime Minister's Brain*, by Gillian Cross, initially published in 1982 and 1985 respectively, and adapted into one six-part serial by Helen Cresswell for the BBC in 1996. The TV programme appeared in Britain at a time when schooling, discipline and curriculum reorganisation, as well as anxieties about the potential criminal uncontrollability of the video-watching young, in the wake of the James Bulger murder by two 10 year olds in 1993, were still very much on the political agenda, which made it a potentially interesting text to discuss for a whole variety of reasons.

The first TV series, as in the books, had a classic fairy tale structure of a group of isolated children outwitting and defeating a monstrous adult; the central protagonist was a young 12-year-old girl, Dinah Hunter, a Cinderella-like character, an initially unloved orphan in a foster-family. The second series, broadcast in 1997, was set in a bio-technical research station, run by a resurrected Demon Headmaster, and involved the same group of children thwarting his plans to 'speed up evolution' by manipulating DNA. Central to the theme of this series was the Head's intention to 'bypass childhood'. The third series in 1998 was set in a university; in this scenario, the once-again resurrected Demon Head took over a powerful university computer in order to pursue world-domination, and his defeat was brought about by a network of children around the UK using the Internet to blow up the computer's circuits with bombardments of childish nonsense-rhymes.

One of the pleasurable aspects of the series was the way in which the story subverted popular discourses about the 'dumbing-down' effect of popular culture on children's minds by showing that it was, in fact, the Head's methods of formal education which produced this effect, while popular entertainment forms, such as game shows and jokes, were seen to be not only intellectually challenging and empowering, but also the instruments of the tyrant's downfall. Much of this highly topical quality is due to Cross's original and prophetic story, published in 1982 when the attack on progressive education methods, now in full-swing in 2000, was only just beginning under Mrs Thatcher's Conservative government. Cross's text (p. 86, 1995 edition) describes Dinah's realisation that the Head was using hypnotism 'to make us learn things parrot-fashion'. Dinah's foster-brother comments: 'A quick way to produce a school full of geniuses', and Dinah corrects him: 'We're not learning to *think*. We're just learning to repeat things. Like robots. It looks good but it's no use at all.'

This deadening of the child's curiosity and creativity is portrayed by Cross (p. 86) as having sinister political implications. As Dinah points out, 'He's got a whole army of people who'll do and say exactly as he wants. Why should he stop there?' When the Head's plan is thwarted at the end of the first book, he turns on Dinah: 'Do you realise what you have done, you stupid girl? You have destroyed this country's chance of becoming the first properly organised, truly efficient country in the world.' The story thus makes particularly explicit the link between particular styles of education, and particular styles of government. The radical aspect of Cross's text, which makes it contemporary in terms of current debates about childhood (see chapter 3) is that childhood and childish playfulness are seen in *The Demon Headmaster* as an integral defence of political liberty against totalitarianism, and, as such, an indispensable ingredient of any libertarian model of a public sphere. Dinah and her child allies between them, are alone able to work towards the downfall of the Head's project, using, with ironic appropriateness, the technology of contemporary childhood entertainment.

As Hodge and Tripp (1986, p. 101), pointed out, 'the problem of reality and its definition has within it a continuing political dimension'. The ability of children to tell the difference between fact and fiction and the issue of who shapes the version of reality that is offered to children, are thus fundamental to debates about televised representations and children's relationship with them. Thus, *The Demon Headmaster*, the biggest popular hit of children's television drama in the 1990s, seemed a particularly appropriate text for detailed examination in the study. The task chosen focused on children's perceptions of what was real and believable, or otherwise, and why, in the Demon Headmaster stories. In order to generate discussion, children, as usual, working in groups, in the whole-school stage were asked to generate lists of unlikely events in an episode from the second series, about the abolition of childhood. In the second, single small-group stage, the group was asked to rank the events generated by the class from the *least* to the most possible, giving reasons for their choices. The list of impossibilities produced by the large group between them fell broadly into two categories. The first category was based on scientific reasoning:

You can't speed up evolution.

There couldn't be a giant egg [referring to the egg which hatched the DNA-manipulated lizard in the DH's biotechnology lab].

There is no giant wasp [referring to a genetically-manipulated wasp which stung one of the child characters].

No one could turn into a lizard [referring to the combination of Dinah's DNA with the lizard's DNA by the Head].

There couldn't really be those giant creepers [genetically manipulated plants which grew so fast that they alerted Dinah and her group to what the DH was doing].

The second group of unlikely events was to do with human motivations and judgements about likely human behaviour:

No-one can take over the world.

You can't hypnotise people.

You can't kill Dinah.

The Demon Headmaster wanted to rule the world – not very likely.

Hypnosis was seen as the most plausible event, and 'turning someone into a giant lizard' the least plausible.

Through this task, children's awareness of 'authenticity' and the kinds of production features which either contributed to it, or detracted from it, were made explicit. So were their readings of the programme's ideologies. Discussing whether it was possible that the Demon Headmaster might kill Dinah, one girl, aged 9, pointed out: 'yes – anything's possible on TV'. The same girl, deploying 'real-world' expectations of human behaviour, also agreed with her group that no 'real headmaster', including their own, would behave like the Demon Head, but this claim became the starting-point for a discussion, going beyond the events in the programme, but obviously stimulated by them, in which the possibilities of adult violence towards children were acknowledged.

The possibility that real life was 'not all sunny' (Bettelheim, 1976, p. 4) emerged from these discussions of the likelihood, or otherwise, of a head teacher killing a pupil:

GIRL 1   I think this one [is not likely] – the Demon Headmaster wanting to kill Dinah. He only wanted to in the programme, I don't think he'd do it in real life.

BOY 2   Yeah [inflection suggesting 'yes, he would'].

GIRL 1   Some headmasters would. It's not just about headmasters . . . Headmasters could want to kill. Not Mr D. [their own headmaster], he wouldn't.

GIRL 1   Supposing he got really psyched up? . . .

BOY 1   Not Mr D., he wouldn't.

GIRL 2   Not Mr D.

The girl who said 'it's not just about headmasters' was recognising the fact that the programme was a parable about power and its abuses which went beyond a story about school. The point was then passed over as several other children came in with a desire to discuss their own head teacher. The children were clearly not fearful of their own head (who at one point walked across the hall where this discussion was taking place, and there was loud laughter). Nevertheless, the possibility that a head could kill a pupil was voted as the second most plausible event in the list, after hypnosis – obviously a recognition of the 'less sunny' possibilities of life.

This group also indicated an awareness of the underlying philosophies of the programme, for instance in a series of exchanges concerning the possibility of getting rid of childhood:

GIRL 1   It would be impossible to get rid of childhood.

BOY 1   It's necessary to start your life. It gives you things like . . .

GIRL 2   Freedom.

BOY 2   You'd have to get rid of every child in the world as well.

Their construction of childhood as a state of freedom recognised the programme's representation of adult institutional authority (in its most extreme form) as a state of repression, and of childhood as a state which was inimical to this. These children also saw childhood as synonymous with individual children: to destroy childhood, as one girl put it, 'you'd have to get rid of every child in the world'. In this, their definition of childhood differs from sociological and anthropological definitions of 'childhood' as primarily a cultural construct. For these children, 'childhood' is synonymous with 'every child'.

From the outset, as with Hodge and Tripp's research, these children's discussions about reality and the boundaries of the possible were focused on modality issues – the extent to which forms and conventions of the medium signified greater, or lesser, degrees of 'reality' and realism. Like some adult scholars, they also hypothesised the ability to tell fantasy from reality as a possible defence against harmful effects. Later in the discussion, the children returned again to the topic of the abuse of power, this time discussing the possibility of turning somebody into a lizard, which Girl 1 saw as unlikely, not in terms of its scientific plausibility, but in terms of the human motivation of the Headmaster:

GIRL 1   Miss, even if you really hated somebody you wouldn't have enough aggression to turn somebody into a lizard.

INTERVIEWER   OK so we believe that people wouldn't go that far? Do you believe that people are basically too good for that?

BOY 1, BOY 2, GIRL 1   Too good, too good, too good . . .

INTERVIEWER   So who do you think is going to win? The goodies or the baddies? [The children had not seen the final episode of the story at this stage.]

CHORUS   The good.

GIRL 1   The good always win.

BOY 1   I'd like to see a programme where the bad guy wins; just once.

The discussion about the modality of the programme – what was likely, and what was not – allowed children to use the fantasy world of the story to examine the boundaries, both of real-world reality and of narrative plausibility, and to test out and extend their limits. The examination of fantasy, and the narrative possibilities it permits, placed the discussions at a safer distance – a place where bad guys could 'come back'. In a story, the possibilities of the bad guy winning are legitimate; in reality, the prospect of Mr D. killing a pupil, was rejected and turned into a joke, although the possibilities of some other headmaster – a 'normal' person with 'evil thoughts underneath' – killing a pupil were accepted.

The goodness of children

In traditional children's narrative, children are the main protagonists in a world where they find themselves without adult support, as is the case in *The Demon Headmaster*. It is a necessary convention of the empowering function of children's fiction, as Hunt (1994) has pointed out, that it is always children, not adults, who are sufficiently open-minded to be contacted by ET, to recognise the corruption of aristocratic power, or to resist the hypnotic enslavement of *The Demon Headmaster*. A basic element of children's narrative is that adults do not listen to children, and this is a basic element of childhood experience also.

The idea that some childhood experiences, such as the experience of not being heeded, are universal, is sometimes treated sceptically. For example, Bazalgette and Staples (1995, p. 96) point out: 'the idea that children can transcend or ignore national, ethnic and religious boundaries has an obvious appeal to anyone wanting to prove that such boundaries are unnatural constructs.' Anyone 'wanting to prove that such boundaries are unnatural constructs' might thus seem to be allying themselves to imperialist or neo-colonialist ideas about European cultures being the standard whereby all other cultures should be measured, which would be unfortunate. However, carrying cultural relativism, and a necessary recognition of cultural diversity, to the point where children's universal experience of being young, small and dependent is downplayed, can be unhelpful to children, of whatever culture. Failure to recognise the universality of being young, small and disenfranchised, could hamper international attempts to challenge, for instance, increasing media globalisation, and the exploitation of young child-labourers in the production of cultural products for also-exploited Western children (see Klein, 2000, on the topic of the Indonesian manufacture of expensive Nike sports shoes for children in urban American ghettoes). To the extent that children's narratives, especially folk and fairy tales, do seem to share common historical and cultural motifs, including the power of the child to make a difference in a harsh adult world, this idea seems a psychologically valuable one: it infuses children's narrative with a sense of hope, and hope is a necessary ingredient for all people at a stage when the largest part of their lives is still to unfold. The togetherness of children is reflected in the 'gang-hut' meetings of much children's fiction, such as those in *The Demon Headmaster*, where children plan with other children their strategies for coping with the tests confronting them.

In our interviews with producers we found some resistance to the idea that there were ideological sub-texts to stories such as *The Demon Headmaster*, which suggested an adult uneasiness, even in the kinds of liberal and enlightened adults who make children's programmes, about the possibility that children's fiction could be political. For instance, in the interview with Anna Home, the then Head of Children's Programmes at the BBC (Davies and O'Malley, 1996, pp. 139–40), Home was asked what sort of values informed producers' decisions about whether to use controversial material. She replied: 'I don't know what "values" means actually.' The interview then goes on:

INTERVIEWER   For instance watching *The Demon Headmaster*, it seemed to me that it had a strong didactic agenda. It's great fun, but there's clearly a worry about people gaining control over other people, about respect for individual freedom,

AH   Yes, but I don't think that anybody sits down and analyses it like that.

In contrast, the children in the discussion groups were eager to discuss the moral and ideological issues, including moral ambiguity, underlying the story. The Durham children speculated about the psychological motivations of the Demon Head, and how it was possible for someone to behave as he did. They came up with the humanistic notion that anyone can turn out to be evil; evil does not have to be the product of supernatural powers, but can be the product of 'normality', a word used repeatedly:

BOY 1   The Demon Headmaster would want [people] to be normal people.

GIRL 2   Yeah, but he isn't a normal person, is he? He wants everybody to be like him.

BOY 1   He's just a normal person who hypnotises people and has normal evil thoughts; he's just a normal person underneath.

In the debate at the primary school in Buckinghamshire, which required children to discuss whether the programme should be banned, moral dimensions also appeared. Inevitably, given the task, the discourse from the children in this school was more focused on audiences and their responses, than on content. But one 11-year-old girl defended the programme, in the terms of Brechtian aesthetics, because it was 'good', and stressed the moral significance of the solitary child/group of children, standing bravely alone against a hostile society:

It is the way it is not just based on straightforward school children finding it out – they are school children but they are a bit different from everyone else. They have their own gang and they don't go to assemblies and things, because they do their own thing – it's not just these children find something out – it's these children are alone and nobody else will believe them.

This group took the opportunity of discussing the 'suitability' or otherwise of *The Demon Headmaster* to draw some distinctions between it and other dramatic genres – they were particularly explicit on the subject of fantasy:

GIRL 1   Children don't just want to watch what is real they want fantasy, they don't just want to watch what happens every day – they know what happens because they see it in their own home – they want to see something that is really unbelievable.

Later on, Boy 2 (below) articulated a key difference between children's and adults' drama for him, drawing on the generic category of 'children's', a category which cuts across other generic categories, such as soap opera, or fantasy, or horror, just as the state of 'childhood' cuts across other demographic categories (see chapter 7). For this boy, when a programme is *classified* as 'children's', children watching are able to feel safe. This sense comes partly from a generic knowledge of children's programmes as stories which do not, as a rule, include terrible, unresolvable events. They are, through being defined as 'children's', fantasies, no matter how many signifiers of realism they may include. This discussion of 'children's' versus 'adults' thus returned to the question of realism again. As the discussion gathered momentum, the question of realism led inevitably to the question of 'use': several children pointed out that the whole function of stories, whether realistic, or fantastic, is precisely to get away from the mundane. The means for doing this, as these media-literate children were aware, were narrative and production features, suspense, narrative 'hooks', and 'letting your mind escape'.

BOY 2   Not everybody wants to watch things that happen every day, because things like *Cracker* or *The Bill* have always got drugs or someone trying to kill someone else, but in programmes like *The Demon Headmaster*, if someone says they are going to try and kill somebody you know they are just making it up. There are programmes like *Byker Grove*, and they are just all about real life, but this is like fantasy and what doesn't happen – you can't really believe it, but you just want to watch it.

GIRL 1   At the end, if you get to a good bit when something is just about to happen – it finishes and so you want to watch the next episode and you can get hooked watching it again.

GIRL 2   You don't just want to watch all soaps and dramas and things, because you want to have something to let your mind just escape.

9 Animation

> In cartoons you can do anything, you can do anything really, you can make anything happen, as long as you can draw it. With films, I really like films, because it's real people and they are doing things sort of like more clear and more firm – the colours – and you can see all the things that are happening and it makes you feel it is true. While in cartoons you know it is only drawings.   Girl, 7, outer-London primary school

As this little girl was able to explain, animation is a form of filmed storytelling in which, instead of actors performing live, still drawings or models are used to portray actions; each frame portrays a minute element of a movement, either drawn, or modelled (as with clay-mation, or model figures) or computer-generated, which when projected at 24 frames a second, simulate movement. Animation as a technique is thus very far from being representationally realistic in the way that photographic images are; as such, the form presents a number of challenges for scholars interested in evaluating children's understanding of and critical responses to media (for example, Hodge and Tripp, 1986). Animation is a genre extremely popular with children, and one which has aroused some concern about the social impact of its exaggerated representations of extreme violence (for example, Gerbner *et al.*, 1978; Kline, 1993). But, as this child's comments make clear, it is a genre whose basic technique makes a profound difference to the way the events portrayed are interpreted: they are '*only* drawings'. Animation, as this girl points out, is not bound by the rules of realism applying to live human characters, and from this many other kinds of judgements follow.

In her introduction to *A Reader in Animation Studies* (1997), Jayne Pilling, its editor, argues that the 'brilliant' commercial and artistic success of Walt Disney, in the 1920s and 1930s, created a model for the form as a children's medium, which has overshadowed other, more adult and experimental possibilities for it. Disney's choice of fairy tales

225

for his animated feature films, and of comic stories based on animal characters (Mickey Mouse, Donald Duck) obviously contributed to animation being seen as particularly appealing to children, but this has led, claims Pilling (p. xi), to a tension between animation seen on the one hand, as a serious branch of cinematic art, and on the other, as 'cartoons for kiddies':

Following Disney's audacious gamble on the animated feature film, animation became defined by the Disney model – that of the cartoon as child/family entertainment and as such, a no-go area for most film critics and theorists other than as material for ideological/sociological analysis.

The fact that child/family entertainment should be a no-go area for critics and theorists is certainly the case, but it is curious that it should be so. As discussed earlier in this book, there is no inevitable reason why media directed specifically at children should not be seen as capable of critical/theoretical analysis. Pilling's collection of essays on animation is a welcome recognition that animation is a serious art-form (although it does not refer to a more recent development in the form: the revival of the prime-time cartoon for adults as a vehicle for social satire and stylistic experimentation – *The Simpsons*; *King of the Hill*; *South Park*; *Futurama*). But, as Pilling says, animation's association with children has meant that not only is animation seen as unworthy of critical attention, but also, because of its commercial success, it has been seen primarily of interest as an economic, political and psycho-social phenomenon, rather than an aesthetic one.

Part of the difficulty of seeing animation as an art-form, and, further, as a serious *children's* art-form (and one theme of this book is that there are such things as children's art-forms with particular criteria which are different from adults'), is, as Pilling asserts, the problem of Disney. Many writers, including Walt Disney himself, have claimed artistic status for his products – Robert Field's *The Art of Walt Disney* appeared as long ago as 1942. Since then, however, the word 'Disney' has become more identified with the hegemonic process of global 'Disneyfication', than with the quality of Disney's stories, or with the developing artistry of his, and the studio's, animation techniques (see, for example, Wasko, 1996). The word Disney, despite the continuing beauty and ingenuity of many of the studio's products, as, for example, the recently restored *Fantasia*, and *Toy Story II*, has become synonymous, not with art, but with industry, not with storytelling, but with empire-building. Disney has become, as Eric Smoodin (1994, p. 3) puts it: 'a type of American cultural icon, the systems builder'. Smoodin (p. 3) likens Disney to Thomas Edison and Henry Ford:

While celebrated for individual artifacts, Disney was actually the master of vast 'technological systems' to use Thomas Hughes's term. These systems involved 'far more than the so-called hardware, devices, machines, and processes', but also the 'transportation, communication and information networks that interconnect them' and the array of employees and regulations that make them run.

This alone should surely encourage the scholarly community to see the necessity of taking children's cultural products seriously. Nevertheless, Disney's success notwithstanding, the animation form has suffered not only from being associated with children and families, but also from being associated with a particularly ruthless branch of the American television industry: toy-led cartoons, and the linking of the commercial profitability of the toy industry, with the provision of programmes for children. As Stephen Kline (1993) has claimed, this has led to a massive deterioration of quality and range in the provision of televised entertainment for children in the United States in the past two decades.

Cartoons on television

Although animation was traditionally associated with cinema, and, for many writers in Pilling's collection, in its art-house forms, still is, television has provided a new source of demand for the animator's art, and cartoons are now the dominant genre on all children's schedules in both the USA and the UK and in many European countries. Animation is also, of course, a staple of TV advertising techniques. The comedy-animal tradition, begun with Mickey and Donald, continued through Warner's Looney Tunes, with their *Tom and Jerry*, still to be found in British children's schedules; it has been carried on by the highly successful Hanna Barbera company, creators of *Yogi Bear* and *Top Cat*, staples of children's TV schedules since the 1960s. Disney's animated feature films, based on traditional tales and motifs, continue to be regularly produced, aimed at a family audience, and with rigorously controlled dissemination of videos, and other products and toys linked to the movies through especially timed cross-promotion in stores and restaurants, including Disney's own theme parks. This style of cross-media promotion – both 'vertical' and 'horizontal integration' – has been profitably followed by other producers of films, programmes and toys. Disney also has its own television channel. The Disney-led association of animation with, first, children and, second, commerce, has, according to Pilling, been disadvantageous to the form's aesthetic status.

A major reason for the centrality of animation in children's television, particularly in the USA, but also in other parts of the world importing

US products, is, according to Kline (1993, p. 279), its relationship with merchandising: 'Contemporary children's culture exists because merchandising interests are willing to invest in the production of children's television.' Kline, writing from the perspective of a concerned, liberal parent, interested 'in the relationship between television and socialization', questions whether such a system is compatible with programme quality: weakness in storylines and character development he argues, are 'cast aside' by programmers: 'producing good fiction and effective marketing are not always harmonious goals'.

Thus the vexed question of 'quality' is raised, with the implication being that the cartoon form is intrinsically inferior to other kinds of storytelling, because so many of its exemplars are formulaic products of marketing-led corporate initiatives. In the discussion of the toy-led, marketing-led world of (American) children's culture, which is by no means a universal culture, and is not accepted as such by those who run broadcasting in the UK and in Europe, concerns about corporate exploitation of children, cynical lack of attention to storytelling quality, effects on child audiences, the flooding of schedules with a majority of animation programmes (Davies and Corbett, 1997) and the deceptively improvisatory nature of the genre itself, are all conflated into one large, single area of concern. These issues need to be separated, and some of the children's comments in the study help to do this.

Criticising cartoons

Jayne Pilling is right that critical theory sees children's material as 'off limits', but at least, as discussed in earlier chapters, in the realm of children's literature, these limits have begun to be challenged. Children's literature suffers from the problem of 'use'; it is perceived to be 'good' when it trains, enculturates, sets good examples, inspires and provides stimulating cultural experiences for the developing imagination. Peter Hunt (1991, p. 5) argues: 'Just as critical theory now concerns itself with everything in and surrounding the text, from personal response and political background to language and social structure, so children's literature is a field which takes in every genre of writing.' In critical theory, argues Hunt (and Pilling's comment supports him) children's literature is a non-subject: 'it is simple, ephemeral, popular and designed for an immature audience'. The existence of children's literature and culture, whether classic fiction, or *Pokémon* and *Rugrats*, teaches us that we cannot analyse or critique children's material, by definition, without considering what it *means* to be a product aimed at children: what are 'children', what do they like, need, think, how do they respond?

Children's culture demands a consideration of the audience, if only to justify the classification of something as 'children's'. It could be proposed – and many children in our study would certainly propose – that critical/theoretical approaches to culture, rather than denigrating 'use' as a criterion of evaluation, do not pay enough attention to 'use'. 'Children's' material teaches us that 'use' must be taken into account. It reminds us that writers and artists and cinematic auteurs are in the marketplace, writing to perceived audiences, and different groups within audiences. It reminds us that it is necessary to recognise how different audiences 'read' cultural material, and position themselves in multiple roles in relation to it: whether as consumer, family-member, 'little kid', 'big kid', school student, boy, girl, citizen, critic/theorist – or respondent in a research study, exploring (usually) only one of these forms of response. In hardly any area of media output, as Pilling's comments suggest, are these tensions between text/market/audience/use, so obvious as in the area of animation.

Kiddies' cartoons and butt plugs

One of the major institutional constraints operating on how animator-artists work is the technology of distribution, another is the lucrativeness and popularity of the form for child audiences, particularly in terms of marketing link-ups. Animators' distributional outlet has to be moving-image technology – television or cinema, or computer technology such as CDROMs or the Web – and these, as in the case of cinema, and, to a lesser extent, television, are almost entirely controlled by large commercial operations, who own both production and distribution facilities. Within these global corporate arrangements, the most hospitable outlet for animators' work is children's programme schedules, not least because, as mentioned, one of the ways in which the comparatively high costs of animation can be recouped, is through toy-licensing deals.

The medium of television generally, and not just 'kiddies cartoons', has nearly always been treated primarily as a sociological/psychological phenomenon whose main interest to the academy has been its effects, or 'social impact'. The tension between these two approaches to the medium is articulated in Mark Langer's chapter in Pilling's reader, on the cartoon *Ren and Stimpy*. This was originally commissioned as a children's show, but, in its attempts to 'push the envelope' towards a more 'adult' form (that is, more explicitly scatological and obscene), it ran into trouble with its distributors, the children's channel Nickelodeon, and its original creator, John Kricfalusi, was sacked from the programme. As Langer explains, this was partly because his obsession with farts and butts was bringing complaints from the Federal Communications Commission, the regulatory body in the USA, and especially because it was scaring away Mattel, the toy company, who had a deal to produce toys based on the show's characters.

Kricfalusi, the creator of the show, first ran into trouble with the Standards and Practices department at Nickelodeon because he wanted to include episodes such as 'Ren and Stimpy Bugger Christmas' and 'Stimpy's First Fart'. Nickelodeon had a deal with Mattel to produce Ren and Stimpy products – but these, of course, had to be aimed at children to be profitable. As Langer (1999, p. 157) points out: 'Positioning *Ren and Stimpy* outside of a juvenile taste group might have jeopardised the popularity of the series among potential Mattel toy purchasers, adversely affecting the value of the licence and the profitability of *Ren and Stimpy* to Nickelodeon.' Kricfalusi's partner in Spumco Bob Camp's idea for possible spin-off products included (Langer, 1999 p. 157): 'Enema bags, butt plugs . . . toys that leak on you and explode in your face – *real* fun stuff!' It is likely that such products would have had enormous appeal to children – but, of course, it is not children who are the primary purchasers in the toy market, but adults. Parents and relatives who might be willing to go along with Teletubbies, or Tamogochi crazes, would probably be less willing to walk into a toy store and ask for 'butt plugs', no matter how much their children might pester them.

Langer also points out the appeal of cartoons for adults, which is different from their appeal for children. In keeping with Pilling's call for animation to be recognised as an art-form, for Langer it is the appeal of 'hipness'. What he calls 'animatophiles' are similar to the fans and creators of comics, and to other marginalised fan groups such as 'Trekkies, transcendentalists, jazz 78 rpm record collectors'. Hipness, says Langer (1999 p. 147), 'derives its meaning and value from the exclusive nature of the code used by a particular taste group. Once it becomes decipherable by the total culture, it ceases to be exclusive and loses its value to members of the group.'

Hipness as a badge of cultural specialism is a valued category for adults, but it is the very opposite of the value of a plaything for children. Children's play is often based on crazes for particular toys, but exclusivity is much less the appeal than inclusivity is. When something becomes a craze for children, it has to catch on among everyone. Being part of a minority group, with exotic tastes, would not carry the same cachet of street-credibility at all. In a playground culture, often based on suspicion and bullying of children who are 'different', hipness can be a distinct drawback. The universality of appeal of favoured toys and programmes among children is what marketers find so valuable. It is only when the *majority* of children become attached to a show or product, as they regularly do, but for a comparatively short time, that the product is worth licensing and selling.

Marsha Kinder (1991), in a critical examination of the postmodern, multi-referential appeal of cartoons, the toy market, advertising and children's fantasy play, proposes 'use' again – a positive, cognitive use for these children's crazes. She argues that they have an intellectual function, permitting cultural cross-referencing and cognitive bootstrapping. Intertextual references can only have meaning and value when a lot of other people 'get' them. It is the cognitive task of developing children to discover the main rules and conventions of what other people 'get'; indeed, this is the process whereby language first develops – the deduction of underlying grammatical rules in the speech of the people around them, such as how to form plurals, which will be generally, if sometimes mistakenly, applied (for example, the way young children talk about 'sheeps' in English). Similarly, storytelling and other cultural products offer lessons in the rules of narrative and cultural text-formation; it is the child's task to infer what these rules and underlying structures are.

There are problematic aspects to this, in terms of delivering child audiences to exploitation from toy manufacturers and their allies, as Kline, and more recently Naomi Klein (2000), in her book about corporate branding, point out. But it does not follow that these relationships, despite distributors' wariness about fart jokes, should be artistically limiting, as only one example of a popular, and brilliant, ratings-topping cartoon – *The Simpsons*, produced for Rupert Murdoch's Fox Channel in the USA – demonstrates. Nor can the link between cartoons and toys always be seen as a harmful one for individual children. Hilton (1996, p. 42) points out: '. . . taking risks, deferring gratification. This is what the toy industry knows so well, its figures offering an enticing invitation to enter the pleasurable, autonomous dilatory space in a familiar narrative.'

It certainly does not make the animators' work unworthy of critical attention. Indeed, *Ren and Stimpy* have followed a fairly well-trodden path (see Pearson and Uricchio's collection of essays on *The Batman*, 1991) in which popular culture forms of storytelling are commissioned and broadcast for the mass, or family audience, become popular with, and extensively critiqued by, this mass audience, and then, much later, when their interestingness has been safely sanctioned by public acceptance, they become noticed by critics. Although not decrying the desirability of professional critical attention to popular forms, such as children's animation, it is necessary to remember, as our children's comments demonstrate, that a lack of published professional criticism does not mean that no criticism has been going on.

Popular culture is always first critiqued by the populace, as David Bianculli (1992) has documented in his account of the way American audiences develop 'tele-literacy'. Sub-groups of this large 'mass audience' for popular culture go on to become fans and 'cultists', developing considerable specialised expertise on a given popular text, such as *Star Trek* or *Xena – Warrior Princess* which may surpass that of academic analysts (see for example, Jenkins' book *Textual Poachers* (1992) and Tulloch and Jenkins (1995) on the fans of *Dr Who* and *Star Trek*.) Academics catch up with these trends quite a long time after the public, including fans, have started them. In fact, the first critics of a popular text even precede the populace; they are its producers and their workmates. John Marsden (interviewed for the BBC study in spring, 1996), Head of Animation at Carlton/Central UK, argued that there were strong opinions among the 'animation community' about national differences in animation styles which, despite globalisation and the ease of dubbing voices, were hard to eradicate. When co-productions *did* try to eradicate them, and to formulate a multinational style, the result, he argued, was an artistic failure:

It's amazing how people still stick to their style . . . *The Animals of Farthing Wood* [a BBC co-produced animated series about woodland animals, made with several European partners] was a mess. I'm sure it worked commercially, but . . . the scriptwriters were pulling in different directions . . . I could see that they'd got everybody chipping in their comments within this Euro development situation, all these different countries got their input, politically correct for those countries – it lost all the spike, all the fun, just a big grey melting pot.

Marsden pointed out that his colleagues at Carlton had learned from this that the best co-production situation, artistically, was two partners. More than this was, he said, 'disastrous'. Marsden's comments, as comments from producers often do, illustrate how inseparable questions of creativity, artistry, technology and distribution can be. Animation, as an internationally popular form, and also one which travels everywhere because of its use of dubbing, is a particularly relevant topic for the kinds of negotiations described by Marsden.

Bulk animation

The quantitative amount of airtime devoted to animation is seen as an important indicator of the quality, or otherwise, of a children's television schedule; the more animation in the schedule (especially the more imported American animation) the more the guardians of public service values are likely to be worried. In a report produced for the British Broadcasting Standards Council (now Commission) Blumler (1992, p. 4) expressed concern that: 'By 1991 the mainstream services (BBC1 and ITV) were devoting over half their scheduling time to animation and other predominantly entertaining formats, compared with between a quarter and a third of the corresponding minutage in 1981.' Blumler's survey looked at the years 1981 to 1991, and in 1997 it was followed up by a report written by a colleague and myself at the London College of Printing, also published by the Broadcasting Standards Commission. In our survey of the five years (inclusive) between 1992 and 1996, we found that the proportion of airtime in British children's television schedules devoted to animation rose on BBC1, from 9 per cent of the schedule in 1981, to 26 per cent in 1992 to 35 per cent of the schedule in 1996 and from 9 per cent to 40 per cent on ITV during the same period (Davies and Corbett, 1997).

Our definition of animation was the one adopted by the industry – a very broad category, based primarily on technique (that is, stop-frame filming of drawings or models), not on genre. The industry's classification of children's animation thus does not acknowledge any distinction between *The Simpsons, Rugrats, Tom and Jerry* or *Noddy*. We acknowledged in our report that this way of categorising programmes was potentially misleading, and should certainly not form a hard and fast basis for judgements about quality. We pointed out that much animation in the UK is almost entirely aimed at the very young, and should really be categorised as 'Preschool' because it included 'gentle, uneventful series' such as *Noddy, Rupert* and *Paddington Bear*. We further argued (Davies and Corbett, 1997, p. 170), with masterly programmes like *The Simpsons* and *Rugrats* in mind: 'When it comes to intrinsic programme quality, too, animation is often unfairly dismissed as generically inferior. Animation as a technique permits experiments in storytelling and effects which can be more innovative and imaginative than much live action programming.'

These provisos were ignored by the very considerable public comment provoked by the report. Among several other correspondents, Mr Anthony Murphy of Brighton wrote indignantly to the *Guardian* newspaper (7 November 1997) claiming: 'obviously the Commission is unaware of the quality included in some modern cartoons, such as . . . *Rugrats* (BBC1)'. Mr Murphy, like many commentators in the public sphere of the newspaper correspondence columns, had not read our report. However, neither the authors nor the Broadcasting Standards Commission regretted the public debate, informed or not; critics' lack of attention to the fine print is an occupational hazard of public comment. The BSC survey, by placing children's programming and its composition decisively on to the public agenda, fulfilled an object not often achieved – the object of making children's issues publicly central in cultural debates.

Another finding less prominently discussed in the press coverage was the contribution of the increase in channels to the decrease in programming diversity (some newspaper groups, such as Rupert Murdoch's News Corporation, have financial stakes in the new channels). In a summary of findings across all channels – the then four terrestrial channels (a fifth, Channel 5 has since been added) and five satellite/cable channels, including Nickelodeon and Disney – we found that the amount of animation had increased overall in direct relationship to the contribution of the new satellite/cable channels. When the output of all the channels, both terrestrial and cable/satellite, was aggregated, 66 per cent of children's programming in 1996 was animation. Drama (on cable/satellite, entirely imported American drama, such as *Sister, Sister*) accounted for 17 per cent of children's output; entertainment programming (for example, games and quizzes) 9 per cent, preschool programming 6 per cent and factual programming a tiny 2 per cent. Thus, allowing for the fact that, within the category of animation, there was a range of genres and a great deal of what diverse writers described as high-quality programming, the fact remained that far from increasing programme diversity and choice, the effect of the new competition to the established channels had been to narrow the overall range of genres – even as defined in these very broad and inclusive categories – in children's programming. This is not what the children who carried out scheduling exercises in our study were calling for.

Children's views on cartoons

The quantitative questionnaire had revealed some intriguing attitudes to cartoons on the part of the children in the sample, which we wanted to pursue. For instance, in the questionnaire responses, animation as a genre seemed to be appropriated by the youngest children specifically for themselves. Although cartoons were popular with all ages of children, only in the case of the youngest, did a majority agree that: 'Cartoons are *only* for little children.' Fifty-four per cent of 5 and 6 year olds (seven out of ten 5 year olds, and 52 per cent of 6 year olds) agreed with this statement, whereas 7 year olds and upwards had a majority of children *dis*agreeing with it. There was emphatic disagreement among 10, 11 and 12 year olds – around three-quarters of this age group said it was 'not true' that cartoons were only for little children. Given that all children liked cartoons, this difference in responses suggested that many of the youngest children categorised themselves 'as little children' (which sevens and upwards did not want to do) and were more likely to see animation as a genre particularly targeted at them.

Other questionnaire data on cartoons had shown age differences too: 75 per cent of 6, 7 and 8 year olds chose *Rugrats* in preference to *Byker Grove* in the two channel choice exercise (see chapters 1 and 4), whereas a majority of 12 year olds (53 per cent) preferred the drama. In the ten-channel choice, the most highly favoured programmes among all age groups were cartoons, or cartoon-like action adventures: among 6 year olds the highest 'ratings' in our simulated choice exercise went to *Power Rangers* (25 per cent), *Ace Ventura* (23 per cent) and *Scooby Doo* (27 per cent). Among 7 year olds, 22 per cent chose *Power Rangers*, 23 per cent chose *Ace Ventura*, and 18 per cent chose *Scooby Doo*. There was a change of taste as the age range went up: among 8 year olds, *Ren and Stimpy* (12 per cent) attracted more votes than *Scooby Doo* (10 per cent) or *Power Rangers* (also 10 per cent). *Ren and Stimpy* was the most popular cartoon with 11 year olds (17 per cent chose it) as against only 4 per cent of this age group for *Scooby Doo*. Buckingham *et al.* (1999 p. 139) point out 'the distinctiveness' of children's audiences, compared to adult ones, by comparing the differences in popularity between the top thirty adult shows watched by adults, and the kinds of adult shows preferred by children – which tend to be 'cartoonish' such as *Mr Bean* and *Gladiators*. Our study further showed that, within the category 'children', there is even further variation in taste for cartoons and cartoonishness, depending on age.

Cartoons turned up several times in the qualitative comments in the questionnaire, too, and again, they were used by children as a way of categorising themselves as 'young' or 'old' in their tastes, for example, this 11-year-old girl from a secondary school in Middlesbrough:

Children's television is brilliant! It has a lot of programmes for young and older children which I like because even though I am 11 coming up 12 next year, I still watch *Rugrats*, *Tom and Jerry*, etc. I'm always watching television.

Others expressed a desire for more access to the 'adult' cartoons, for example these two, from a Milton Keynes primary school:

I wish that *Superman* and *The Simpsons* could be on every day when I got home from school. (Child (gender not specified), 9, inner-city primary school, Milton Keynes)

I think you should put . . . *Beavis and Butthead* on BBC and Sky 1 at 8 till 9 p.m. (Boy, 11, inner-city primary school, Milton Keynes)

A 9-year-old girl in an inner-London primary school, one of those who agreed 'cartoons are only for little children', was a Disney fan. The only programmes she mentioned were Disney's, and clearly, for her, the cartoon form meant something different from what it meant to those who were fans of *The Simpsons* and *Rugrats* – programmes she did not wish to discuss at all:

I like to watch Disney films, my best Disney films are *Pocahontas, Pinocchio, Cinderella, Beauty and the Beast, The Aristocats* and that's all.

Talking about *Rugrats*

As the fieldwork drew to a close, it had become obvious to us that the decision to exclude children under 8 years of age from qualitative tasks, primarily at the request of teachers who felt that organising discussion groups among the younger children would not work well, was too conservative. A number of 6 and 7 year olds, in discussions following the questionnaire, had shown themselves eager and able to debate some of the issues raised in it. Because cartoons were seen to be popular in the questionnaire stages of the study, we felt that we should devote one of the qualitative tasks to the genre, and we decided to use the two-stage task format in one of the last schools to be visited in the study, where the teachers felt confident that their 6–7 year olds could cope with it.

An example of what was generally agreed (as in the correspondence following the 1997 BSC report) to be 'quality' cartoon programming in the current schedule was *Rugrats*, acquired for its first showing in the UK by the BBC, from Nickelodeon USA in 1994, and also later shown on British Nickelodeon in a 'windowing' arrangement – whereby a programme is shared between two channels. *Rugrats* is a story-length American cartoon, produced by Klasky Csupo, part of the Viacom group; it is based on a group of children and babies; adults are featured only in the background. The animation style is distinctive and somewhat grotesque; it is certainly unusual, by comparison with the formulaic, cheaper (because based on fewer drawings) styles of the staple Hanna Barbera tradition, and we were interested to see whether children noticed the 'look' of the programme.

Although *Rugrats* is now a firm favourite with British children, as with children elsewhere in the world, it took a while to become established, as Teresa Plummer Andrews and Michael Carrington (both interviewed for the Broadcasting Standards Commission study in spring, 1997), who bought it for the BBC, explained:

MC And then you get *Rugrats*, which is a unique style. It's huge.

TPA I have to tell you when we bought it was, '. . . we don't know about this'.

MC It established itself over two years.

TPA It took a long time, also when you look at it; it was so different, and the concept was so different, but it was a real flyer. It took two years of *Live and Kicking*, of pushing . . . to establish it.

The children who discussed *Rugrats* were the youngest group in the study – a group of 6 to 7 year olds. The goal of the exercise was first to pay some serious critical attention to the cartoon form, and, second, to provide an opportunity for the 'little kids' to give opinions on a genre which they had so emphatically claimed as their own. The group – in an outer-London infants school – were first shown an episode of the show in a whole-class group. They were then asked to perform a *Ready Steady Cook* type voting exercise, in which they held up one of three colour-coded cards saying either 'Brilliant', 'OK' or 'Not Very Good', to rate seven different aspects of the programme. These were: the characters: Angelica; Josh (both older children – Angelica is a 3 year old, one of the regulars, and 'a bully' according to her creator, Arlene Klasky); 'The Babies' (Tommy, Chucky, The Twins, all toddlers dressed in nappies/ diapers); the story; the jokes; the music; the drawings. The most popular elements of the show were then put in order, again by counting the votes from the whole-class group, listing them on the board and discussing them in a whole-class feedback session.

The most highly rated elements of the programme were The Babies, with 24 'Brilliants' and 1 'Not Very Good', and the drawings, with 19 'Brilliants', 3 'OKs' and 3 'Not Very Goods'. Josh, a 'bad guy', was the most unpopular character with 24 'Not Very Goods' and only 1 'OK' – an example of children's flexible use of the word 'good' to mean, in the case of character, morally good, or admirable, and in the case of production elements, like drawings, to mean well executed. Angelica, the bossy 3 year old, received 6 'Brilliants', 17 'OKs' and 2 'not very goods'. According to an article by Mimi Swartz in *The New Yorker*, 30 November 1998 (p. 60), Angelica is seen as something of a role model in American culture generally, but these children's reception of her was lukewarm. As a regular character, she appeared to be acceptable – 'OK' – but was not generally perceived as 'brilliant' as The Babies. The music received 15 'Brilliants' and 8 'OKs'. Interestingly, given the importance of humour in *Rugrats* – much of it based on the typically adult 'paedocratised' idea of babies being able to talk and act with adult agency (a feature of much advertising on both British and American television) – the jokes were the least approved ingredient after Josh. Ten children thought they were 'Not Very Good' and only 8 thought they were 'Brilliant'.

After the voting – much enjoyed – the children discussed with one of the researchers why The Babies received so many 'Brilliants'. There was a chorus of responses, emphasising pro-social values, 'kindness', and also their centrality in the story. *Pace* Langer, these children's responses illustrate the point that, for the very young, 'cool', or 'hipness', is a less admirable quality than 'kind' – and moreover, the two qualities were seen to be opposed: 'Because they are funny . . . Because they are kind and funny . . . They are in the whole story all the way through . . . They are not cool, they are kind . . . They are the main characters.'

The drawings were the next most highly rated element of the programme, and, in the discussion about why this was, the quality of realism and reality again emerged as a central value. Asked why the drawings were popular, the comments were: 'Because Chucky looks real, very animated.' The interviewer pursued this:

INTERVIEWER   Do they look like real people?

CLASS   No, because they are in a cartoon, but sometimes they make you feel that it is a real story.

INTERVIEWER   So they are well done, they are well animated?

CLASS   They are not real.

INTERVIEWER   What do you mean, they are not real?

CLASS   They are not like popular pictures.

INTERVIEWER   Not like popular pictures. Do they have real people in them?

CLASS   No they are drawings. Well, The Drawings – they draw Chucky, they draw on a piece of paper, they draw a different one and then they flip it.

Although the drawings were popular, one child argued that 'they are not as good as in other cartoons' – perhaps recognising their distinctive, caricatured quality, so different from the standard children's animation style. (This was before the advent of the current 2000 craze, *Pokémon*, with its ultra-minimalist drawings). The interviewer pursued the question of the difference between animation and live action, and asked whether *Rugrats* would be as good if it had 'real people' performing it. Their responses invoked issues of quality, and also technique and the relationship of technique to 'reality'; there was also a (rare) awareness of implications of cost, although animation in fact costs as much as costume drama to produce – something of which these children were only hazily aware:

CLASS   [If it were real people] the voices would be different, it wouldn't be so good.

INTERVIEWER   Any other ideas?

CLASS   If it were real the colours would have changed.

INTERVIEWER   How would the colours change?

CLASS   It is like a black and white film years ago . . .

It it were real it wouldn't look very good, because of the colours and if it was real there would be buildings and cars . . .

If it was real they would need more money so it wouldn't be as good.

After this, as in all the other exercises, a small group of children, one representative from each small group in the whole-class stage, reordered the grouping and discussed their reasons for doing so. The task thus forced some critical consideration of the programme; children were being asked to say which elements of it were 'best'. What were interesting, as in all the tasks, were the reasoning processes children used, and the elements of justification – whether aesthetic, moral, sociological, or institutional (as, for example, scheduling slots) – which were invoked to support their judgements. In many cases, as here, children moved away from the specific 'ordering' task to speculate on other aspects of the material which had caught their interest. The girl quoted at the head of the chapter was particularly interested in exploring differences between films (with 'real', that is, live-action, people in them) and cartoons, which are drawings, through aesthetic impression: 'colours are more clear and more firm' in live action; in cartoons they are 'only drawings'. Another boy, in the same conversation, pointed out the wider creative possibilities of cartoons, particularly in the treatment of fantasy violence, something that some adults might disapprove of, but which would have pleased John Kricfalusi:

BOY 1   I like cartoons, then you can do more stuff with it, like if things come out from your head, you can't really do it on yourself, things coming out from you.

INTERVIEWER   What kind of things coming out?

BOY 1   Like the brain or something.

In the second stage, more attention was paid to the story, which one girl described as 'really good'. Asked why, the quality of 'originality' emerged:

GIRL 1   Because in the end it felt really real and it made it sound really funny and different jokes from other stories that are being made.

INTERVIEWER   OK, why was this story different?

GIRL 2   It was different, because you know the people haven't just copied anything else have they, they have made it on their own, it is quite different from the other cartoons that people may have seen.

The interviewer then asked them to compare the cartoon with other storytelling genres, such as the fantasy *The Queen's Nose*, the realistic soaps, such as *Grange Hill* and *EastEnders* and the children's comedy, *Julia Jekyll and Harriet Hyde*. Asked if these shows were cartoons, the group answered: 'No. They are films. They have got real people in them.' It was at this point that Girl 1 came up with her definition of the difference between cartoon characters and real people, quoted at the beginning of the chapter. All the children strove to enlist modality concepts to explain the differences. Reality cues could be both technical – the use of drawings – and likelihood of narrative, as Girl 1 explains. This girl – obviously a rather exceptional 7 year old – was already aligning herself with the point of view of older children in the study, looking for social usefulness and helpful examples in her drama:

GIRL 2   *Rugrats* is a cartoon. *Grange Hill* is like with real people and it is like it is really happening. On cartoons it is not quite like it is happening, it is not quite happening to them, but like *Grange Hill* it does really happen, they are real people.

GIRL 1   I do watch *Grange Hill* because it is about a school and of course I go to school and I watch it, it is quite good, because it is a bit like a cartoon. It has got lots of things happening in it, things that go wrong, also I like the characters, but also in *Rugrats* as I said before anything can happen really – so I like both. I think *Grange Hill* is better, because when we go to middle school if we watch that, we might learn things.

One of the boys – the one who talked about 'things [coming] out from your head' – then diverted the conversation back to technique, emphasising the wider issue of production quality, and demonstrating his own technical knowledge:

BOY 1   Cartoons are better because if, say, they do a mistake they can just rub it out but if it is real people and they do a mistake they can't like just rub it out, they have to get another tape and do it again.

According to John Marsden (interviewed for the BBC study in spring, 1996) of Carlton/Central 'there is a huge future for animation'. Interestingly, like Jayne Pilling, but from a producer's rather than a critic's perspective, he came back to the topic of Disney, and the potential threat, or alternatively, stimulus, that Disneyfication could be for the animation form. On the one hand, because Disney would only allow their own products to be seen on their own channel, 'there's going to be a lot of people, including ITV, looking for animation product. It's going to help . . . animators that aren't attached to Disney.' On the other hand, as he acknowledged: 'Disney know this and they are buying up animation studios like crazy.' This, he argued, was frustrating to animation artists who wanted to maintain control over their own work and their own styles. Some British animators have set up as independent studios and have contracted only to produce particular scenes for Disney pictures, but, said Marsden:

They suck in the animators that way and they pay them money that's impossible to match. A lot of good animators have been vacuumed up by Disney and the likes of Disney . . . the reverse thing that makes people come back into the fold is that they in turn get frustrated by the discipline imposed on them . . . The strong ones with the passion and the flair will resist that.

It could be argued, too, judging from the comments of our infants' school critics, that, to please an audience with this degree of discernment when they are only seven (assuming that the discernment is maintained), only strong programme-makers 'with passion and flair' have any chance at all of surviving in the competitive storytelling market of the twenty-first century.

Conclusion: children and television drama – narrative closure?

I think it [the questionnaire] is great. Thank you for bringing it in.

Boy, 8, inner-London primary school

The research described in this book began in 1995, with representatives of the BBC's Policy and Planning Department asking me to carry out some empirical research for the Corporation on children and television drama, from my then base at the London College of Printing. As with other media and academic projects, both the research, and the Corporation itself have been affected by the tide of history. Five years later, in spring 2000, when the write-up of the research in this book was finally completed, it was announced that the Policy and Planning Department of the BBC would be abolished, in structural changes to the BBC, by the new Director General, Greg Dyke. More significantly for the research, these changes also included the abolition of the Children's Department as a separate and autonomous programming section within the BBC. (A development discussed in more detail in chapter 2.) I do not know whether the demises of both these departments are linked, or whether they are merely coincidental, but the conjunction is poignant. Without them, the research described in this book might not have been carried out.

Of course, there would be those within broadcasting (and perhaps within the academy too) who would say, 'So what?' Many media professionals do not see the point of academic audience research, which (unlike ratings) takes years, and is often written in jargon which they feel that nobody else can understand. We certainly met people within the BBC and other media organisations who held this view. Interestingly, they did not include most of the people who worked directly for children. Most of these people saw nothing inappropriate about academic researchers, with more time and intellectual distance from the programmes than they themselves had, talking to child audiences about their tastes and opinions, and suggesting interpretations of these opinions, based on academic theory and knowledge. The creative professionals were eager to co-operate with the study, and eager to hear about the findings as they came out.

The final report of the original research, complete with full sets of data (Davies, *et al.*, 1997) was sent to the (now defunct) BBC's Policy and Planning Department in 1997, and a copy went to the (now-assimilated) Children's Department. It would be good to think that the outpouring of confidences of the nearly 1,400 children in our study to their 'Dear BBC' did not fall on totally deaf ears, but the report arrived on executives' and producers' desks at a time of distraction by other developments. There were several changes of staff in Policy and Planning, and in 1997 the Children's Department was in the process of undergoing a number of changes of headship, including the retirement of its long-standing Head, Anna Home. A number of senior children's drama producers, interviewed by us in the early months of the research, had lost their jobs at the BBC by the end of it, in the course of these developments.

Following Home's retirement, there was a split (as elsewhere in the BBC) between commissioning and production of children's programmes, resulting in two children's heads, one for commissioning programmes, from both in-house and independent programme-makers, and another for producing and making them within the BBC; there was a further regional production 'head', in Scotland. This split between the commissioning and production of programmes has now been brought to an end by Greg Dyke's new dispensation, for which creative producers are likely to be thankful. The impact on the children's service, of the rejoining of commissioning and production, allied to the dissolution of Children's as a separate department, remains to be seen.

The research described in this book has thus been affected by, and has tried to take account of, the various upheavals to which British and global broadcasting have been subjected in the last five years – and it has also tried to take account of the burgeoning academic output on the subject of theories of childhood during this period. Purely as a piece of 'market research', the findings as initially presented to the BBC (Davies *et al.*, 1997) can be straightforwardly summarised. They showed that, when it came to drama, children liked realism; they demanded good examples; they saw distinctions between children's and adults' drama, and liked a range of both; they did not privilege drama over other genres when forced to choose; they mentioned hundreds of titles, both adults' and children's, as programmes they liked or disliked; there were differences between younger and older children, with a 'watershed' at around 9 to 10 years, when children began allying themselves with older, rather than with younger, audiences; there were very few marked differences between boys and girls in the statistical analyses, although there were slightly more boys than girls among science fiction and action-adventure enthusiasts, and slightly more girls than boys among soap and traditional drama enthusiasts.

One of the most surprising findings was that it was children in the least-privileged schools who most valued traditional, 'élitist' forms of drama – drama based on books, and historical drama, in other words, expensive drama. This is a counter-intuitive finding in terms of traditional sociological ideas about child audiences who are supposed to be populist in their tastes, unless paternalistically forced to consume 'higher' cultural forms like classic children's books. This finding is also counter-intuitive for a market-based broadcasting system with aspirations to maintaining a public service reputation, while making, and saving, money. In such a system, towards which the BBC, along with all other broadcasters, is moving, there is no economic advantage to be gained by making very expensive programmes which would only be appreciated by a few (or even a lot of) poor children. If more 'down-market' programming had emerged as what these less-privileged children really wanted, the results of the research would have been more consistent with the current broadcasting *zeitgeist*. Broadcasters could fulfil their public service responsibilities to serve the interests of children by giving less-privileged children what they were asking for, at the same time as providing commercially attractive, and cheaper, programming for all children.

In terms of academic discourse about children over the last five years, another timely text has just arrived on my desk, which summarises some of the many scholarly preoccupations about childhood, including children's relationship with the media, from the last two decades. David Buckingham's *After the Death of Childhood* (2000b) summarises current public and scholarly concerns in its opening paragraph (p. 3): 'in recent years debates about childhood have become invested with a growing sense of anxiety and panic'. In support of this, he cites a number of phenomena – press reports about child murders; 'home alone kids'; abduction by paedophiles; sex tourism; child crime, drug-taking and teenage pregnancy; moral panics about the influence of 'video nasties'; pornography on the Internet; problems with the '*idea*' (Buckingham's italics) of childhood, as represented in Hollywood's paedocratisation (to use John Hartley's (1998) word) of adult characters like Forrest Gump, or adultification (to use Neil Postman's (1982) word) of children, like Little Man Tate; the strangeness of pop-star (and former child prodigy) Michael Jackson with his obsession with Peter Pan, and his association with child-abuse scandals; and the 'authoritarian and punitive' responses of politicians and policy-makers to all these concerns. Buckingham's summary is a good illustration of the generally dystopic ways in which 'childhood' has been characterised and debated by scholars in the five years during which the research described in this book was taking place.

After the initial report was delivered to the BBC, and I had gone to work in the School of Journalism, Media and Cultural Studies at Cardiff University, the London College of Printing hired a Research Fellow, Dr David Machin, to continue jointly working with me on the project – in particular to bring an anthropological, discourse-analysis perspective to bear on the qualitative data. These data, the transcripts of all the discussion tasks, had been reported in only brief descriptive terms in the BBC Report and needed more analytical work. David was struck by the, to him, unexpected and counter-intuitive quality of much of the data: the tendency of all children, in all the discussion tasks, to require pro-social 'good examples' from all the programmes they talked about, even those which had only the most tenuous link with socially responsible goals, such as *Man O Man*, or *Top of the Pops*. Our research question became: what is going on in this kind of discourse? Why did children feel the need to use socially responsible language in choosing schedules, or rejecting programmes to save money? What were the origins, for them, of these kinds of representations? What did this kind of language suggest about how children saw themselves, not only as media consumers, but also as potential decision-makers on behalf of other children?

Obviously, the tasks had not been designed with the goal of producing anthropologically or sociologically significant research, but only to elicit children's judgements about television drama. However, the nature of the tasks meant that other kinds of social and political criteria had to be employed by the children in trying to decide between competing interest groups in designing their programme schedules. Children were not explicitly instructed to be 'sensible' or 'morally responsible' in the task designs – indeed, in requiring role-play and an element of performance (with colour-coded play-equipment, such as badges, cards and labels for all the groups), the tasks had been specifically designed to be playful, while at the same time encouraging collective and democratic decision-making. The judgements the children produced were a by-product of exercises designed to find out how they prioritised different forms of television storytelling, and to give them reasonably enjoyable ways of telling us which would not disrupt their class routines. However, through the processes of collaboration and debate, determined by the children themselves, which required eventual consensus, a consistent bias towards social responsibility was produced. We do not believe that this research shows that children are always sensible and moral. Furthermore, we were and are aware of the way in which people taking part in research 'discursively position' themselves, to use David Buckingham's phrase, to create a particular desired impression. The discursive positions chosen by these children, as they negotiated in groups – whether 'authentic' or not' (although I would have problems accepting any suggestion that the children were actively 'lying') – are what is so revealing. What these data suggest is that, when it comes to cultural constructions of childhood, the constructs of 'children as spokespersons for other children' employed by the children in our study, are very far from being the focus of 'anxiety and panic' described in Buckingham's account. As such, the children's constructs of childhood and its public characteristics and needs, and how to present themselves as representatives of those needs, were divergent from current adult constructs.

Evidence for this disjunction between what children (given the circumstances of the tasks) think childhood represents and what the adults responsible for them (given similar circumstances) think it represents, was found towards the end of the project. Again, this was as an unexpected by-product of a different kind of exercise. I gave a presentation about the research to a group of media education teachers in Wales, on an in-service training weekend, in the autumn of 1999. Since role-play had proved to be so revealing a technique with children, I decided to use it with the teachers too. I gave them the Children's Channel scheduling task as an exercise and asked one group to do it as themselves, and another group to role-play and to do it as 'nine-year-old children'.

The group of adult teachers pretending to be children was as illuminating in its comments as the children on the space ship in the pilot study had been, in its assumptions about how children would perform such an exercise. In the first place, the teachers decided, as a group, to behave anarchically, rather than co-operatively, and generated the following comments, all interrupting each other, and failing to set up any procedures for democratic consensus as the children in the study had done:

TEACHER/CHILD 1   Are we choosing for ourselves or others?

TEACHER/CHILD 2   We pick our favourites, as 6 to 9 year olds.

TEACHER/CHILD 3   I'm pretending to be my 9-year-old daughter.

TEACHER/CHILD 1   Wouldn't there be a rebellious streak?

TEACHER/CHILD 4   It's not supposed to be balanced – we're only nine.

Unlike the children, the teachers made no attempt to make a schedule based on time of day, nor to accommodate their schedules to different age groups, nor to ensure diversity of content. Their assumptions about how children as schedulers would behave were of a group which was anarchic, self-oriented, undisciplined and lacking in the ability to take responsibility for others. It was the exact opposite of what the child audience had shown itself to be in the role-playing tasks in the study. Given the public discourse about childhood, and the many problems associated with modern children which these well-read media teachers would be aware of, it was obvious that these teachers thought that children-as-schedulers would be socially irresponsible and would think entirely about their own media gratifications, rather than about media uses, or about the needs of others. The group of teachers acting as themselves obviously did not adopt the personae of self-willed 9 year olds, but they still assumed that the most popular programmes for a children's schedule would be cartoons and entertainment – fun and gratification, rather than balance, diversity and social improvement.

If these assumptions about how children are likely to behave when they are consulted politically are widespread among the adults responsible for educating and serving them, then a self-fulfilling prophecy will mean that cultural representations offered to children will assume what these teachers seemed to assume: that children are self-oriented, and unable to accept the needs, rights and tastes of others, unable to act responsibly, politically or morally. If children are not seen as potential citizens, even by the kinds of teachers who take special in-service training courses about media education, then children generally are going to have an up-hill task in overcoming these adult expectations, which is rather worrying for the rest of us.

There are, however, some grounds to resist despondency about this disjunction between teachers and children. Adults generally have *not* completely given up on childhood as a special and valued period of life – nor on children as special and valued people. If there are causes for 'anxiety and panic' about childhood among adults, they are causes for concern by standards of comparison with what could be, and what adults believe *ought* to be. The 'sacred garden' of childhood, as Buckingham (2000b) describes it, is not 'sacred', nor is it mythological. It is real, both as a period of intense, formative experience which each adult carries inside him or her, and as an ideal of nurturing which helps to determine what we believe 'ought to be'. It is also real as a period of social interaction with family, neighbourhood, peers, friends, culture, and media in a whole variety of ways, often negotiated (as the children in this study indicate) with considerable assurance, despite the many pitfalls and hurdles – as well as support systems – set up by these families, peers and other groups.

The other ground for optimism (maybe) is the often-noted tendency of children to be 'subversive' of adult culture. A possible irony of the findings of this research is that, at the beginning of the twenty-first century, almost the only way children can find to be subversive of adult society, is apparently by being socially responsible. Their culture tells them constantly that they are a problem and a source of panic and anxiety: OK then, say these children, the hell with what adult culture says about us: we're going to be *good*.

One of the most provocative characteristics of the data in the study is thus that, when children were put in positions where they were 'in charge' or where they were 'consultants to the BBC', they were often concerned to 'protect' the presumed susceptibilities of other children, especially 'little kids', and to require socially responsible messages from all kinds of programming, including the most frivolous genres. Paradoxically, when children were given the voice that libertarians lament is denied to them in the public sphere, in this study at least, they often used this voice to express distinctly non-libertarian opinions. If children ruled the world, or managed the broadcasting industry, how well would some of the liberties of expression and interpretation and freedom from censorship, so cherished by adults, survive? And, if they would not survive, what should adults do? Stand back and let children destroy cherished liberties, in the name of children's rights, or intervene to provide more enlightened alternatives, through discipline, control and regulation?

The final conclusion of this study is that, whether children are demonic tearaways, or socially responsible young puritans, or – as is most likely – sometimes one, and sometimes the other, the 'lugging' and 'civilising' processes required from adults in bringing them up, socialising them, and entertaining them will not cease to be necessary. These efforts will always work best as a collaborative process in which, as in the way adults talk to new babies in grammatical sentences, children, whatever they are like, are treated *as if* they were sensible people.

Appendices

Appendix 1

Schools used in the sample and
characteristics of their intakes (self-reports
from schools)

Profile of schools (self-descriptions), including special needs factors

REGION	TYPE OF SCHOOL	No of pupils	Av. class size	% of council housing	Social class	% on free meals	% of single parent	BBC Special needs support	CHILDREN & TV DRAMA Ethnicity	% other langs	SCHOOL Problems with English	PROFILES Media Ed.	Special needs Index	% of sample
Glamorgan	outer city sec	1500	30	30%	LM/M	10%	10%	11%	white European	100% Welsh	don't know	Y12, 13	0	2.0%
Cardiff	inner city prim	360	31–35	don't know	mixed	don't know	don't know	12%	34%	34% E2L	22%	Rec to Y6	3	7.4%
Cardiff	inner city prim	350	28	mixed	WC	33%	don't know	28%	50%	50%	don't know	no	6	9.3%
Co Durham	rural primary	28	28	60%	WC	12%	10%	15%	white	0%	0%	Y5, Y6	2	4.7%
Middlesboro	inner city sec	1112	20–28	don't know	WC	23%	don't know	6.30%	12% Asian	12%	minimal	Ys 10–13	3	3.8%
Co Durham	rural secondary	871	26	60%	WC	15%	don't know	16.00%	98% Caucasian	1%	10%	no	2	3.9%
Harrow	outer London prim	360	30	70%	WC	23%	30%	10%	mixed	8%	3%	no	4	2.0%
Harrow	outer London prim	357	30	mixed	WC/LM	19%	don't know	7%	46% ethnic minority	25%	11%	no	2	5.8%
Harrow	outer London sec	950	25	don't know	mixed	19%	approx. 25%	35%	45% white, 18% Indian, 9% Afro-Caribbean 5% Somali, 23% other	40%	10%	Ys 9–11	5	1.8%
London	inner London sec	500	28	90%	WC	41%	don't know		Bengali/Anglo/Asian	65%	3%	Y10, 11	6	3.3%
Islington	inner London prim	300	28	95%	WC	70%	don't know	40%	25% white, 25% Bengali, 50% other & mixed race	65%	55%	no	7	10.9%
Milton Keynes	inner city prim	400	30	97%	WC	52%	very high	35%	white	>1%	don't know	no	6	8.9%
Bletchley	outer city prim	334	30	15%	MC	1%	20%	11%	largely white	1%	0.50%	no	0	12.8%
Bucks	rural primary	215	31	15%	LM/M	0%	36%	20%	predominately white	0%	0%	no	1	10.3%
Oxfordshire	rural secondary	1400	29–30	don't know	mixed	tiny %	20%	25%	99% white	0%	10%	Y12, 13	1	4.3%
Didcot	outer city prim	300	30	don't know	WC/LM	0%	0%	0%	most white European	n/a	n/a	no	1	6.5%
Exeter	outer city prim	390	27	70%	WC	22%	30%	29%	WASP	0.1%	29%	no	4	2.2%

WC Working class
LM Lower middle
M   Middle class

Appendix 2

Questionnaire for children aged 8 and over

A Questionnaire

"What you think about television"

**Please fill in this questionnaire
to help the BBC find out what <u>you</u> think about
children's television.**

ABOUT YOU

Please finish these sentences:

I am ----------- years old

My birthday is ------------------

My school is called -------------

My class is ---------------------

**Please tick the
answer for you:**

Are you a boy?   yes / no

Are you a girl?   yes / no

Please tick the answer for you:

I have an older brother   yes / no
I have an older sister   yes / no
I have a younger brother   yes / no
I have a younger sister   yes / no

YOUR IDEAS ABOUT TELEVISION

Please put a tick in the box which applies to you:

For example:

I like watching Blue Peter	True ✓	Not true	Not sure
News is boring	True	Not true	Not sure ✓

Programmes for children are better than programmes for grown-ups	True	Not true	Not sure
There are too many programmes for little children	True	Not true	Not sure
I like watching programmes with teenagers in them	True	Not true	Not sure
Cartoons are only for little children	True	Not true	Not sure
I want more programmes for children my age	True	Not true	Not sure

YOUR IDEAS ABOUT TELEVISION - continued

Please put a tick in the box which applies to you:

Children's television helps me with problems in my life	True	Not true	Not sure
I like stories about people who lived a very long time ago	True	Not true	Not sure
Children need their own programmes in CBBC and CITV after school	True	Not true	Not sure
Made-up stories with actors dressed up are better than programmes with real people	True	Not true	Not sure
Children's television helps other children with problems in their lives	True	Not true	Not sure

YOUR IDEAS ABOUT TELEVISION - continued

I like stories about science fiction and the future	True	Not true	Not sure
The stories on children's television are too babyish	True	Not true	Not sure
I would like to see more stories from books on children's television	True	Not true	Not sure
Children don't need their own programmes; they can watch programmes like EastEnders and The Bill	True	Not true	Not sure

WHAT YOU THINK ABOUT DRAMA

Please tick one answer:

Drama is: a) someone telling / reading a story
           b) a story with actors / people dressed up
           c) an exciting event
           d) something that couldn't happen in real life
           e) (your idea) --------------------------------

Please tick which of these programmes is a drama programme:

East Enders	Drama	Not drama	Not sure
Grange Hill	Drama	Not drama	Not sure
Gladiators	Drama	Not drama	Not sure
Newsround	Drama	Not drama	Not sure
Men Behaving Badly	Drama	Not drama	Not sure
Live and Kicking	Drama	Not drama	Not sure
Just William	Drama	Not drama	Not sure

CHILDREN'S OR ADULT'S PROGRAMMES?

Please tick which programmes are specially for children:

East Enders	Children's programme	Not children's programme	Not sure
Grange Hill	Children's programme	Not children's programme	Not sure
Gladiators	Children's programme	Not children's programme	Not sure
Newsround	Children's programme	Not children's programme	Not sure
Men Behaving Badly	Children's programme	Not children's programme	Not sure
Live and Kicking	Children's programme	Not children's programme	Not sure
Just William	Children's programme	Not children's programme	Not sure

TELEVISION WITH
2 CHANNELS

Imagine you are watching a television with only TWO CHANNELS. These two programmes are on at the same time. Please tick which ONE you would choose to watch:

1.   Rugrats
2.   Byker Grove

TELEVISION WITH
2 CHANNELS

Imagine you are watching a television with only
TWO CHANNELS. These two programmes are
on at the same time. Please tick which **ONE** you
would choose to watch:

1. Rugrats
2. Art Attack

TELEVISION WITH
3 CHANNELS

Now imagine you are watching a television with
**THREE CHANNELS. These three programmes
are on at the same time. Please tick which ONE
you would choose to watch:**

1. Rugrats
2. Byker Grove
3. Friends

TELEVISION WITH
5 CHANNELS

Now imagine you are watching a television with
FIVE CHANNELS. These five programmes are
on at the same time. Please tick which **ONE** you
would choose to watch:

1. Rugrats
2. Byker Grove
3. Friends
4. Art Attack
5. Home and Away

TELEVISION WITH 10 CHANNELS

Now imagine you are watching a television with **TEN CHANNELS**. These ten programmes are on at the same time. **Please tick which ONE you would choose to watch:**

1. Rugrats
2. Byker Grove
3. Friends
4. Art Attack
5. Home and Away
6. Garfield
7. Power Rangers
8. Ace Ventura: Pet Detective
9. Scooby Doo
10. Ren & Stimpy

WHAT YOU WATCH ON TELEVISION

Please tick a box:

Do you have a television in your bedroom?	Yes	No	Not sure
Do you have satellite or cable?	Yes	No	Not sure
Do you watch Nickelodeon?	Yes	No	Not sure
Do you watch the Disney Channel on television?	Yes	No	Not sure
Do you watch the children's channel TCC?	Yes	No	Not sure
Do you watch the Cartoon Network?	Yes	No	Not sure
Do you watch Children's BBC (CBBC)?	Yes	No	Not sure
Do you watch Children's ITV (CITV)?	Yes	No	Not sure
Do you watch Children's Channel 4?	Yes	No	Not sure

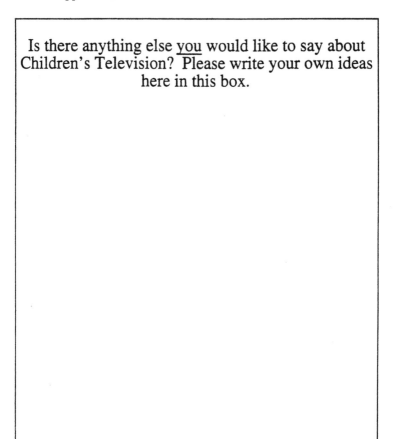

Is there anything else <u>you</u> would like to say about Children's Television? Please write your own ideas here in this box.

Well done, you have finished! And thank you very much for your help.

References

Acker, S. R. and Tiemans, R. K. (1981). 'Children's perceptions of changes in size of televised images', *Human Communication Research*, 7(4), 340–6.

Ang, I. (1993). *Desperately Seeking the Audience*. London: Routledge.

(1996). *Living Room Wars: Rethinking Media Audiences for a Postmodern World*. London: Routledge.

Aries, P. (1962, reprinted 1996). *Centuries of Childhood*. London: Pimlico Press.

Arnold, M. (1963). *Culture and Anarchy* (first published 1896). Ed. J. Dover Wilson, Cambridge University Press.

Bandura, A., Ross, D. and Ross, R. (1963). 'Imitation of film-mediated aggressive models', *Journal of Abnormal and Social Psychology*, 66(1), 3–11.

Barker, M. (1989). *Comics: Ideology, Power and the Critics*. Manchester University Press.

Barker, M. and Petley, J. (eds.) (1997). *Ill Effects: The Media Violence Debate*. London: Routledge.

Barwise, P. and Ehrenberg, A. (1996). *Television and its Audience*. London: Sage.

Bazalgette, C. and Buckingham, D. (eds.) (1995). *In Front of the Children: Screen Entertainment and Young Audiences*. London: British Film Institute.

Bazalgette, C. and Staples, T. (1995). 'Unshrinking the kids: children's cinema and the family film', in Bazalgette, C. and Buckingham, D. (eds.), *In Front of the Children: Screen Entertainment and Young Audiences*. London: British Film Institute.

BBC (1995). *People and Programmes: BBC Radio and Television for an Age of Choice*. London: BBC.

(1996). *The BBC and Children*, report on Governors' seminar. London: BBC.

Bellah, N. R., Madsen, R., Sullivan, W., Swindler, A. and Tipton, S. M. (1985). *Habits of the Heart: Individualism and Commitment in American Life*. University of California Press.

Bettelheim, B. (1976). *The Uses of Enchantment: the Meaning and Importance of Fairy Tales*. New York: Random House.

Bianculli, D. (1992). *Tele Literacy*. New York: Continuum.

Birt, J. (1999). *The Prize and the Price: The Social, Political and Cultural Consequences of the Digital Age*. The New Statesman Media Lecture, Banqueting House, Whitehall, London: 6 July 1999.

Blumler, J. G. (1992). *The Future of Children's Television in Britain: an Enquiry for the Broadcasting Standards Council*. London: BSC.

267

Blumler, J. G. and Hoffman-Riem, W. (1992). 'New roles for public service television', in Blumler, J. G. (ed.), *Television and the Public Interest: Vulnerable Values in West European Broadcasting*. London: Sage/Broadcasting Standards Council.

Bourdieu, P. (1984). *Distinction: A Social Critique of the Judgement of Taste*. Cambridge, MA: Harvard University Press.

Brown, J. A. (1991). *Television 'Critical viewing Skills' Education: Media Literacy Projects in the United States and Selected Countries*. Hillsdale, NJ: Lawrence Erlbaum Associates.

Bryant, J. and Anderson, D. (eds.) (1983). *Children's Understanding of Television: Research on Attention and Comprehension*. New York: Academic Press.

Bryant, J. and Zillman, D. (eds.) (1994). *Media Effects: Advances in Theory and Research*. Hillsdale, NJ: Lawrence Erlbaum Associates.

Buckingham, D. (1993). *Children Talking Television: The Making of Television Literacy*. London: Falmer Press.

(1995). 'The commercialisation of childhood? The place of the market in children's media culture', in Drummond, P. (ed.), *Changing English*, 2 (Autumn 1995), 16–20.

(1996). *Moving Images*. Manchester University Press.

(1997). 'Electronic child abuse? Rethinking the media's effects on children', pp. 32–47, in Barker, M. and Petley, J. (eds.), *Ill Effects*. London: Routledge.

(2000a). *The Making of Citizens: Young People, News and Politics*. London: Routledge.

(2000b). *After the Death of Childhood*. Cambridge: Polity Press.

Buckingham, D., Davies, H., Jones, K. and Kelley, P. (1997). 'Towards a political economy of children's broadcasting', paper presented at the Manchester Broadcasting Symposium, University of Manchester, April 1997.

(1999). *Children's Television in Britain*. London: Britich Film Institute.

Carpenter, H. (1985). *Secret Gardens: A Study of the Golden Age of Children's Literature*, London: George Allen and Unwin.

Cassell, J. (1998). 'Storytelling as a nexus of change in the relationship between gender and technology: a feminist approach to software design', in Cassell, J. and Jenkins, J. (eds.), *From Barbie to Mortal Kombat: Gender and Computer Games*. Cambridge, MA: MIT Press.

Cassell, J. and Jenkins, J. (eds.) (1998). *From Barbie to Mortal Kombat: Gender and Computer Games*. Cambridge, MA: MIT Press.

Caughie, J. (1991). 'Before the golden age: early television drama', pp. 22–41, in Corner, J. (ed.), *Popular Television in Britain: Studies in Cultural History*. London: British Film Institute.

Comstock, G. and Paik, H. (1991). *Television and the American Child*. San Diego, CA: Academic Press.

Connolly, M. and Ennew, J. (1996). 'Introduction: children out of place', *Childhood*, 3(2), 131–47.

Corner, J. (ed.) (1991). *Popular Television in Britain: Studies in Cultural History* London: British Film Institute, pp. 22–41.

Criticos, C. (1997). 'Media education for a critical citizenry in South Africa', in Kubey, R. (ed.), *Media Literacy in the Information Age*, Current Perspectives Information and Behavior, volume 6, New Brunswick, NJ: Transaction.

Cross, G. (1982). *The Demon Headmaster*. Oxford University Press.

(1985). *The Prime Minister's Brain*. Oxford University Press.

(1995). *The Demon Headmaster* and *The Prime Minister's Brain*. London: Puffin/Penguin.

Curran, J. (1991). 'Rethinking the media as a public sphere', pp. 29–57, in Dahlgren, P. and Sparks, C. (eds.), *Communication and Citizenship: Journalism and the Public Sphere*. London: Routledge.

Davies, M. M. (1982, reprinted 1993). *The Breastfeeding Book*. London: Frances Lincoln/Century.

(1989). *Television is Good for Your Kids*. London: Hilary Shipman.

(1997). *Fake, Fact and Fantasy: Children's Interpretations of Television Reality*. Mahwah, NJ: Lawrence Erlbaum Associates.

Davies, M. M. and Andrewartha, G. (2000). *Under the Gunge: A Production Study of the Carlton/ITV Children's Game Show*, Mad for It. London: Report to the Broadcasting Standards Commission.

Davies, M. M. and Corbett, B. (1997). *The Provision of Children's Programming in the UK, between 1992 and 1996*. London: Broadcasting Standards Commission.

Davies, M. M. and Machin, D. (2000a). 'Children's Demon TV – reality, freedom, panic: children's discussions of The Demon Headmaster', *Continuum: Journal of Media & Cultural Studies*, 14(1), 37–50.

(2000b). ' "It helps people make their decisions": dating games, public service broadcasting and the negotiation of identity in middle childhood', *Childhood*, 7(2), 173–91.

Davies, M. M. and O'Malley, K. (1996). 'Children and television drama: a review of the literature', London: London College of Printing (unpublished report to the BBC).

Davies, M. M., O'Malley, K. and Corbett, B. (1997). 'Children and television drama: an empirical study with children aged 5–13 years in England and Wales'. London: London College of Printing (unpublished report to the BBC).

Davis, John M. (1998). 'Understanding the meanings of children: a reflexive process', *Children and Society*, 12, 325–35.

Dorr, A. (1983). 'No shortcuts to judging reality', in Bryant, J. and Anderson, D. (eds.), *Children's Understanding of Television*. New York: Academic Press.

(1986). *Television and Children: A Special Medium for a Special Audience*. Beverly Hills, CA: Sage.

Dorr, A., Graves, S. B. and Phelps, E. (1980). 'Television literacy for young children'. *Journal of Communication*, 30(3), 84–93.

Dorr, A., Kovaric, P. and Doubleday, C. (1990). 'Age and content influences on children's perceptions of the realism of television families', *Journal of Broadcasting and Educational Media*, 34(4), 377–97.

Durkin, K. (1985). *Children, Television and Sex Roles*. Milton Keynes: Open University Press.

Eisenstein, E. (1979). *The Printing Press as an Agent of Change*. Cambridge University Press.

Evans-Pritchard, E. (1937). *Witchcraft, Oracles and Magic among the Azande*. Oxford University Press.

Feuer, J. (1986). 'Narrative form in American network television', pp. 101–14, in McCabe, C. (ed.), *High Theory/Low Culture: Analysing Popular Television and Film*. Manchester University Press.

Field, R. (1942). *The Art of Walt Disney*.

Fiske, J. (1989). *Understanding Popular Culture*. Boston: Unwin Hyman.

Furby, L. (1991). 'Understanding the psychology of possession and ownership', *Journal of Social Behavior and Personality*, **6**, 457–67.

Gardner, H. (1991). *The Unschooled Mind: How Children Learn and How Schools Should Teach*. New York: Basic Books.

Geertz, C. (1973). *Interpretation of Other Cultures*. London: Hutchinson.

Gerbner, G., Gross, L., Jackson-Beeck, Jeffries-Fox, S. and Signorielli, N. (1978). 'Cultural indicators: violence profile, No. 8', *Journal of Communication*, **28**, 176–207.

Gerbner, G., Gross, L., Morgan, M. and Signorielli, N. (1994). 'Growing up with television: the cultivation perspective', pp. 17–41, in Bryant, J. and Zillman, D. (eds.), *Media Effects: Advances in Theory and Research*. Hillsdale NJ: Lawrence Erlbaum Associates.

Goodnow, J. J. and Collins, W. A. (1990). *Development According to Parents: The Nature, Sources and Consequences of Parents' Ideas*. Hillsdale, NJ: Lawrence Erlbaum Associates.

Gunter, B. and Furnham, A. (1998). *Children as Consumers: A Psychological Analysis of the Young People's Market*. London: Routledge.

Gunter, B. and McAleer, J. (1990). *Children and Television: The One-eyed Monster?* London: Routledge.

Habermas, J. (1962, translated T. Burger and F. Lawrence, 1989). *The Structural Transformation of the Public Sphere: an Inquiry into a Category of Bourgeois Society*. Cambridge, MA: MIT Press.

Harris, P. L., Brown, E., Marriott, C., Whittall, S. and Harmer, S. (1991). 'Monsters, ghosts and witches: testing the limits of fantasy–reality distinction in young children', *British Journal of Developmental Psychology*, **9**, 105–23.

Hartley, J. (1992). *The Politics of Pictures: The Creation of the Public in the Age of Popular Media*. London: Routledge.

(1998). ' "When your child grows up too fast": juvenation and the boundaries of the social in the news media', *Continuum: Journal of Media and Cultural Studies*, **12**(1), 9–30.

Hawkins, R. (1977). 'The dimensional structure of children's perceptions of TV reality,' *Communication Research*, **4**(3), 299–321.

Hazard, P. (1947). *Books, Children and Men*. Boston, MA: The Horn Book.

Hendrick, H. (1997). 'Constructions and reconstructions of British childhood: an interpretative survey, 1800 to the present', pp. 34–62, in James, A. and Prout, A. (eds.), *Constructing and Reconstructing Childhood: Contemporary Issues in the Sociological Study of Childhood*. London: Falmer Press.

Hilton, M. (ed.) (1996). *Potent Fictions: Children's Literacy and the Challenge of Popular Culture*. London: Routledge.

Himmelweit, H. (1958). *Television and the Child: An Empirical Study of the Effect of Television on the Young*. London: Oxford University Press.

Hodge, B. and Tripp, D. (1986). *Children and Television*. Cambridge: Polity Press.

Hoggart, R. (1958). *The Uses of Literacy*. London: Penguin.

Holland, P. (1997). 'Living for libido; or Child's Play IV: the imagery of childhood and the call for censorship', pp. 48–56, in Barker, M. and Petley, J. (eds.), *Ill Effects*. London: Routledge.

Home, A. (1993). *Into the Box of Delights: A History of Children's Television*. London: BBC Books.

Hunt, P. (1991). *Criticism, Theory and Children's Literature*. London: Blackwell.

(1994). *An Introduction to Children's Literature*. Oxford University Press.

Hunt, P. (ed.) (1992). *Literature for Children: Contemporary Criticism*. London: Routledge.

James, A. and Prout, A. (eds.) (1997). *Constructing and Reconstructing Childhood: Contemporary Issues in the Sociological Study of Childhood*. London: Falmer Press.

James, A., Jenks, C. and Prout, A. (1998). *Theorizing Childhood*. London: Falmer Press.

Jenkins, H. (1992). *Textual Poachers*. London: Routledge.

(1998). '"Complete freedom of movement": video games as gendered play spaces', in Cassell, J. and Jenkins, H. (eds.), *From Barbie to Mortal Kombat: Gender and Computer Games*. Cambridge, MA: MIT Press.

Jenks, C. (ed.) (1982). *The Sociology of Childhood*. London: Batsford.

Kermode, M. (1997). 'I was a teenage horror fan: or "How I learned to stop worrying and love Linda Blair"', pp. 57–66, in Barker, M. and Petley, J. (eds.), *Ill Effects*. London: Routledge.

Keys, W. and Buckingham, D. (eds.) (1999). *Children's Television Policy: International Perspectives, Media International Australia: Culture and Policy*, **93** (November) special issue.

Kinder, M. (1991). *Playing with Power in Movies, Television and Video Games: From Muppet Babies to Teenage Mutant Ninja Turtles*. Berkeley, CA: University of California Press.

Kitzinger, J. (1990). 'Who are you kidding? Children's power and the struggle against sexual abuse', in James, A. and Prout, A. (eds.), *Constructing and Reconstructing Childhood: Contemporary Issues in the Sociological Study of Childhood*. London: Falmer Press.

Klein, N. (2000). *No Logo*. London: Flamingo/Harper Collins.

Kline, S. (1993). *Out of the Garden: Toys and Children's Culture in an Age of TV Marketing*. London: Verso.

Kubey, R. (ed.) (1997). *Media Literacy in the Information Age*. Current Perspectives Information and Behavior, volume 6, New Brunswick, NJ: Transaction.

Langer, M. (1999). 'Animatophilia, cultural production and corporate interests: the case of *Ren and Stimpy*', in Pilling, J. (ed.), *A Reader in Animation Studies*. Sydney: John Libbey.

Lewis, J. (1980). *The Politics of Motherhood*. London: Croom Helm.

Livingstone, S. and Bovill, M. (1999). *Young People, New Media*. Report of the research project: Children, Young People and the Changing Media Environment. London: London School of Economics.

Lohr, P. and Meyer, M. (eds.) (1999). *Children, Television and the New Media*. Luton: University of Luton Press.

Lurie, A. (1990). *Don't Tell the Grown-ups: Subversive Children's Fiction*. London: Bloomsbury.

Machin, D. and Carrithers, M. (1996). 'From "interpretive communities" to "communities of improvisation"', *Media, Culture and Society*, **18**(2), 343–52.

McLuhan, M. (1964). *Understanding Media*. New York: New American Library.

McNeal, J. U. (1992). *Kids as Customers: a Handbook of Marketing to Children*. New York: Lexington.

Meehan, J. (ed.) (1995). *Feminists Read Habermas*. London: Routledge.

Messaris, P. (1994). *Visual Literacy: Image, Mind and Reality*. Boulder, CO: Westview Press.

Meyrowitz, J. (1984). *No Sense of Place: The Impact of Electronic Media on Social Behavior*. New York: Oxford University Press.

Moore, C. and Frye, D. (1991). 'The acquisition and utility of theories of mind', in Frye, D. and Moore, C. (eds.), *Children's Theories Of Mind: Mental States and Social Understanding*. Hillsdale, NJ: Lawrence Erlbaum Associates.

Morley, D. (1980). *The Nationwide Audience*. London: British Film Institute.

Newson, E. (1994). 'Video violence and the protection of children', *The Psychologist*, **7**(6), 272–6.

Oswell, D. (1995). 'Watching with mother in the early 1950s', in Bazalgette, C. and Buckingham, D. (eds.), *In Front of the Children: Screen Entertainment and Young Audiences*. London: British Film Institute.

   (1997). 'Early children's broadcasting in Britain, 1922–1964: programming for a liberal democracy', *Historical Journal of Film, Radio and Television*, **18**(3), 375–93.

   (1998). 'The place of "childhood" in Internet content regulation: a case study of policy in the UK', *International Journal of Cultural Studies*, **1**(2), 271–91.

Palmer, E. (1988). *Television and America's Children: a Crisis of Neglect*. Oxford University Press.

Palmer, P. (1986). *The Lively Audience*. Sydney: Allen and Unwin.

Pearson, R. E. and Uricchio, W. (1991). *The Many Lives of the Batman*. London: Routledge.

Petley, J. (1997). 'Us and them', pp. 87–101, in Barker, M. and Petley, J. (eds.), *Ill Effects*. London: Routledge.

Pilling, J. (ed.) (1999). *A Reader in Animation Studies*. Sydney: John Libbey.

Postman, N. (1982, reprinted 1994). *The Disappearance of Childhood*. London: W. H. Allen.

Propp, V. (1968, reprinted 1994). *The Morphology of the Folk Tale*. University of Texas Press.

   (1984). *Theory and History of Folklore*. Manchester University Press.

Prout, A. and James, A. (1997). 'A new paradigm for the sociology of childhood', pp. 7–33 in James, A. and Prout, A. (eds.), *Constructing and Reconstructing Childhood*. London: Falmer Press.

Qvortrup, J. (1997). 'A voice for children in statistical and social accounting: a plea for children's right to be heard', in James, A. and Prout, A. (eds.), *Constructing and Reconstructing Childhood: Contemporary Issues in the Socio-logical Study of Childhood*. London: Falmer Press.

Radway, J. (1984). *Reading the Romance: Women, Patriarchy and Popular Literature*. Chapel Hill: University of North Carolina Press.

Reith, J. C. W. (1924). *Broadcast Over Britain*. London: Hodder and Stoughton.

Rice, M. L., Huston, A. C. and Wright, J. C. (1983). 'The forms of television: effects on children's attention, comprehension and social behaviour', in Meyer, M. (ed.), *Children and the Formal Features of Television: Approaches And Findings of Experimental and Formative Research*. Munich: K. G. Saur.

Richards, M. P. M. (1974). *The Integration of a Child into a Social World*. Cambridge University Press.

Richards, M. P. M. and Light, P. (eds.) (1986). *Children of Social Worlds*, Cambridge: Polity Press.

Rose, J. (1984). *The Case of Peter Pan*. London: Macmillan.

Rowland, W. (1997). 'Television violence redux: the continuing mythology of effects', pp. 102–24, in Barker, M. and Petley, J. (eds.), *Ill Effects*. London: Routledge.

Schneider, C. (1987). *Children's Television: The Art, The Business and How It Works*. Chicago: NTC Business Books.

Seiter, E. (1993). *Sold Separately: Children and Parents in Consumer Culture*. New York: Rutgers University Press.

Singleton Turner, R. (1994). *Television and Children*. London: BBC.

(1999). *Children Acting on Television*. London: A. and C. Black.

Smoodin, E. (ed.) (1994). *Disney Discourse*. New York: Routledge.

Springhall, J. (1998). *Youth, Popular Culture and Moral Panics: Penny Gaffs to Gangsta Rap 1830–1996*. New York: St Martin's Press.

Staples, T. (1997). *All Pals Together: The Story of Children's Cinema*. Edinburgh: Edinburgh University Press.

Starker, S. (1991). *Evil Influences: Crusades against the Mass Media*. New Brunswick, NJ: Transaction.

Steedman, C. (1990). *Childhood, Culture and Class in Britain: Margaret McMillan, 1860 – 1931*. London: Virago.

(1995). *Strange Disclocations: Childhood and the Idea of Human Interiority 1780–1930*. London: Virago.

Swartz, M. (1998). 'You dumb babies! How raising the *Rugrats* children became as difficult as the real thing', *The New Yorker*, 30 November 1998, 60–7.

Tulloch, J. and Jenkins H. (1995). *Science Fiction Audiences: Watching Dr Who and Star Trek*. London: Routledge.

Tulloch, M. (1995). 'Evaluating aggression: school students' responses to television portrayals of institutionalised violence.' *Journal of Youth and Adolescence*, 24(1), 95–115.

Turner, G. (1990). *British Cultural Studies: An Introduction*. London: Unwin Hyman.

Twitchell, J. B. (1992). *Carnival Culture*. New York: Columbia University Press.

Tyler, A. (1972). *The Clock Winder*. New York: Ballantine Books.

Warner, M. (1994). *From the Beast to the Blonde*. London: Vintage Press.

Wasko, J. (1996). 'Understanding the Disney universe', in Curran, J. and Gurevitch, M. (eds.), *Mass Media and Society*. London: Arnold.

Wertsch, J. V. (1991). *Voices of The Mind: A Sociological Approach to Mediated Action*. London: Harvester-Wheatsheaf.

Willett, J. (ed.) (1964). *Brecht on Theatre*. New York: Hill and Wang.

Winn, M. (1985). *The Plug-In Drug*. Harmondsworth: Penguin.

Wolfe, T. M. and Cheyne, J. A. (1972). 'Persistence of effects of live behavioural, televised behavioural and live verbal models on resistance to deviation', *Child Development*, **43**, 1429–36.

Woollett, A. and White, D. (1992). *Families: A Context for Development*. London: Falmer Press.

Wright, J. C., Huston, A. C., Reitz, A. L. and Piemyat, S. (1994). 'Young children's perceptions of television reality: determinants and developmental differences', *Journal of Developmental Psychology*, **30**(2), 229–39.

Young, B. M. (1990). *Television Advertising and Children*. Oxford: Clarendon Press.

Zipes, J. (1986). *Don't Bet on the Prince; Contemporary Feminist Fairy Tales in North America and England*. Aldershot: Gower.

Index